NAVAL FIGHTER PILOT

LT. CDR. R. J. CORK DSO, DSC, RN

✸ ✸ ✸

A. H. WREN

NAVAL FIGHTER PILOT
LT. CDR. R. J. CORK DSO, DSC, RN

The story of the Fleet Air Arm's unsung hero
and the men with whom he served

A. H. WREN

HERON BOOKS
OF LICHFIELD

First published in 1998 by
Heron Books of Lichfield

© 1998 A. H. Wren

ISBN 0 9532250 0 3

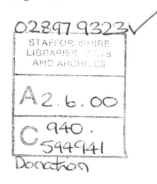
Typeset by MPG Books Ltd.
Printed and bound in Great Britain by
MPG Books Ltd, Bodmin, Cornwall.

ACKNOWLEDGEMENTS

This book was suggested by my father, who, as a Fleet Air Arm pilot himself, felt that one of its most famous sons had been neglected for too long. He had seen a few articles and brief references in books, but these he felt 'wouldn't have filled a single chapter if laid end to end', let alone do justice to the life of a naval hero. So if anything of value were to be written it could only come from a major research effort, involving many individuals. All these contributors are listed below. To all of them I give my thanks:-

Mr. G. Aitken*, Group Captain D. Bader DSO and Bar, DFC and Bar *, Captain G. C. Baldwin CBE, DSC RN, Mr. A. J. Bennett, Mr. D. Bond, Wing Commander F. Brinsden, Mr. A. Bromley, Mr. R. Brooke, Mr. J. V. Brownlee, Mr and Mrs. M. Busby, Commander G. R. Callingham RN *, Mr. R. Chamen, Major V. B. G. Cheesman DSO, MBE, DSC RM (Rtd), Captain P. C. S. Chilton AFC RN *, Mr. W. G. Coleman, Mr. J. Collins *, Mr. B. Cork MC, Air Commodore J. Coward AFC, Commander W. Cowling RN (Ret), Commander R. M. Crosley DSC and Bar RN (Rtd), Air Marshal Sir Denis Crowley Milling KCB, CBE, DSO, DFC and Bar, Captain R. L. B. Cunliffe RN *, Wing Commander W. Cunningham DFC, Mr. G. P. Davies, Mr. S. Elmes, Mr. C. Facer*, Chaplain E. D. G. Fawkes *, Mr. V. R. Foster, Air Chief Marshal Sir Christopher Foxley Norris GCB, DSO, OBE *, Mr. J. E. Gardner OBE, DSC, Wing Commander A. Grant, Herr Gerhard Granz, Mr. B. A. Graves *, Mr. R. Greenwood, Captain N. G. Hallett DSC and Bar RN *, Wing Commander H. J. L. Hallowes DFC, DFM and Bar, Commander R. C. Hay DSO, DSC RN (Rtd), Wing Commander P. Hancock, Mrs. K. Hanson, Mr. G. Hiscox, Mr. A. Hobson, Lt. Cdr. K. Holme RN(Rtd), Lt. Cdr. L. G. Hooke VRD RNR, Sir Michael Hordern, Mr. W. Houlton, Wing Commander P. Howard Williams, Wing Commander B. J. Jennings DFM, Air Vice Marshal J. E. Johnson CB, CBE, DSO and two Bars, DFC and Bar, Captain N. L. D. Kemp DFC, Mr. J. Large, Mr. D. Lawrence, Mr. W. Lawson, Major A. E. Marsh RM (Rtd), Mr. P. Medcraft*, Mr. J. G. Millard, Mr. D. Millington, Lt. Cdr. E. Monk DSM and Bar, Mr. W. K. Munnoch, Mrs. I. Nice, Mr. W. O'Neill, Group Captain R. W. Oxspring DFC and two Bars, AFC, Mrs. F. Parsons, Mr. R. Picken, Mr. H. Popham,* Ms. K. N. Roberts, Mr. D. A. Rogers, Mr. D. Rylatt, Herr. W. Schutel, Mr. W. Scott, Captain T. W. B. Shaw DSC RN *, Sir Edward Singleton*, Mr. A. Spicer, Mr. F. Starkey, Commander J. Sykes RN, Mr. E. J. Trerise, Mr. A. M. Tritton DSC and two Bars, Mr. C. Tuckey, Group Captain S. Turner DSO, DFC and Bar *, Wing Commander G. Unwin, Mr. G. Wallace*, Mr. A. E. Watson, Mr. R. W. Williamson *, Mr. V. Wood, Mr. F. R. Yuill, Mr. J. Zollo.

Many institutions, associations and other groups also helped in producing this book. They are:

The Imperial War Museum.
The Naval Historical Branch, MOD.
The Battle of Britain Fighter Association.
Upton Grammer School.
Eton College.
The German Embassy.
Gemeinschaft de Jagflieger.
SAGA Magazine.
Navy News.
RAF News.
Trincomalee P. Coy RM Engineers Association.
Naval Secretaries Dep't, Officers Mobilization Section, Ministry of Defence.
ICI.
The Burnham, Hitchin, Taplow and Dorney Community newspaper.
The MOD Library, Whitehall.
The New Zealand Defence Force.
The New Zealand High Commission.
The Commonwealth War Graves Commission.
The Napier Daily Telegraph.

Very generously three authors allowed me to quote extensively from their books. My thanks to them for permission to illustrate this work with sections from these moving and absorbing stories:-

"Carrier Pilot" by Norman Hanson.
"They Gave Me A Seafire" by Mike Crosley.
"Sea Flight" by Hugh Popham.

There are a number of official documents quoted in this book all covered by Crown copyright. I would like to thank the MOD for granting me written permission to use this material.

It is sad to relate that many people who offered me such tremendous support whilst writing this book died before seeing the finished work *. Principal amongst them my father, who died of cancer on July 1st 1993. This book is dedicated to him.

PROLOGUE

In near darkness the gull winged fighter sped in from over the sea, its grey green camouflage blackened by the night sky. Dawn was just breaking through the upper reaches of the atmosphere, casting a pale glow over the Corsair's canopy, briefly reflecting the outline of the pilot's head, shrouded and made anonymous by helmet and goggles. The light moved backwards along the fuselage to pick out the initials 'RC' emblazoned along its side. An affectation, some might say, but one the pilot had earned the hard way. In any case few would begrudge him this small sign of self publicity.

As the aircraft banked, its pilot watching the distant rays of sunlight, the words 'Royal Navy' appeared from their place beneath the tailplane.

In anticipation of an early arrival over China Bay he lost height and swept in a wide, gentle curve over the heavily forested land to the north of the airfield. In the distance he saw the flare path around the single runway lit and probably wondered who was awake to see him safely home.

After one cautious pass along the runway he swung his aircraft round and lined up again to land, curving in, left wing held low, flattening out at the last second, waiting for the ground to claim him for the last time. Oblivious of any danger ahead, death sought him out in a moment of searing, unexpected pain. Unobserved in the darkness a second Corsair was moving along the runway, hidden by the darkness. Both aircraft came together with a violent explosion that reverberated across the airfield into the surrounding trees, sending birds shrieking into the sky. The few witnesses present saw the two aircraft crumple into each other and, as metal and flesh became one, fuel tanks detonated bathing everything in a deep orange glow, incinerating all that remained of these two young men.

A Crash Team rushed to the scene, but the intensity of the fire beat them back and their equipment seemed to have little or no effect on the inferno. So they stood helplessly watching the wrecks disintegrate until anything combustible had burned and the funeral pyre could be extinguished.

Within hours the few, pitiful remains had been removed leaving a blackened scar on the runway.

Whilst memories were fresh senior officers tried to piece together events, to find some cause or reason. But their efforts were hampered by so many imponderables, not least amongst them the identity of the first aircraft and its pilot. The few scraps remaining provided no clue. Yet it was a machine and man who could so easily have been identified if the letters 'RC' had survived. Later in the day HMS Illustrious steamed into Trincomalee, its flying programme frustrated by the elements, only to receive a flash signal about a flying accident at nearby China Bay.

Some secretly suspected that the lone Corsair flown off that morning, before all other flights had been cancelled, might have been involved. If so a brief exchange of messages confirmed their worst fears and the death of Lieutenant Commander R. J. Cork DSO, DSC RN, Wing Leader and war hero, was relayed to the ship's company by tannoy.

Few who knew him believed that this veteran, who had survived four years of war, much of it in the frontline, could die so needlessly in a flying accident. Yet, in the rush of war, death was commonplace and life an easily expended commodity. Pilots were, in any case, accustomed to death and learned very early in their training that it could strike without warning, when least expected and with great violence. But Dickie Cork was one of the best and, if he could die in such a simple way, what chances did the rest have ? Even before their war against Japan had started they were faced with a terrible reminder of their own mortality and the slim chance they had of survival to the war's end. Dickie Cork had lived with the spectre of death for a long time and appreciated, more than most, how lucky he had been to survive until 1944, though a sense of invulnerability often coloured a pilot's view of life.' Yet he must have been aware, when requesting transfer to a frontline unit in late 1943, from the comparative safety of training duties, that he was stretching his luck to the limit. Nearly all his friends from 1939 were long dead, POWs or in second line squadrons, but he chose to carry on, ignoring all advice.

Some would think this foolhardy, whilst others saw in his actions the unmistakable signs of war weariness and the lack of concern for safety this condition could foster. Both views might well have held elements of truth, though in each case they overlooked the basic character of the man. Committed to a worthy cause, he would instinctively go on longer and fight harder than those around him. But it was a game of high risk and in the end he tempted fate once too often and paid a terrible price for such bravery. Over the years memories of this gallant officer faded, briefly flickering into life when prompted by occasional references to him in books and newspapers. But in these accounts he remained an aloof, enigmatic figure hidden behind a shield of half remembered encounters and the barrier of rank. Those who survived saw Cork as a man in shadow, a reflection behind a glass canopy - real, but insubstantial. They thought about what sort of man he had been, little realising that his life reflected their own and all those other young men who flew, fought, lived and died with the Fleet Air Arm.

CHAPTER ONE

BORN IN WAR

Freezing winds blew across Europe from the east bringing rain and snow to the entrenched armies. The winter had been a bad one and this cruelly belated cold spell increased the misery still further.

Along the front from Flanders to the Somme, where British and Empire forces held the line, the appalling weather lowered physical resistance and illness claimed as many lives as enemy fire.

As the misery increased, so the number of desertions accelerated. The well advertised execution of father of four, Sapper Frederick Malyon, 12 Company Royal Engineers, as dawn broke on the 4th, did little to dissuade others from trying this precarious means of escaping the next 'Big Push', five days later in front of Arras.

Throughout the hours of darkness, unseen by enemy observers on the ground or in the air, horses and vehicles dragged equipment and ammunition forward, sounds muffled by sacks and the threat of downward rushing artillery shells. Since 1914 the Germans had held the high ground and could, in darkness or light, wreak death and destruction on their enemy.

Even before the battle had begun British casualties rose at an alarming rate. In one division alone, the 56th (London), 27 men lost their lives in the early hours of the 4th, when caught by long range gunfire. But in a war where deaths were counted in thousands, the loss of 27 men only warranted a brief mention in the Divisional War Diary. The receipt of telegrams a few days later in 27 homes gave these events a more profound meaning.

As dawn broke, the first reconnaissance patrols took to the sky, pilots and observers swathed in layers of clothing, exposed skin covered by whale oil to counter the effects of the intense cold. Scout planes patrolled higher up looking for victims amongst the slow two-seaters, but they saw few and engaged even less. The only consolation for those who could climb high enough was a view beyond the battlefield to England, evoking thoughts of home and family.

At those heights the sun shone brilliantly, illuminating and revealing distant scenes. For hours on end, the sky above the Channel was clear and from 15, 000 feet many ships could be seen ploughing back and forth across this short stretch of water. From such a distance they seemed like toys, but each was crammed with soldiers returning from leave or 'going out' for the first time. Where France could be glimpsed through sudden, cavernous breaks in the cloud, it appeared as a gigantic patchwork of fields, roads providing the occasional narrow border. Only the battlefield broke up this rhythmic pattern, leaving a muddy, vivid scar stretching endlessly into the distance.

At midday, the clouds over Southern England parted briefly revealing to those high flying men the distant sight of Dover and Kent, whilst London stayed resolutely hidden by rain and mist. The day saw no sunshine in the city and chill winds swept from the east without respite, drawing smoke and pollution into the countryside beyond. During the few moments of stillness, the rumble of distant guns could be heard on the wind.

The same wind blew through the eaves of the House of Commons, where the last afternoon before the Easter recess was spent debating the parlous state of Britain's air forces, carefully split, by divisive intent, between the Admiralty and Army. Neither recognised the needs of the other and each developed its own air arm independently. By recognising these shortcomings, parliament set in train a series of events that would result in the creation of the RAF in April 1918. Yet in so doing, they would ignore the changing face of naval warfare, from battleship to aircraft. A move that would in a few short years condemn many Fleet Air Arm pilots to fight a war in antiquated and hopelessly outclassed machines.

As darkness descended, hospital trains continued to creep along the web of commuter lines surrounding London, finally darting into the city. For the last few days, hospitals in France and Belgium had been clearing out those wounded soldiers who could be moved. Their beds would be needed by the end of the week for those mutilated in the coming offensive.

On a clear day the smoke from these trains could be traced, from the air, all the way back to the south coast. On the 4th they appeared wraith like through the mists, their lights shaded and just visible in the dark, reflecting back onto the blackened walls and houses as they passed, flickering like a beacon.

Outside the main line stations, ambulances waited to collect the casualties. Early in the war the concourse had been crowded with onlookers to see the wounded come home, but now the sight was commonplace and daily casualty lists publicized the horrors of war well enough to deter all but the most dogged voyeurs.

From these stations wounded were driven through the streets of central London. After the battlefield the noises and sights glimpsed through curtained windows of a city largely unaffected by war would have seemed alien. There had been no Zeppelin raids for many months, so the streets were lit up as though no threat existed and theatres, music halls, clubs and restaurants all did a roaring trade. At the Alhambra in Leicester Square "The Bing Boys Are There" played to a packed house, even though its' leading lady, Violet Lorraine, was absent with a head cold. The same virus struck some of the cast appearing in "Maid of the Mountains", whilst at His Majesty's Theatre a small backstage fire threatened to disrupt the evening's performance of "Chu Chin Chow". It went ahead, but suffered a second disruption when several Royal Flying Corps officers, worse the wear for drink, tried to join the cast on stage. Amidst much shouting and laughing, they were eased gently onto the street, sobered by the sudden chill breeze.

The air filled with snow flurries and the plaintive, incoherent shouts of news sellers echoed through the busy streets, their billboards providing a brief translation "AMERICA DECLARES WAR ON GERMANY". Workers scurrying home, their collars drawn tight around necks, may have noted this news. After so many months of war, where progress was measured in yards and the increasing length of casualty lists, few would have regarded this with more than a passing interest. Life for many was held in limbo by the war and few had the desire to look too far into the future. Despite this, life went on and each day children were born to whom the Great War would be just a distant memory.

As the clouds closed in and the sun was obliterated from view on that cold April day, a son was born to Harold and Ethel Cork, in the western suburbs of the enshrouded city. Within days, his birth would be registered in nearby Brentford and Richard John Cork had, in blissful ignorance of the world around him, begun a journey that would end tragically 27 years later in distant Ceylon.

If we are the product of the age in which we live, then the Great War must surely have moulded young Richard Cork's life. The society in which he grew up had been distorted by its' violence and many unspoken traumas and his own family had not escaped unscathed from four years of a most bitter war.

In 1914 Harold Cork, a Kent man, had been an active member of a Territorial Regiment, the 1/9th London (Queen Victoria's Rifles), his employers allowing him special leave to attend training camps each August. In the long hot summer of 1914 the Regiment was looking forward to two weeks in Dorset, around Lulworth Cove, but the situation in Europe deteriorated so quickly that all regiments were recalled by telegram to their home bases. For the QVR's this meant breaking their journey at Wimborne Station and returning to London.

The move was premature and until October officers and men returned to their homes, reporting each day to their Headquarters in Davies Street for instructions and new kit. The end of their 'Phoney War' came suddenly:

> "Twenty-four hours leave was granted to the whole battalion to enable the men to say goodbye to their friends and relatives, one half leaving at a time. When the day of departure, November 4th, arrived there ensued a scene long to be remembered by those who took part in it. The battalion paraded and was marched through the town to the Dock Gate. The SS Oxonian was seen in the gathering darkness, and the men were marched straight aboard and led to their allotted quarters. The vessel bore the appearance of a whitewashed maze, but investigation showed that it had been used for transporting cattle and had not been altered for the transport of men.
>
> She slipped away as soon as darkness fell and crept out to sea without any light showing. The night was quiet but cold. No lifebelts were issued or directions given in case of danger or disaster and the few boats available were assigned to the crew exclusively, so we were told. Everything, however, turned out well; the passage was calm and uneventful, though everyone was thankful when Le Havre was sighted at 6 o'clock on the 5th and we were put ashore four hours later."
>
> *Sgt. W. W. Crossthwaite, QVR.*

So Harold Cork went to war in a cattleboat, just one amongst thousands snatched from the routine and peace of civilian life. Ill equipped and ill trained, they were expected to fill a void created by the onrush of German forces through Belgium and France. Within days they were in the trenches at Neuve Eglise:

> "There were a few shells going over and a good many snipers at
> work, but nothing much happened as we marched forward. The
> mud was awful, right up to our knees in places and at one point
> we had to cross a stream and got very wet in the process. It was
> a bright moonlit night, but with clouds every now and then, and
> we went along very slowly and quietly, the men doing very well
> and making no noise.
> We finally reached the trench which was ours to hold for two
> weeks and relieved the K. O.Y. L. I. The following morning we
> discovered, in between bouts of shellfire and sniping, that the
> Germans were only 60 to 70 yards away.
> Our own trench was most unpleasant, with a foot or two of
> black water at the bottom and a wet wall of sandbags in front. I
> don't think we were very miserable that first night, the novelty
> of it all was so obsessing, but the iron entered our souls later,
> and the time came when we got to know trenches to which
> these were a rest home. "

Sgt. W. W. Crossthwaite, QVR.

Life now followed a pattern that would become only too familiar in the
years to come. For most, each day was simply a matter of survival. Mail from
home broke the monotony and lifted the spirits, but the wet and cold gradually undermined morale. Only comradeship and the promise of a bath and
a dry bed kept most going. For better or worse trench life became timeless
and soldiers lives became confined to a small strip of featureless land. All
they could do was endure and make the most of small events, especially if
they coincided with rest periods.

> "Christmas 1914
> I think every man had a good time under the conditions. We had
> been on and off in the trenches for the last two weeks and start-
> ed our rest on Christmas Eve. On Christmas Day we had a
> church parade, football match, a good dinner with Christmas
> pudding and then messed about generally, ending up with hot
> punch round a big fire at night. "

Rfn. S. Gubbins, QVR.

With the coming of Spring the QVR's came out of the line held since
November and marched north towards Ypres, going into trenches 70
yards from the German line on March 31st.

> "We are on historic ground here. There has been extremely
> heavy fighting for some time. Every building is wiped out by
> shell fire, only the foundations and a pile of brickbats where
> a house once stood, and in the woods there is hardly a tree
> whose top has not been lopped off by the fire. The zone
> spreads out for half a mile each side of the trenches leaving
> behind it dead trees, dead horses and dead men. A captive
> balloon hangs in the air close by directing shell fire down on
> our heads. The trenches run along a small rise in the ground
> that is called Hill 60.
> Hill is, perhaps, rather an exaggerated term for what is really
> only a slight eminence about 60 metres in height, but is the
> highest point of a ridge overlooking Ypres. "

> *Captain S. J. Samson, QVR.*

The German Army held Hill 60 and could observe all that happened
on the plain below. 2nd Army, on whose front this weak spot lay,
planned to take the 'Hill' as soon as the weather improved and mining
under the enemy's trenches had been completed and explosives laid.
When the attack came the QVR's would be in the forefront of a battle
so typical of the Great War - terrible losses for a few yards of ravaged
earth.

> "April 17th
> 250 yards of enemy trenches seemed to be struck by an
> earthquake. They and the occupants ceased to exist. We went
> 'over the top' and dashed across into the debris where a terri-
> ble struggle ensued. We took the hill alright but a lot of us
> were hit in in the process. The whole cutting (leading to the
> trenches) is full of dead and wounded and, of course, it's the
> same in the trenches.... "

> *Captain Culme Seymour, QVR.*

The battle ebbed and flowed for four days as each side threw more and more reinforcements into the line:

> "Dawn (21st) gradually appears and the enemy begins bom-
> barding with hand grenades. One by one I see my pals fall.
> Maisey and Pearson a little way to my right are lying never to
> move again. What a roar and tumult. Maxim guns are hammer-
> ing away, shrapnel bursting above us and blinding flashes fol-
> low the explosion of hand grenades. My rifle becomes too
> hot to hold and I throw it aside and pick up another. I feel no
> longer a human being. Simply, mechanically I continue firing. "

> *Rfn. C. Woolcock, QVR.*
> *(KIA 6/4/1917)*

By now elements of the QVR's held the hill by themselves. Reserves
were minimal and fresh reinforcements were held up in the back areas.
One by one all officers had fallen and few NCOs remained on their feet,
but the regiment kept up a dogged defence until the 2nd Cameroon
Highlanders arrived. In darkness surviving QVR's trudged wearily away
from the frontline:

> "Till now my nerves have stood me well; but as I recall the
> fearful sights I have witnessed, and realise the majority of my
> pals are gone I give way and breakdown, sobbing like a child.
> Presently I pull myself together and have a little food."

> *Rfn. C. Woolcock, QVR.*

As his surviving comrades came to terms with these horrors, Harold
Cork began fighting a longer, sterner battle. He now lay, semiconscious,
in a Casualty Clearing Station near Poperinghe awaiting emergency
surgery to save his life. Within days, as his condition stabilized, an ambu-
lance took him to Boulogne and home. 232 of his fellow QVR's were
not so 'lucky' and Hill 60 remained their final resting place. As the hospital train steamed through the English countryside to London, Harold
may have considered his good fortune in escaping the guns.

Life in peacetime had followed a fairly settled course, but wartime's
sudden intervention profoundly changed this order. Soldiers lives in the
Great War hung by the thinnest of threads and the random element of
chance unexpectedly and irrevocably changed millions of lives. Against

long odds, Harold had survived and would not see frontline service again. In time he met and married a girl from Devon, Ethel Wood, and in the years that followed, Dickie Cork, his sister, Pauline and brother, Brian, arrived. A new generation for whom the war had played such a dominating role. It took life and gave life randomly in ways unimagined in 1914. It also left a legacy of injuries, trauma and grief that changed attitudes and societies. The generation growing up between the wars were a product of these events and would see their lives coloured and shaped by this massive upheaval.

CHAPTER TWO

GROWING UP BETWEEN THE WARS

Very few families escaped tragedy in the Great War. So it was in the Cork and Wood households. Apart from her husband's injuries, Ethel Cork had to cope with the loss of one brother and the disablement of another. So Peace, when it came in 1918, was not greeted with universal celebration; the depth of suffering made such a reaction impossible. Instead relief, tinged with great sadness, pervaded most thoughts.

Demobilization began within days, but vast numbers remained in uniform throughout 1919, kicking their heels in camps around Britain and France waiting for bureaucracy to release them. It was a frustrating time and ill feelings were heightened by the knowledge that few jobs might exist outside. Servicemen released first had an advantage, or so those still in uniform thought. In reality the economy could not sustain such an influx of men and swiftly broke down under this extreme pressure.

Though his injuries were severe, Harold Cork recovered sufficiently to stay in the army until early 1919, but his remaining service was spent in England, with a period in Ireland in the aftermath of the Easter Uprising.

With a young family to support, employment was essential and he was able to return to work shortly after being demobbed. It must have been a strange experience, out of uniform, without military discipline, to be back once more in civilian life. Yet his scars were a constant reminder of less stable times.

Almost in celebration of peace and a return to 'civvy street', Ethel gave birth to a second child, Pauline, born in her grandfather's house in Hampshire. Dick, by this time, had developed into a lively two year old and photographs show him dressed in the fashions of the day, with his blond hair grown long. Two years later, when his brother was born at a

Nursing Home near Maidenhead, these styles had given way to something more robust.

School provided a new outlet for his energy and he seemed to spend
a great deal of time fighting in the playground, dragging in some innocent parties on occasions, as Brian Cork later recalled:

> "I remember my first day at school, because he (Dick) was a
> bit aggressive at times and was always involved in fights and
> things. So I arrived at school and there was one particular
> boy that he was normally having arguments with and I
> remember him saying to this lad coming home, 'my kid broth-
> er could take you on'. Whereupon this boy lashed out and
> blacked both my eyes, which I didn't think was a frightfully
> good way of spending my first day at school. Meanwhile this
> boy had shot off down the road."

A child could not perceive the problems of an adult world recovering from war, life being centred upon home and school. High unem-
ployment rates and poor living conditions were a disturbing reality,
causing great discontent through many levels of society. Against this
background families struggled to survive and few could afford luxuries,
looking, instead, to better times ahead.

As the decade passed there were signs of recovery around London.
Developers saw the opportunity presented by the many railway lines
spreading out from the city into the countryside and began construct-
ing thousands of new homes to relieve pressure on an increasingly con-
gested capital.

Seeing the opportunities this presented, the Cork family moved to
Buckinghamshire in late 1927. A month later, after the Christmas holiday, Dick started at the local Grammar School. His arrival coincided
with that of a newly qualified teacher, John Collins, who recalled these
days many years later, a few weeks before his death in 1991:

> "I began my teaching career in the late 1920s with eagerness
> and joy. It was at Slough that I really began to think of teach-
> ing as a full time job and revelled in the challenges it offered a
> naive young man.
> Certain boys and girls loomed large before my eyes as I
> watched them develop into young men and women. They
> were a grand generation, though ill-starred by history they

were growing up in a world about to fight a terrible war and many would fall. Those I remember most tend to be the ones larger than life. Dickie Cork was one of these, with his ready smile, good looks and lively personality.

He wasn't a very gifted boy towards literary studies, yet he was thorough and careful in his work, though he never achieved high standards in the classroom. But he was true to his family, willing, generous minded, staunch and true. All strengths not really appreciated by schools then or now, but in the real world, of immeasurable worth.

I'm sure Dick was a late developer in many ways, particularly in classroom matters. His mind was really too active to be restricted by a desk and the life outside with all its excitement beckoned. There were many boys like that and I'm sure the war, when it came, proved a godsend for those lively lads. "

If he longed for more excitement there were few outlets except, perhaps, on the sports field, where excess energy could be expended. By 1930 he began making regular appearances for Gray House. Being much younger than the other boys he found himself at a disadvantage and for a while was consigned to second teams until his skills were recognised, as House records relate:

"26.2.30 2nd XI beat Henschel House 14 0

Too hectic to be of much interest from the point of view of good play. Gray kept in Henschel House's area throughout match. Cork, at outside right, scored four times.

19.3.30 2nd XI beat Milton House 11 0

A very satisfactory result. Cork scored an excellent goal.

13.12.30 1st XI drew with Milton House 7 7

The team was handicapped by the necessity of including several reserves at the last minute. Cork (right half) bolstered a weak defence; without him the score would have been higher."

So the weeks and months passed. If he found classroom life tedious, the sports field provided some excitement and new friendships gave life fresh impetus. Arthur Blake, a dark haired, handsome, athletic boy whose family lived close to the Grammar School, became his close friend. They had much in common and their personalities complimented each other, as a mutual friend later described:

> "They were the very best of friends and always seemed to be together, laughing, joking and generally having great fun. Dick was always self assured, confident and fairly forthright, whilst Arthur was a little shy and reserved and placed great reliance on his friend. Dick led and Arthur happily followed, but there was no sense of superiority because Dick had the most profound respect for his comrade.
> I remember them both being very competitive and house matches between Gray and Herschel (Arthur's team) resounded to their friendly rivalry. If anything, Arthur had the edge in cricket and soccer, whereas Dick excelled at rugby. But as they grew older and stronger, both became excellent sportsmen, with little to choose between them.
> Outside school, the two appeared inseparable and with others from their circle of friends would often be seen around Slough and Burnham having great fun and, as all kids do, getting into scrapes. There was no nastiness in them at all, just a love of life."

If adolescent life held the promise of a future full of hope, then it would prove to be illusionary for those reaching maturity in the 1930's. Events in Europe were moving quickly and the inexorable rise of Nazism in Germany sounded a profound note of warning to those astute enough to hear it.

In Britain, these events seemed far distant and few thought of "that little man with the Charlie Chaplin moustache" as a threat. The atmosphere at home still mirrored attitudes prevalent before the '14/18 War inward looking with a reliance upon the illusion of an Empire and a great navy. Society saw no threat from outside and seemed content with disarmament and appeasement.

For Dick, Arthur and their friends these formative years were ones to be enjoyed. If the Australians were touring, the Boat Race was on, the sun was shining and there was fun to be pursued, so be it they were young and such serious issues could wait. Sadly, though, these distractions also meant that he achieved little at school and records report a struggle to keep up. A decision had to be made about his future and it was decided he should leave when 15. His thoughts are not recorded, but it may have come as a relief, as John Collins recalled:

> "There was something very poignant about a child with great ability struggling to impress in the classroom. In Dick's case development was delayed and at 18 or 19 he would have shone, but at 15 his physical energy and sense of fun got in the way.
> He, like many others, left early with the struggle far from over. Though, strangely, they were, in many ways, better equipped to deal with life outside than those who went to university. Their real strength lay in their personalities and not a text book and to restrict these lively young people was unfair. The outside world could be a frightening place, but these youngsters soon adapted to its ways, free from the rigidness of school life."

In the weeks prior to his departure, he attended a number of interviews and the school diary records that "he was apprenticed to the confectionary trade". There may have been a last minute change of heart, because just after Christmas he started work with Naylor Brothers of Slough. Arthur remained at school for another two years, eventually joining the same company as his friend.

At first, this new world was interesting, but within weeks the routine began to pall. Adjustment, at such a young age to work would be difficult. There were lighter moments, of course, and being amongst a fairly large group of young men was some compensation. Whilst horseplay was frowned upon, few youngsters could resist the temptation to indulge in the occasional prank, usually at the expense of someone else's dignity. Dick, as many of his friends later admitted, was always at the centre of this gentle mischief and his laughter was often heard in the distance, as some dreadful fate befell a work mate.

Free from the constrictions of school his life was gradually changing. He was treated as an adult, more or less, had his own income, but the day's revolved around a small world between Burnham and Naylors. Working hours were fairly long and winter's short, dark evenings gave him little opportunity to enjoy sport. Summer, when it came, held the promise of family holidays and long, balmy evenings. Something to look forward to unrestricted by work. Not that Naylors were bad employers in any way, as Cyril Tuckey, a friend of both Dick and Arthur, relates:

> "Naylors were a very friendly family concern where everyone
> knew everyone else. The offices were a bit spartan, a carpet
> in the centre of each room with stained boards around the
> outside, but comfortable and quite lively for all that.
> I remember Arthur and Dick well. Although great friends they
> were completely different in character, Dickie being the play-
> boy type and Arthur much more solid in character, but they
> complemented each other so well. "

Time passed and with it the desire for fresh challenges grew. Sport
had always played a major role in his life and now he looked to the playing field for competition. Through friends at Naylors he and Arthur
joined Windsor Rugby Club and began playing matches regularly for the
junior teams. Physically he had now developed into a very strong young
man and could stand the rigours of the game. During the late 1930's he
played whenever work allowed and had great success as a wing three-
quarters, whilst Arthur joined the scrum as prop. Ronnie Bennett, a fellow player, later recalled the impact these two made on the team:

> "I knew both of them and their families well. Arthur was my
> best friend and Dick a great one too. I worked in the same
> office as them as well as playing in the same rugby team.
> Thanks to them we had great seasons just before the war and
> broke all records. They provided strength and speed and
> always gave of their best.
> They were marvellous fellows, so full of life. "

Their sporting interests were expanding and included rowing, then
a great attraction to those living along the Thames, west of the city, with
Henley so close. They joined Eton Excelsior Rowing Club in 1936 and
trained throughout the winter for the coming season, where their
efforts were rewarded with selection for the senior eight :

> "Arthur stroked the senior eight and Dick rowed at number
> 7. We won eights at Staines in both years and reached the
> semi-final of the Thames Cup in 1938 there were also wins at
> Molesey and Maidenhead. Dick was a keen, fit and fearless
> sportsman and an oarsman of considerable ability, who with

Arthur Blake formed the foundation on which the senior
crew was formed."

Ronnie Bennett.

"After the races everyone relaxed at the pub and slept in the
club's boathouse at Eton. After a thick night the boatsman,
whose name was Sellars always known as 'Celery' came
round with hot tea and Andrews Liver Salts, which soon
brought us back to life."

Cyril Tuckey.

Throughout 1938 both Dick and Arthur yearned for something to
happen that might break the predictable circle that surrounded their
lives. There had to be something more worthwhile to do and their imag-
inations roamed far and wide in search of likely goals. Their conversations gave voice to these ideas and they buoyed each other up with the
promise of better things to come. Vague, undefined thoughts became
firm plans, though many were discarded as impractical. The Rhodesian
Mounted Police advertised for officers in mid-1938 and applications
were considered, but after much thought this idea dropped from view
to be replaced by something closer to home.

Events in Germany dominated headlines and many now realised that
war could not be avoided. Britain's Armed Forces, starved of cash for 20
years, campaigned for men, money and more equipment. The tide was
turning in their favour and the government grudgingly responded to
these demands. New tanks, guns, ships and aircraft would take time to
design and build, but manpower could be increased fairly quickly. In an
effort to boost numbers, the Royal Navy and Royal Air Force introduced
Short Service Commissions to attract young men who lacked formal
qualifications, but had the right physical and mental attributes.
Advertisements appeared in the press and on hoardings around Britain,
the largest at Waterloo Station, where it dominated the concourse for
many months.

Dick, Arthur and thousands of others heard the call and saw the
opportunity for which they had searched. Yet as their plans took shape,
other possibilities came to mind, inspired by boyhood memories of aircraft and pilots. The late 1920's and 30's were aviation's Golden Age and
its pioneers were revered for their record breaking flights. Amy

Johnson, Lindbergh and many others became household names, whilst Alan Cobham brought flying to many doorsteps with displays and brief flights for those who could afford the fare.

If this was not enough Burnham's Minister, Hugh Reid, himself a former fighter pilot, having flown SE 5As with 41 Squadron in 1918, took great delight in seeing and encouraging Dick and Arthur to follow in his footsteps. So the die was cast and the two friends submitted their applications to the Royal Navy, hoping above all else to join the Fleet Air Arm.

CHAPTER THREE

STILL NO NEWS ?

Although the prospect of war cast a dark cloud in 1938, the year began well for Dick. His skill on the rugby field came to the notice of county selectors and he very proudly wore Berkshire's colours on three occasions. His performances were solid, if unspectacular, and held out promise of greater things in the future. At the same time training with Eton Excelsior took on fresh impetus as the regatta season approached. Henley beckoned and the senior eight looked forward to the challenge with anticipation.

Under the direction of Eton Excelsior's ex-Cambridge Blue, H.O.C. Boret, the crew quickly developed, spurred on by Brian Cork now cox. Although one of the youngest in the team, he kept a tight grip on them, urging greater exertions, when the need arose. These efforts were rewarded with victory at Staines early in the season.

The rowing programme at Henley began in earnest on July 23rd, when Eton Excelsior were drawn against a team from the Civil Service Boat Club in the first round. The weather overnight had been poor and the day seemed to hold little promise of improvement. The wind turned during the day and came strongly from the south west, acting as a brake to the crews as they forged down the Thames, passed Temple Island on towards Lion Meadow. Record times seemed unlikely in these conditions, but the 'eights' were good and some fine racing was expected. Excelsior came home one and a quarter lengths ahead.

A day later they defeated Emmanuel College, Cambridge, by two and a half lengths, then Reading University fell in a time of 7 minutes and 33 seconds. The semi-finals beckoned and Excelsior found themselves up against the London Rowing Club, a dominant force in racing, as Dick and the rest of the crew well knew.

July 26th dawned dry and fine, with banks of cloud well to the west.

The wind was slight and drifted across the river from the north east, adding natural impetus to the hard working crews. Excelsior arrived early on the course and spent the morning preparing themselves. Their heat was the first in the programme and as they toiled on the river they could see the enclosures filling with spectators, colours multiplying with a profusion of blazers and summer dresses. As the sun beat down sounds from the Royal Artillery Band reached the crews; familiar tunes picked out above the hubbub of background noises. As Excelsior readied them selves for the start, the crowd broke out their picnic baskets and looked down the course.

Responding to the Umpire's instruction "Go!", tensed muscles exploded into action. Oars bit deeply into the water, blades lifting, tilting then falling in rhythm, as speed picked up and the boats ploughed through the water. This explosion of effort became suffused with time and the world seemed to stand still as the crews fought for some small advantage. Spectators, many wearing blazers and white trousers, ran along the embankment, cheering and trying to keep pace with the boats. Only those on bicycles managed to keep up. Their shapes caught the sunlight and reflected down onto the river beneath them blurred images frozen in time by photographers lining the far bank.

Both crews fought gallantly to the end, the London Rowing Club team just nudging ahead for victory in the last few lengths.

Although disappointed, thoughts of a holiday in Cornwall raised their spirits. Within days the two friends, with Dick's parents, sister and a mutual friend, Isabelle, travelled to Looe. In a letter to his parents, Arthur described their last holiday before the war:

> Thursday,
> Looe,
> Cornwall.

> Dear Mum,
> We arrived late on saturday tired, but happy. A quick tour of
> the town and we settled into the Jolly Sailor pub, tucked
> down a side street behind a garage and fire station. We spent
> the evening playing skittles and enjoying a few drinks !
> The weather has been grand and the sea warm enough for
> swimming without rigor mortis setting in after a few minutes,
> but the occasional chill breeze definitely freshens you up.
> We spend the days lounging around and the evenings in the

Jolly Sailor, rushing back through East Looe over the bridge to the other side of town as dinner time approaches. We just make it by the skin of our teeth with Mr Cork gently chiding us.
We took two sailing boats around St George's Island out 'into the deep blue sea'. In between trying to handle sails and such like Dick managed to take some photographs. We posed for him trying to look as though we knew what we were doing, but the impression couldn't last because I got caught in the rigging. I wonder how we'll fare in the navy as a pair of sailors. Still we weren't seasick.
Dick and Isabelle seem very keen on each other and he talks incessantly about her when apart. It will be interesting to see what might develop there ! Anyway see you at the weekend, love to all.

Arthur

With their holiday over and winter descending, Dick and Arthur's thoughts turned, once again, to the Navy and the lack of response to their applications. As the weeks passed, so feelings of restlessness increased and the inactivity began to pall. Their dissatisfaction was not helped by friends asking if they had received any word from the Admiralty. The cheeriness of their reply "still no news" began to wear thin and more impatient responses remained close at hand for the less wary. Eventually their patience was rewarded with the arrival of OHMS envelopes directing them to attend medicals, "time and place to be confirmed".

Neither had any qualms about their fitness as they were both very keen sportsmen, as Brian Cork recalled:

"The medicals were very stringent, because they could pick and choose. But they played rugger and rowed a lot and to row at that level you had to be damn fit. Its just not rowing one race, you could have three heats and a final in one afternoon 4 races in the space of three or four hours. On the basis of fitness they got through with flying colours.
One of the tests involved holding their breath for as long as possible. Arthur broke the record, I believe, with about two and a half minutes on the clock and Dick wasn't far behind."

As expected, they passed and attended interviews, a couple of weeks later, at the Admiralty in London.

Dressed in best suits, white shirts, plain ties and highly polished shoes, they sat waiting for their allotted times to arrive, eventually being ushered into a vast oak panelled room by a young Lieutenant. Ahead of them, behind a long, very substantial table, sat a daunting array of senior naval officers, with gazes fixed upon each young volunteer who entered. A gentle hand guided the nervous candidate to a single chair facing these 'interrogators' and a few, seemingly endless, seconds passed before the chairman spoke. "Why do you want to join the Navy? Have you had any sailing experience ? What sports do you play? Why do you want to fly? Have you flown before? How do you know it will suit you?" All safe ground and easy to answer with a little preparation and thought.

Interviews over, both could breath more easily whilst waiting for the Navy to consider their fate. So back to work while the service pondered their suitability and decided how many of these young men would be required by the Fleet Air Arm. Peter Radford, a fellow applicant in 1938, later summed up the tension he felt whilst waiting for the Navy's decision:

> "The interview was bad enough, but the wait that followed
> was even worse. I couldn't summon up any interest in my job
> and snapped back at any imagined slight or disagreement.
> Eventually my father took me to one side and told me to 'wind
> my neck in', but it wasn't as easy as that. I had concentrated all
> my plans for the future on becoming a pilot and the thought
> of failing was almost too much to bear. But fail I did and was
> inconsolable for weeks afterwards, so totally had I set my heart
> on flying.
> In my case it didn't last long, because in September '39 I volun-
> teered for the RAF and saw service on bombers throughout
> the war. With hindsight I suppose I was mad to have taken it
> so seriously, but I was young and desperately wanted some
> excitement. As it turned out I got more than I bargained for."

For Dick and Arthur, the result was worth waiting for, as both received acceptance letters granting them Short Service Commissions. Whatever else the future held, the break with peacetime life was nearly complete. If they had any qualms, these were soon lost in the rush to start a new life, so full of potential.

CHAPTER FOUR

LEARNING TO FLY

A determination to succeed in this new life burnt bright in Dick's heart. Without realising it, the Navy and its traditions were making their mark on his personality and needed little prompting to absorb him totally. His and Arthur's arrival at Greenwich, for basic training, completed this transformation.

The college, regal in looks, situated on the southern bank of the Thames, epitomized everything for which the Royal Navy stood and profoundly affected anyone walking through its gates; none more-so than impressionable young recruits.

Even though the college was a brief train ride away from Burnham, the last few days before departure were full of activity. Kit was acquired, bags packed, and farewells said. The two young men were going through a ritual that marked the end of their civilian life and so the occasion had to be played out to its natural conclusion.

On arrival Dick and Arthur were assigned to Pilots Course Number 6, which was large by pre-war standards, reflecting the number of men applying for Short Service Commissions. Having 'come onboard' on May 2nd, 37 fresh faced young men paraded together the following morning for a pre-course peptalk. If some balked at thoughts of strict discipline and regimentation, they consoled themselves with the thought that it would not last long. Others looked forward with keen anticipation, desperate to make the right impression. In 1940, when his brother was about to begin officer training himself, Dick wrote to him offering words of encouragement, describing his own experiences:

> "There is one thing you must remember and that is when
> you get there work like mad and try and get somewhere near
> the top of your term. It probably doesn't matter much at the

moment as long as you pass, but if you want to stay in the
Army after the war, which you may want to do, its going to
be most important.
You can do it if you want, but for God's sake work like mad
for this its really worth while and you'll enjoy it no end
when its over and above all be as smart as you can in saluting everyone and calling them 'Sir', even if you make a mistake saluting everyone and salute an instructor in the shape
of an RSM or something. I did at first and saluted the door-
man on the gate when I first went to Greenwich. No one
minds and they prefer you to be that way rather than the
other. Sorry to moan like this only I'm awfully keen on you
getting your commission. "

Dick clearly reveals much about his own aims and ambitions in these
few lines and gave vent to plans of his own to remain in the Navy after
the war. In 1940, despite months of fighting, his resolve to stay and
make a career in the service was unshaken. The war had not deflected
him from this course and a maturity of judgement now replaced his
boyish ambitions.

At Greenwich his commission as acting Sub Lieutenant was confirmed. Badges were sewn on pristine uniforms and he and Arthur headed for nearby photographic studios for those stylized portraits that
ended up in albums or framed on shelves in their parents homes. A
moment of pleasure to be savoured, before the serious business of
becoming Naval Officers began.

The days passed quickly with each hour filled with drill, lectures and
sport, whilst evenings revolved around the Wardroom bar, with occasional mess dinners and dances in the Painted Hall. The best of these
was the Mid-Summer Ball, to which Dick invited Isabelle, who was soon
to leave for Canada as an instructor with the League of Health and
Beauty. A civilian lecturer at the college described the Ball in his diary
the next day:

"These occasions are always great fun and quite glamorous.
The Navy dressed up the Hall and anterooms in great style,
with flowers and bunting in profusion, and the girls all
looked gorgeous in their ball gowns. The naval uniforms
completed this colourful scene and the evening went well,
helped by a liberal amount of drink.

> The service band, who had practised so hard for the occasion, did sterling work and kept up a steady flow of good dance music. Though a moments pause was unavoidable when a couple of young trainee naval airmen over did it and threatened to mingle too closely with the musicians. Luckily they kept their balance, but were seen later by the Commander slumped in a darkened corner of the Wardroom."

Isabelle and Dick enjoyed the evening and her dance card reflected some of the fun they had. The Fox Trot seems to have been a favourite and they danced to the tunes "Deep Purple", "Romany" and "Could Be". Arthur and an old friend from Eton Excelsior days, David Harrison, himself an officer with the RAFVR, danced briefly with Isabelle, but for most of the evening she and Dick remained together.

A closeness in their relationship had developed and both regarded this impending separation with some sadness, although it was only for a short time, or so they thought. Being a low priority passenger the start of war meant that she was unable to get a berth on an eastbound ship and so was stranded in Canada.

In late August basic training came to an end and the recruits were posted to No 20. Elementary Flying Training School at Gravesend. In the first few days instructors assessed each mans flying ability; rejecting those who lacked aptitude and grading those that remained as fitted to become pilots or observers. The only environment in which this could be tested was in the air and each candidate was allotted a small number of flying hours to prove their worth. Those with the necessary skills would go solo fairly quickly and move onto more advanced manoeuvres, but some would struggle and need more intensive tuition. They were slower to adapt, yet once the barrier had been breached, they often turned out to be the better pilots.

After kit had been issued, each recruit was assigned to an RAF instructor and, after briefing, sat around the airfield enjoying the hot summer sunshine waiting for these experienced pilots to beckon them towards one of the waiting Tiger Moths. As each aircraft took off trainee pilots, still waiting their turn on the ground, watched assiduously, looking for any weakness and comparing each performance with their own efforts.

With his first flight over, Dick scribbled a letter to David Harrison describing this experience:

"We waited around on the ground for some minutes with the
engine ticking over, waiting a signal to take off. I was only a
passenger with an NCO pilot in charge and so just watched
the proceedings, having been told most clearly not to touch
anything unless told to. I must admit I lost my bearings completely in the air and apart from the Thames could not identify a great deal, even though it was a bright day.
I must admit I expected to see a bit more from a few thousand feet. But even London, which is big enough after all, was
hidden in a heat haze. Still it was a tremendous feeling to be
in the air after so many months.
The instructor let me handle the aircraft after a while, but I
was a bit ham fisted and 'controlled' it abysmally. After a few
minutes things improved and I was able to keep her straight
and level.
Poor old Blakie was a bit green when he got down and
blamed it on the instructor !"

Over the next few days, the instructors carefully taught each pupil
the basic techniques of aircraft handling taxying, take off, turning, spinning and landing. Gradually those who would make pilots developed a
level of sensitivity that allowed them to balance the controls, gauge
height and speed and, most importantly, feel the aircraft. Others found
it more difficult and fell by the wayside; one in three by the end of the
course.

Dick quickly developed a rapport with the Tiger Moth and on August
31st, after 7 hours and 10 minutes of dual instruction with Flight
Sergeant Hymans, was ready to go solo. A great moment in any pilots life
and one fraught with uncertainty for both pupil and instructor:

"After a brief flight, in which we went through all the usual
manoeuvres, all of which I completed to the instructor's
apparent satisfaction, we taxied in and he jumped out leaving
me by myself.
'Take off, one circuit and land. OK and for God's sake don't
do anything stupid!' he shouted over the engine's noise and
that was it. I couldn't decide whether to jump down beside
him or sit tight and give it a go. But for all my inexperience I
felt fairly confident and was convinced that this 'simple'test
was well within my capabilities. So I did all the basic checks,

looked around for other aircraft in the circuit and prepared for take off.

I must admit I felt very alone without that reassuring figure in the aircraft with me and for a moment, all those recently learned lessons were forgotten and I was all 'fingers and thumbs'. But even after only a few hours flying, I had begun to handle the controls instinctively and so trusted these instincts to take charge. I took off into wind after a few moments thought, feeling the aircraft lift gently into the air, adjusting the controls to counter a slight drift to port. I kept my eyes on the horizon, glancing down occasionally to check instruments and my position in relation to the airfield. As a novice, I continued to be surprised at the speed with which I could lose my bearings and so kept an eye on the airfield, determined to keep it well in view at all times.

I followed the instructor's directions to the letter, turned to port after flying straight and level for some minutes, ran parallel to the airfield before turning again to make my approach. All my landings had been a bit bumpy up to then, but by some chance (not to be repeated for sometime) I got my height and speed just right and put her down with scarcely a murmur.

It seemed an event of such great achievement that I expected a round of applause, but my moment of triumph was dashed by my instructor who gave me an unsmiling and barely audible 'Not bad', and then launched into a brief, but pointed account of the things I could have done better. Only later did I hear from a friend that he had paced back and forth during my flight, offering unheard (to me, of course) encouragement, exploding with a relieved 'Good lad', as I put her safely down.

My first solo marked a great turning point in my time with the Navy, because I felt that I had arrived as a pilot and could hold my head up with the rest. I knew that there were many more stages to go through before my Pilot's Badge was awarded, but to have soloed remained a very special land mark. "

Sub Lieutenant (A) B. A. Graves RNVR.

As Dick put his Tiger Moth down successfully after his first solo flight, events further east were taking Europe closer to war. Hitler's forces, massed on Poland's borders, advanced on September 1st, crushing a brave, but hopelessly outclassed enemy. Britain and France, bound by treaty to help, threatened Germany with war and set its leaders a time limit in which to withdraw. Inexorably they were drawn into the conflict and, on the 3rd, war was declared. Pilot training suddenly became more serious and the young men at Gravesend comprehended the reality of their position for the first time.

As the crisis worsened the Air Ministry activated contingency plans and pulled second line units back from the areas threatened by invasion. 20 EFTS, in Kent, was one of these and moved, under emergency orders, to an airfield near Birmingham. Instructors flew the aircraft, whilst bags and equipment went by road. Some trainees went by car, whilst others 'thumbed lifts' in the Tiger Moths' spare seats. Those left behind, took the train up to town, enjoying a night or two in London, before catching an express from Euston to the Midlands.

Within four days everything was ready and flying could begin again. For the rest of the month, into October, Dick flew most days, when the weather allowed. Gradually, tests became more complex and their skills more finely tuned. Cross country navigation, aerobatics, instrument flying, recovery from a spin and forced landings were all practised under Flight Sergeant Hymans' guiding hand. After 55 hours and 30 minutes flying time, the Chief Flying Instructor put Dick through his paces and marked him 'average' as a pilot, stamping and signing his Logbook accordingly.

He enjoyed flying the Tiger Moth, but the gap between this training biplane and operational types was immense. Progression to aircraft with performance that ran closer to those in front line service was imperative. The Harvard, an American built advanced trainer, was the ideal stepping stone and Dick and Arthur transferred, in early November, to No. 1 Flying Training School, based at Netheravon on Salisbury Plain in Wiltshire to learn to fly this machine.

Assigned to 'B' Flight, in the care of Flight Lieutenant Hammond, Dick flew the Harvard, for the first time, on the 8th. He acclimatized well and soon delighted in the greater speed and precision of this stubby nosed, radial engined aircraft.

Accidents had occurred frequently at 20 EFTS, but the Tiger Moth had been fairly forgiving and the casualties light as a result. The Harvard, with its greater power and weight, was more of a handful and on November 11th, they experienced their first fatality. Having accompanied Dick on a series of stalls and powered approaches, Hammond took Sub Lt. Copsy up for a repeat performance. All went well for a few minutes, until the pilot lost control and dived straight into the ground, killing both men instantly. What remained was removed by the crash team, in a 'blood wagon'. A very grisly reminder of the dangers they faced each day, as many later recalled:

> "One day several months into our training we watched a
> Harvard take off, something we had seen so often that it hardly
> registered any more. But the aircraft's engine was stuttering and
> the pilot (one of our course) was struggling to get her airborne,
> so we watched with some concern.
> At about 500 feet the engine gave 'up the ghost' and we looked
> on as B...... broke the cardinal rule and turned back to land,
> rather than carrying straight on. The Harvard lost flying speed,
> went into a spin and crashed without recovering. His death was
> violent, instantaneous and very messy.
> We didn't see his body removed but the following morning a
> 'sympathetic' instructor led us into a hangar, where the
> Harvard's remains lay on the floor, and told each of us to look
> into the cockpit. Even with B......'s body removed the sight
> was gruesome and the instructor's voice reminding us not to
> turn back if the engine fails provided a very salutary backdrop
> to this sad scene. It was a lesson I never forgot."

> *Bernard Graves.*

As 1939 gave way to 1940, Dick's hours on Harvards and, later, Fairy Battles grew rapidly. The programme was intense and allowed little time for a social life in the depths of Wiltshire. Local pubs did a roaring trade when flying was ruled out due to poor weather and each student relied upon post from home for light relief. Dick had been separated from Isabelle for seven months and greatly missed her. Letters from Canada lifted the gloom, but the war, having come between them, now disrupted post across the Atlantic. In a letter to Isabelle, Arthur described his friend's predicament and gives a moving insight into their lives and thoughts at that time:

> "My dear Isabelle,
> All that breaks the silence in this cabin is the scraping of
> pens. My conscience is pricked, for I hear such a lot about
> you and nothing much else from Dickie, and I think that a

scratch from my own humble pen would not come amiss.
I must open with a request. Please endeavour to ensure that
your letters to Dickie arrive at pretty regular intervals, 'cause if
he doesn't hear from you almost every day it seems he's like a
bear with a sore head, and as I have to fly with the blighter
now, it would make life a little more pleasant. You've simply no
idea with pouted lips, frowning brow and whining monotone
he tells me "Havn't had a letter from Canada for so many days",
and I have to set to and convince him that you havn't met
someone else, or that the mail boat or something has been
sunk. When the overdue letters do arrive, sometimes two at a
time, there's no holding him. We almost get sloshed on the
strength of it. I do wish you could be here to see his face light
up, I bet you wish you were too.
Dicky tells me that you're getting a bit browned off with
regard to Canada, and keeps trying to organise things, but this
blasted war seems to complicate things no end. It seems a bit
'ard, but as the prophet says "all good things come to he that
waits", and I feel assured that the time will come when I am
sinking a meditative "younger" with you and Dickie "somewhere in England", preferably the one and only Jolly Sailor Ah
! happy days.
We were just looking through the snaps this very evening, and
I realise that the ones you took are not in my collection, so if
you feel inclined sometime, I should be glad if you could let
have the negatives, so that I may return them to you with
another letter.
You know, it seems so long since I saw you, actually, it is a tidy
period, and I have such a lot to talk about have another drink
with you, brandy this time; that's better!
Now I expect you know almost as well as I do, what we have
been doing, but just in case, I might mention that Dickie and I
are co-pilots when the occasion arises now. Its rather fun.
Today, we went formation flying just Dickie and I in our little
yellow planes. Dick leading and myself formating on him. Did
we beat up the countryside, shades of Henley. I do hope we
can stick together, but that's rather asking a lot, still, here's hoping.
I learnt from Dickie that you had hurt your back. I might suggest a little more soda on these occasions, but trust that it is

absolutely OK now. The jolly old spine can hurt more than somewhat as old Bevan used to say. Hear he's married to Muriel now -
good show.

This marriage business seems to be in the air, do you think you
could bring back some nice Canadian blond for me, there's simply no one left in England now. Do your best you know my taste.
We lead a pretty dull life here, the wretched petrol rationing
complicates movement to a certain extent, but I suppose we
mustn't grumble having just returned from a week's leave, given
entirely on the spur of the moment owing to the bad weather
conditions. It was good seeing the old places and London town
again, but it only brings home how many of the blokes are scattered about the country. Its extraordinary how things can change
in such a short time, all because of some perishing human, or
would it be more correct to say "inhuman". But still, let us not
dwell on the miserable side "Have another brandy - grand!"
Ah, Isabelle, I sigh for the good old days before the war, but life
must go on, and so lots of people say "Everything happens for a
purpose", and it undoubtedly has worked out that Dickie and
yourself should be so far away from each other, just for this little
space of time, until more favourable days. So please don't feel so
miserable about being stuck out there, just think of it as something that's got to be done "part of the drill" shall we say. In any
case I often say to Dick, that he is jolly lucky to have someone
that cares for him as much as you do to write to. I'm sure it's an
added incentive to work hard. So don't forget to look around for
that blond for me, and remember, I'm pretty fussy, but I think I
can leave the matter in your hands.

I'm sending this letter by ship, as Dickie tells me it is just about
as quick, if not quicker than air mail, so I hope it doesn't take too
long and don't forget I collect foreign stamps.

Incidentally, I had a Christmas card from your mother in which
she quoted "Ah! the thrill of seeing your name". Gladdened my
heart to no little extent, so please give her my love next time you
write, and I'm sure Dickie won't mind if I send my love to you.

Your very dear friend,
Arthur"

Dick and Arthur were reaching the end of basic training and in early March, received word that their Pilots Badges had been awarded. With pride, and some show, they sewed bright new wings to their left sleeves, above Sub Lieutenants rings. A few moments satisfaction before moving closer to the serious business of flying operationally and preparing for war.

Across the World, in New Zealand, many young men were also responding to this call to arms and volunteered for service. In Napier, Murray Anderson, an 18 year old, wasted little time in putting his name down and within days, found himself on the Royal New Zealand Navy's Reserve List waiting call up. 'Mudge', as his family called, could not wait to be part of the war and waited impatiently for a letter to arrive that would transform his life.

Mudge's sister Freda, retains the most vivid memories of this gentle, dedicated young man:

> "Mudge was born in 1922 and attended Napier Boys High
> School with his brother Dick, until our father was taken ill.
> Both boys and I had to leave to help run the poultry farm.
> Later Mudge went to work in Woolworths and in his spare
> time belonged to the Royal Port Nicholson Yacht Club. He
> had a small yacht called 'Dauntless' and sailed, whenever he
> could, around Wellington Harbour with two of his friends as
> crew. But he loved sport and took part in anything that was
> going on. When he was only eight years old he won a covet-
> ed swimming cup. Swimming was his great love, though later
> he participated in cycle races as well.
> He was always a cheerful, happy person and ours was a
> devoted family. He was good looking and had a lovely smile,
> that I still remember so well. He had a beautiful baritone
> singing voice and was much in demand at various local gath-
> erings."

In a just world, Mudge Anderson and Dickie Cork would not have met, but fate would link them, irrevocably together in death, four years later.

CHAPTER FIVE

THEIR LORDSHIPS ARE DETACHING YOU

As the course at Netheravon drew to a close, flying exercises became more complex, bringing the young pilots closer to operational standard. The spring days were full of with activity as Harvards and Battles were put through their paces and Salisbury Plain and its many picturesque villages resounded to the sound of engines howling overhead. When darkness fell the noise lessened, but still the busy schedule continued, as pilots grappled with the intricacies of night flying.

When not flying, pilots adjourned to local pubs, passing the time talking 'shop' and discussing the war. On one April evening, as the course drew to a close, Dick and some other Navy pilots, after a few pints, set down, in cartoon form, their impression of each member of the Flight. Some nicknames were recorded, each reflecting some aspect of that person's character, looks or flying skills, whilst others appear in a form registering some personal idiosyncrasy. In the picture Harvards buzz all around a cartoon Netheravon, L/S Chester smokes an oversize pipe, laying down a smokescreen as he goes by, Midshipman Elwell reads 'Flight', whilst 'Half Roll' Shuttleworth, Peter 'don't look now' Nicholls and 'Tiny' Devonald with monster legs outside the fuselage fly by. In the top right hand corner a sign warns 'Watch out boys, Mad Dickie coming', an oblique reference to the close, fast manoeuvres Dickie Cork took joy in performing, to the alarm of the unwary. At the end of the evening, Dick carefully pocketed the cartoon and sent it, with his next letter, to Isabelle in Canada.

So far their flight training had been directed by the RAF. Now, after many months away, these young pilots returned to their parent service, and were posted to HMS Raven on April 21st. They arrived in the midst of a storm leaving clothes and kit badly soaked.

At Raven, on the edge Southampton Airport, Dick and Arthur joined

759 Squadron, and then 760 Squadron, to learn about deck landings and the vagaries of Fleet Air Arm life. Meanwhile the German invasion of Western Europe had started, the Wehrmacht surprising the Allied armies, who fell back in disorder. The British Expeditionary Force (BEF), to the north of the line, found themselves battling across the 'killing grounds' of the Great War, Flanders and the Somme, an irony not lost on most of its Commanders, who had been young men in 1914.

Overhead the RAF were heavily engaged, committing large numbers of bomber and fighter squadrons to the battle. Flying hundreds of missions in a matter of days, with airfields overrun and retreat a daily occurrence, these squadrons were soon reeling under the strain and casualties rose alarmingly. Churchill wished to stand firm beside the French and Belgians, and considered throwing more squadrons into the fray, at the cost of Britain's defence, but in this he faced tough opposition from Hugh Dowding, Fighter Command's C in C.

During the 1930's one idea dominated British planning at some stage London and other major industrial cities would be bombed. To counter this, a network of fighter squadrons and airfields were planned; aided by the development of radar. As more squadrons and pilots crossed the Channel, to make good losses, Dowding saw his force being 'frittered away' on a lost cause. Better, he argued, to withdraw and keep a sufficient number of fighters in Britain to meet the expected attack. Dowding was, of course, correct, but he was preaching a message that ran contrary to the spirit of Allied cooperation. Yet his cautionary words won the day and Churchill deferred his decision to commit more fighters to France, but, as Dowding ruefully observed, Fighter Command had been dealt a telling blow even before the Battle of Britain had begun. Squadrons in France had been decimated and those in Britain stripped to provide reinforcements.

The most pressing need was for pilots, but the flying schools could not cut corners. Half trained men could hardly handle a Spitfire let alone an experienced opponent. So the Air Ministry looked for other ways of boosting numbers. Coastal Command and Bomber Command released some aircrew to Dowding, whilst Czech and Polish pilots, who had escaped the Nazis, were formed into new squadrons. But the number made available by these measures, was pitifully small by comparison to the losses in France. The Fleet Air Arm remained one of the few untapped sources and the Admiralty were canvassed for support. In the event, they agreed to release 50 or so pilots to the RAF. A small number, perhaps, but a highly trained and resolute force that would prove itself in the coming battle.

At Raven, these debates were a world apart from the lives of Dickie Cork and his young comrades, although they were aware of the seriousness of Britain's position from each day's press reports. As the evacuation from Dunkirk reached its hectic conclusion, Arthur wrote to his family describing the impact war was having on their lives:

> "Each day we fly in different sorts of aircraft, practising all sorts of tricks. Dick and I have taken a particular shine to a biplane, the Gladiator, which, as they say is 'real flying'. Some of the boys prefer something a little bit more substantial, but the single-seaters look best to me no one else to worry about.
>
> The news from France looks bad and seems to be getting worse. I wonder whether we will be involved in the near future. One of our prophets of doom thinks we should all be on carriers in a week or two, 'safely' twiddling our thumbs, but I have my doubts. As you can imagine the rumours abound.
>
> One of our non-flying types put his head round my door this evening and quoted 'from a reliable source' the latest bit of gossip, in his words, 'Their Lordships are detaching you to the ...... (can't mention who !)'. I'm not sure how much reliance we can place on this and so I will wait and see what happens, but I expect to be here for some considerable time yet...."

The rumour proved to be correct, as Dick and Arthur soon discovered. After landing his Skua on June 10th, having put it through its paces for photographers from 'Flight' magazine, Cork was handed a posting notice transferring him to No. 7 Operational Training Unit at Harwarden one of several OTUs hastily formed by the Air Ministry to prepare pilots for frontline service.

Their first impressions of the place were not good, as another recruit described when writing home:

> "It's been raining all day and the field is muddy and very churned up. We are living in hastily erected tents all clustered together in groups and they smell of decay an impression enhanced by their colour and general bearing !

Every one is a bit fed up, because it seems that the RAF have dumped the Navy types in the worst possible position, with little thought for our wellbeing. The cry 'its the war' rings a little hollow at present and so we can't wait to reach squadrons where things are bound to better. Our only saving grace is that we are flying the best aircraft in the world by far and will certainly give the enemy a bloody nose with it, when our time comes...."

This view was confirmed by J. A. Kent, a very experienced fighter pilot who also passed through the OTU's hands in June:

"Neither of us (he and one 'Babe' McArthur, another test pilot) were too impressed with the station which was a sea of mud, and the accommodation was under canvas which we both loathed. So it came as a horrible shock when the CO said he felt that there had been a mistake and we must have been posted in as instructors and not pupils. Mac and I talked very fast and managed to convince the CO that we really were pupils. We did not mind the discomfort for a few days if it was to get us onto operations, but the thought of being based there for an indefinite period was too much.
I quite understood the Station Commander's reasoning when I met the instructors as hardly any of them had been on operations and mine had served in a squadron for over three years.
Everything was confused during this period and the training syllabus was very sketchy it consisted mostly of formation flying and dogfighting exercises.... But many of the new boys never had the chance to fire their guns (due to a lack of ammunition) until they went into action for the first time, a sobering thought when one considers the task before them. It was a great tribute to their grit and determination that they carried themselves into the violent battles of the next few months, and inflicted the damage they did, with virtually no instruction or practice in air fighting. "

These OTUs were certainly put together quickly, in the worst possible conditions, but the RAF still managed to equip them with Spitfires and Hurricanes. By early June they had 39 of them on strength. But such was the shortage of pilots in Fighter Command that the course lasted a mere two weeks and effort was concentrated upon familiarisation and not tactics. As a result some left with only 10 hours fighter experience, unprepared for what lay ahead. Cork was luckier than most and managed 23 hours and 15 minutes on Spitfires in eleven days.

Flying a Spitfire for the first time could be an alarming experience :

"As I looked forward from the cockpit the Seafire's (the Navy's version of the Spitfire, on this occasion a Mark 17) nose seemed to stretch away from me into the distance, obliterating my forward view, and I felt constricted on all sides by the smallness of the cockpit. By sticking my head over the side, I could just see down the fuselage. All the warnings imparted by more worldly wise souls, came back to me and I realised the problems I might have on take off and landing. With the engine warmed up, I waved away the ground crew, gunned the engine and took her down the runway, swinging the aircraft from side to side to see where I was going. The noise and vibration were tremendous and for the first time I realised just how powerful this machine was, after the Harvards, Oxfords and Ansons I had flown up to that time. Acceleration on take off surprised me and I kept my head well out of the cockpit trying to see anything ahead. But this was nearly my undoing because the wind whipped my goggles from my face and these whacked me over the back of my head. Without protection for my eyes, I was momentarily blinded and quickly ducked my head back into the cockpit to get my bearings. I was in the air, without fully realising how this had happened, but found myself in a dive, heading for the Wardroom, packed with officers enjoying their gins before lunch. I quickly brought the Seafire's nose up and turned out towards the sea, taking a big breath of air as Crail slipped behind me.
After a shaky start, I relaxed and began to enjoy flying such a marvellous aircraft; its sensitivity, manoeuvrability and power. For half an hour I put her through her paces ending up by putting her into a steep dive towards the Isle of May, winding her up to top speed. Climbing away I performed a couple of rolls and a few loops before settling down to land.
Even though I had coped with my first flight, I found, on

landing, that my legs were like jelly and for the first time in
my life I headed for the bar and downed a double whisky."

Bernard Graves.

'A' Flight and 'B' Flight conducted basic training on Spitfires and
Hurricanes respectively. So there was the natural expectation, amongst
recruits, that they would fly the type flown at Harwarden operationally. Both Dick and Arthur flew Spitfires and hoped for a joint posting.
They even canvassed the instructors for their support, but the pressure
they applied may well have been counter productive, because they
were posted to different squadrons Dick to 242 and Hurricanes, with
two other Navy men, Jimmy Gardner and Pete Patterson, and Arthur to
19, flying Spitfires.
    In a letter to a close friend, Dick bemoaned the vagaries of the post-
ing system:

> "Having spent two weeks in and out of Spitfires, flying over
> the Welsh Hills, the RAF decided to post me to a Hurricane
> Squadron somewhere in East Anglia. You would have thought
> it a simple matter for them to have allowed me a few flights
> on one before sending me off operationally on the type. It
> really makes you wonder if they know what they're doing.
> Meanwhile Blakie is cock-a-hoop because he'll be flying a
> Spitfire, his smile has to be seen to be believed, though like
> the rest of us he is uncertain what to expect, especially if the
> organisation here is anything to go by! They'll probably have
> us flying Tiger Moths dropping bricks on the German hordes
> as they mass on the other side of the Channel before we've
> finished.
> It is a shame that we won't be going together."

    Meanwhile Arthur wrote to his parents, trying to play down the task
he and Dick faced by minimizing the dangers they faced:

> "Well our postings came through and, sadly, we will not be
> together in the same squadron. It will be very strange to be
> apart after all these years. Still I expect our paths will cross
> and we will have a few drinks to toast old times.
> The papers seem so full of stories about the German Air

Force and how strong it is, but our boys will be more than a match for them when they come. So you needn't worry about me, I will be flying a marvellous aircraft in a splendid squadron, so I'm sure I can give a good account of myself in the weeks to come. You needn't worry about me, no matter how hard the battles, my training will stand me in good stead. As Dick says they will be so terrified when they see us coming that they will turn tail and head for home begging a prior engagement."

The need to reassure family and friends, as they fought a battle in the full glare of public scrutiny, was paramount. Little could be hidden and many young men would fight and die as their countrymen looked on, unaware of the torment they suffered, as gunfire and burning petrol invaded their cockpits, mutilating and killing, in seconds or minutes of unremitting horror and pain.

If Dick and Arthur contemplated their chances of survival, both could take comfort from knowing that they were going to good squadrons, led by men of undoubted courage and skill. If there was anything that might increase their chances of survival, then the quality of those around them would certainly feature high.

After his initial disappointment, Dick prepared himself for whatever the future might hold. He knew little about 242 Squadron and grilled instructors at Harwarden for more information. The few meagre details they could add hardly increased his knowledge; it was Canadian by origin and had flown in France during the retreat. Even the Commanding Officer's name was unknown not surprising when even he had been drafted in, without fanfare or ceremony, a week before Cork's arrival. Many men would find themselves in similar positions in the months to come, as Fighter Command tried to make good its losses.

The squadrons returning from the Continent were in a poor state, tired, with few spares or supplies to speak of, most equipment having been lost in the rapid retreat across France. Their aircraft were badly in need of attention and morale was at a very low point. A period of rest and recuperation was desperately needed, but such a luxury, in the face of an enemy determined to carry the battle across the Channel, made this impossible. Everything hung on the speed with which squadrons could be rehabilitated. Quick action and positive leadership were needed, none more so than in 242 Squadron.

From East Anglia they fought over Dunkirk, before transferring to

France to prop up crumbling defences. They arrived too late to be of any real use and spent a torrid few days fighting a rearguard action across Northern France all the way to St Nazaire, where the ground-crew managed to scramble on a boat sailing to Falmouth. As the vessel slipped from its berth, a number of 242's Hurricanes swept overhead giving some protection from enemy aircraft. Two miles out, they dipped their wings and sped off over the Channel to England.

Although populated by Canadians, losses were so great that most replacements came from the RAF, diluting this connection. The hard core that remained resented Fighter Command's attempts to Anglicize them. So Douglas Bader's appointment as Commanding Officer was met with some hostility. They need not have worried, in Bader they had a leader and a man without parallel.

In the six days before Dick's arrival, Bader had begun to rebuild the squadron, charming, coercing or berating any opposition. In his own distinctive way he brought the squadron to readiness and, at the same time, laid to rest the ghosts of unfulfilled ambition and rejection that had pursued him since the crash in which he lost his legs, some eight years earlier. He felt that the years in between could now be erased.

It was at this point that the three Naval Officers, fresh from OTU, joined 242, uncertain and wary in a 'foreign' service. But any lingering doubts they may have had, were swept away by the strength of Bader's personality; in his squadron few would be without purpose or commitment for long. The three newcomers were soon swept along in the wake of such a dominant force, though his approach inevitably upset many less forthright souls.

Something of this influence came through in a letter Dick wrote to David Harrison, as he also waited a posting to a fighter squadron:

> "Well Blakie and I said goodbye to each other in London and made our way to our own squadrons, which as it happens won't be too far apart, so we might meet for a few drinks.
> I had hoped to be flying Spitfires, but the old Hurricane will do, though the rumour is they were outclassed by the 109s in France, but saw off everything else ! I expect we will find out whether this is true over the next few weeks.
> Our new CO is quite a character and one who leads from the front. He lost both legs before the war and against all odds made it back into the RAF. His energy is endless and he drives pilots and groundcrew on relentlessly, extolling greater effort

all the time. He is a'Hendon' specialist and likes to keep us all
tightly together in formation, so there is little room for error.
But it gives us all a marvellous feeling of unity.
Life on the ground is fairly relaxed and the 'boss' takes time
to tutor us in combat techniques. He's seen action himself,
flying Spitfires over Dunkirk, and is a great advocate of the
tactics used in the Great War. He sees little difference
between then and now, except we fly higher and faster.
I hope you're as lucky with your squadron as I have been
with mine. I'm sure, wherever he is, Blakie has found a nice
quiet corner and has settled in nicely, with a glass in one
hand and newspaper in the other."

The pressures of war seemed to allow little time for friendships away
from the squadron. Isabelle was still in Canada, with little prospect of
return and the separation made it difficult for their friendship to flour-
ish. The fondness remained, but loneliness began to erode the relationship and more than the Atlantic began to separate them from each
other. Their letters, whilst loving in tone, now arrived with ever longer
intervals in between. In reality the war had intervened and thrown
their lives on rapidly diverging courses. If Dick found this separation
difficult, he did not reveal his feelings and threw himself into the task
at hand, spending as much time as he could in the air, revelling in the
comradeship of this revitalized squadron.

Meanwhile Bader continued to pursue perfection, determined to
take 242 to the forefront of Fighter Command. But his uncompromising
stance made him few friends outside the squadron, as Jimmy Gardner
later recalled:

"He wasn't the most diplomatic of people. He had very
strong opinions and stuck to these no matter who he was
talking to, a senior officer or otherwise. What he said had to
go and that was that. There wasn't any point in arguing with
him, he had made a statement and that was it. I found it difficult in that way and wished he had been more relaxed and
reasonable, because I'm sure he could have achieved just as
much, if not more that way. But it was in his character and
there would be no changing him.
Yet in many ways he was just what the squadron needed,
especially with the mix of nationalities we had. His main task

had been to get the Canadians under control, because they hadn't sorted out their commitments and were a bit wild. They were pretty typical of their countrymen who hadn't been to Europe before. They were quite fiery and spent their spare time playing poker and gambling or going on leave into Norwich, whenever they had the chance. But they were good pilots who responded well to Bader's direct approach and ultimately gave him their total respect. In the end, I suspect, they would have followed him anywhere. As the weeks passed, Dick and I became very close friends. We were similar in age and had a lot in common, not least of all being 'dark blue boys' in the squadron. He was a very fine type, large in stature and very handsome, with an unerring ability to get on with everybody, almost the complete opposite to Bader, yet the two of them got on famously."

During their first week with 242, the three 'dark blue boys' flew many hours on Hurricanes, singly and in groups. Occasionally Bader rehearsed squadron manoeuvres - tight formation flying, aircraft clustered together in groups of three, with the whole unit gathered in the smallest possible area. This proved a nailbiting experience, requiring complete concentration, to avoid collision. However, it created a cohesion and confidence throughout the squadron, though, as a tactic, it would prove something of a liability as the coming battle would reveal.

On July 6th, disaster nearly struck. Coming into land, after a 50 minute practise flight, Dick overshot the airfield, landed heavily, writing off his aircraft. Embarrassed more than hurt he expected a 'rocket' from Bader, but received only a perfunctory 'look out next time, we can't afford to lose you'. Such an attitude spoke of someone who had seen the same thing happen many times before and had committed the 'sin himself.' Bader realised that castigation could only breed resentment. It was a lesson that Cork would not forget. An expensive aircraft had been destroyed, but an even more valuable pilot had been saved. As it was, he had jarred his back and received a number of cuts and bruises, sufficient to keep him on the ground until the 8th. But the pace was hotting up elsewhere and within days the Luftwaffe met the RAF head on, in the first phase of the Battle of Britain. 242 were ready, but to Bader's annoyance they were kept in reserve guarding the Midlands. It would be sometime before they would see action.

CHAPTER SIX

"AND THE SKY WAS FULL OF BLACK CROSSES"
(JULY - AUGUST 1940)

As Cork recovered from his injuries, the Luftwaffe's attacks grew more intense. Unsure of the enemy's strength they tried to entice the RAF's fighters into the air to test their response and their mettle. But the defences would not be drawn, preferring to conserve their strength for the major onslaught that lay ahead. As these small battles raged over the coastal areas, British convoys still took passage through the Channel, avoiding the longer, safer voyage northwards along the west coast. To the Germans, these ships were an inviting target and were frequently attacked. Fighter Command countered with patrols over the coast during daylight hours.

On July 10th 242 Squadron flew their first convoy patrols. Three Hurricanes being sent out until relieved by another Flight. Dick saw nothing on his first patrol, but later that morning Jimmy Gardner had more luck:

> "We ('Green' Flight) went into the cloud at 2,000ft and at about 20,000ft we were still flying wingtip to wingtip and it was getting very bumpy. In the end I felt I just had to break-away, which I did, otherwise I might have run into the other aircraft. I then circled my way down to the ground looking for a gap in the cloud. To be frank I had never attempted blind flying in my life, but that's the way it was in war, you just got on with it.
>
> I came out over a small convoy of freighters going up the East Coast and there was a Heinkel 111 bombing them, its greenish grey camouflage showing up against the sea and clouds. I was able to latch onto him as he quickly dived back for the Dutch Coast having spotted me. I must admit I had to

go full throttle and then break the emergency boost to get
more power and catch him up. I fired when in range and he
went down halfway between the English and Dutch Coasts. I
suddenly found my windscreen covered in oil and thought
that with all that extra power I had damaged my engine. I
was pretty perturbed so headed back home very quickly. But
I realised, as I turned west, that it was oil from the Heinkel I
had been shooting at and not mine.
Either way it meant that I didn't spend enough time on the
scene and didn't see the Germans get into their dinghy.
After all the excitement I was rather disorientated. I roughly
knew the way I had been going, but in concentrating on the
aircraft ahead I hadn't kept a very accurate course. But I
knew if I headed back northwest, England would be there
somewhere…."

Gardner made it home safely and received his comrades' congratula-
tions. The Heinkel's crew were not so lucky and were posted missing
by their unit, III/KG 53. Only later would they learn that all four were
dead.

In a letter to Arthur, in late July, Dick described these early patrols and
day to day life in the squadron. Both 242 and 19 Squadrons remained
on the periphery of the battle and both men balked at their lack of
involvement:

"Well here we are enjoying the good weather in sunny
Norfolk! The company is good and the beer not too bad, if it
wasn't for the occasional flight, we might be on holiday. Not
seriously, of course. We spend the days hanging around dispersal waiting for a convoy to pass or in the vain hope of a
'scramble' to help the lads 'down south'. Pretty much the
same as you.
We hear reports on the radio of activity elsewhere and begin
to wonder why we are kept back here. I expect Fighter
Command know what they are doing, but the situation seems
so desperate that you would think every aircraft would be
needed by now. Anyway 'the boss', who is very hot on this
issue, keeps up a steady barrage on those he feels might be
able to get us involved.
Convoy patrols are becoming a bit tedious. We seem to spend

most of our time weaving back and forth over the ships, occasionally chasing shadows picked up by radar and finding nothing when we get there. But Jimmy Gardner (who sends his regards by the way) managed to catch one a few days ago and despatched it in fine style. Several others have repeated this performance since then, but no luck for me yet.

I heard the other day that two lads from No 6 Course have been killed on bombers. I'm still trying to find out who they were, perhaps you have heard ?

Its funny to think that this time last year we were still at Greenwich, hadn't seen an aircraft and weren't even sure who to salute. How things have changed, but everything has been altered so much by the war. I had a couple of days leave and was surprised to find so few of the old crowd at home, most now in uniform, dispersed around the countryside. I went to see your mum and dad, finding them in good spirits, but anxious about you. There wasn't much I could say to reassure them, because they obviously realise the dangers we face, read all the press reports and see how things are going for themselves, but I did my best.

I still hear from Isabelle though the post across the Atlantic is still very erratic. She sounds really fed up and still sees little chance of making it home in the near future. I do miss her...."

After five weeks together, new and old pilots had grown accustomed to each other. Dick had, in particular, made an impression upon the Canadians, who had tried to shock the more 'straight laced' British officers, as Stan Turner recalled:

"I think they found our ways a little odd at first, but we were a lively bunch and wanted to keep our Canadian connections. Dick treated us like wayward younger brothers, smiling benignly when the horseplay started. At first this led to much ragging, which he took in great spirit, but as we got to know him, realised a tremendous sense of fun lurked behind a cool exterior. Once he understood that he didn't have to be on his best behaviour all the time, things livened up considerably, though he never got the hang of poker, and always knew where to draw the line when things got out of hand.

As a pilot, he was good and would stay fastened to your wingtip or tail for hours on end if necessary. Even though we had experienced combat in France and knew what we were doing, Dick managed to give us all a hard time in mock dog-fights, so his success later on didn't come as any surprise. If he had remained in the RAF, rather than return to the Navy, he would have been one of our top scorers. He had the killer instinct.

During those long hot August days, when we seemed to spend a lot of time sitting around waiting for something to happen, we'd often talk about the war. Most seemed happy to survive and didn't give a great deal of thought to the future, just in case they didn't make it. Dick was certain he'd survive and seemed to carry an air of invulnerability around with him to prove the point. This was usually an act, but with him looked quite genuine. We tried to make him see the error of his ways he seemed unaffected by our 'advice'.

All in all a good man to have around. "

Throughout July and August 12 Group's Squadrons had few oppor-tunities to participate in the battle, though there were occasional moments of excitement. On August 19th, enemy aircraft attacked Coltishall and a stick of bombs exploded demolishing a hangar, killing two men. Bader led Cork and seven other Hurricanes in pursuit, but could not catch the low flying bombers, which took advantage of cloud cover to make good their escape.

Low cloud again covered Coltishall and heavy rain fell on the 20th. Six Hurricanes were scrambled and ordered to patrol their base in case the Germans took advantage of conditions to strike the airfield again. Bader was not at dispersals when the six took off, but arrived shortly afterwards, angry that they had been sent up in such appalling condi-tions. Minutes later Midshipman Patterson's aircraft was seen to dive vertically into the sea, a victim, it would seem of the weather, rather than enemy action. When the section landed and the loss was reported, Bader vented his anger on the controllers for sending out his pilots in impossible weather conditions.

Dickie Cork was absent on leave in London, when this tragedy occurred, but as one friendship came to an end, another was about to be renewed. Confined to the periphery of the battle, 12 Group's Commander, Air Vice Marshal Leigh Mallory, laid down plans that would allow his squadrons to support 11 Group if the need arose. At Coltishall, his fighters would be too far north, but at Duxford, and its satellite field, Fowlmere, they would be close enough to reinforce the hard pressed southern squadrons.

Dick flew to Duxford and Fowlmere on the August 27th to familiarize himself with these airfields and spent a few hours with Arthur Blake, whom he had not since July. 19 Squadron had been based at Fowlmere for some days and had already seen action. On the 25th they had been scrambled with 66 and 310 Squadrons. Out over the Thames Estuary they fell upon a large force of bombers and fighters. Arthur, tucked in behind another Spitfire and waded into the attack. Minutes later he emerged unscathed, but shaken by the violence of his first combat, as he later reported in a letter to David Harrison, himself now learning to fly Hurricanes at No. 6 Operational Training Unit:

> "So much for the peaceful life. Just when I was just beginning to think I would see the war through without firing a shot in anger, all hell broke loose and I found myself in the thick of things.
> For weeks we have been practising and I thought myself an expert, but the real thing has shown me to be a beginner still. Oh well! at least I lived to tell the tale, though I'm still not sure how I managed to avoid being hit. The enemy seemed to be everywhere and all I could do was twist and turn, firing at anything that passed. Believe it or not I didn't use my sights I'd forgotten to switch them on in the excitement! I don't think I did much damage and probably got in the way of others, so not an auspicious start. Anyhow one of our Sergeants got two MEs, so not all was lost.
> Dick flew in yesterday and ambled over to dispersal where we sat and chatted for some time. It was good to see him again and hear all the news. Like me he seems to have led a quiet life up to now and is waiting 'patiently' for something to happen. The way things are going we should be in the thick of things before long.... "

August 30th dawned with clear skies and the promise of hot weather. As sleepy eyed commuters made their way to work from the Home Counties through suburbs still untouched by war, squadrons came to readiness. Aircraft, having spent the night in mechanics' hands, undergoing repair, were marshalled into position,with guns loaded and tanks full. Those pilots who could face food sat over their breakfasts before making their way to dispersal; few lingered, anxious to be ready before the first plots of the day appeared on radar and interceptions were ordered.

At Coltishall the morning papers were scanned for indications of activity in their area. Once again headlines proclaimed great success amongst the southern squadrons, but stories widely circulated within the RAF, suggested a grimmer picture and it seemed inevitable that reinforcements from 12 Group would soon be required.

Shortly before dawn, servants roused pilots and as they shaved and dressed, Bing Crosby's voice drifted down from Willie McKnight's room as he played records from his treasured collection.

The airfield was heavy with dew and condensation soon covered the pilots shoes as they checked their aircraft, each indistinguishable in camouflage from the other, except for code letters painted in white along each fuselage. L and E were common to all, but they were followed by an individual letter. Bader flew 'D', 'A' McNight, 'L' Cork and so on. But to personalize their aircraft still further, each pilot had some emblem painted on the cowling or below the cockpits of each aircraft. A boot kicking Hitler, the Grim Reaper, flags spelling out 'England Expects' (Jimmy Gardner), whilst Dickie Cork had a Naval crown.

The flight to Duxford passed without mishap, Douglas Bader offering encouragement over the R/T as Coltishall fell away beneath them. Skirting London's defensive ring of silver grey balloons, he took his squadron in a wide sweep towards their rallying point, hoping that they might see some action on the way. But the flight passed quietly and each Hurricane landed safely, mechanics swarming over the visiting aircraft, refuelling and making them ready for action.

As the day wore on, enemy raids stayed well to the east, hitting ships sheltering in the Thames Estuary and, then, sector airfields in Kent and Surrey. 11 Group committed 16 squadrons to counter these attacks, whilst 12 Group attempted to protect their airfields; a pattern repeated in the afternoon as two more massed attacks developed. Airfields were again the target and Fighter Command soon realised that 11 Group's squadron would need reinforcement;many of its aircraft being on the ground, refuelling and rearming as the second wave approached.

242 were amongst the squadrons scrambled and at 16.26 hrs were ordered to patrol over North Weald. Ignoring instructions from the controllers, Bader turned his squadron away from the impending attack into

the west so that they might gain height and come in with the sun behind them. A risky business in which a delay might let the Germans press home their attack unchallenged. 242 were in luck and completed their manoeuvre in time to strike.

As they climbed above incoming raids, the sun glinted on the wings of distant, unidentified aircraft, partially hidden in a heat haze. Blue Section were ordered by Bader to investigate and quickly sped of to intercept these anonymous shadows, leaving only eleven Hurricanes to tackle anything that might turn up.

Over the R/T Flying Officer Christie (Green 1) reported a "vast number of twin-engined enemy aircraft heading east" and all eyes looked down trying to spot the threat. The formation, stepped up from 10 to 20,000 feet, came on in groups of 70 to 80, moving faster now, having dropped their bombs on targets in Surrey, untroubled by the RAF.

Bader snapped out instructions, ordering one section to tackle the top most group, taking the remainder down with him, line astern, to break up the main body of enemy aircraft. The ME 110s and HE 111s broke away from the downward rushing Hurricanes. Bader hacked down two 110s, one disintegrating, the other bursting into flames. McKnight destroyed three, whilst the remainder accounted for another seven, before the skies suddenly cleared and no more targets remained.

In combat instinct and training kept the lucky ones alive. Those too slow to react, became casualties, their agonies marked by smoke chains spiralling downwards. Only Douglas Bader seemed more aware than most of the battle's course and his account reflects this wider perspective:

> "After diving into the attack and breaking up their formation
> the ME 110s seemed only capable of climbing turns to a nearly
> stalled position then trying to get on our tails. It didn't work
> and we quickly began to hack them down.
> Apart from those I accounted for, one pilot sent a Hun
> bomber crashing into a greenhouse. Another went headlong
> into a field full of derelict cars, turned over and caught fire.
> One of my chaps sent a twin-engined job down into the
> reservoir near Enfield and another went down amongst hous-
> es nearby. A 'dark blue boy' from the squadron (Cork) claimed
> one of these and then watched a second victim go down
> with its engine flat out, crash into a field and disintegrate into
> tiny pieces.

We hadn't shot them all down, of course they didn't hang
around long enough for that, but apart from the twelve
destroyed there were many others badly shot up who probably never got home. Like the one seen staggering out over
Southend with one engine out and the other smoking.
Later that evening LeighMallory came through by phone to
congratulate us on our success and I pressed home the point
that with more aircraft we could have done substantially
more damage. It was a strategy close to his heart and that
day's work seemed to support his view that 12 Group should
operate with larger formations. Within days this idea became
reality. "

Dick emerged unscathed from his first combat and two days later
described the encounter to David Harrison:

"The suddenness and speed of the fight took me by surprise
and it was all I could do to keep up with my Flight
Commander. As we came down, the sky seemed full of black
crosses and whichever way we turned Nazi bombers seemed
to block our way, but we hit them hard and sent them skid-
ding in all directions.
Their 'fighter escort' was pretty useless and seemed more
concerned with protecting themselves than the poor old
bombers, who had to fend for themselves. In the ensuing
fight we managed to destroy 12, but most of this action and
much of my own contribution remains a blur, though at night
the details become much clearer.... "

242's pilots returned to Duxford to find the whole squadron intact.
Yet celebrations were muted as they trooped towards squadron offices
to recount and record their experiences. To an outsider, the situation
seemed unreal, as each pilot played down the impact of combat. Some
appeared nonchalant, whilst others smoked. A reporter present that day
recalled this image:

"Their air seemed so casual and supper appeared to hold
greater importance for them than the battle in which they
had so recently fought. One young Canadian (Willie McNight)
whistled quietly as he sat beside the Intelligence Officer com-

pleting the form, looking for all the world like a high school boy doing his homework. A Navy pilot (Dickie Cork) sat quietly to one side, head back, eyes shut with the afternoon sun warming his face. One was left to marvel at the resilience of these men and their willingness to fight and die with such little fuss."

Dick sat for sometime over his report looking for some basic thread to describe the patrol and eventually settled upon a simplistic narrative:

"Whilst flying sections line astern sighted enemy at 1705 approx. Attacked ME 110 in company with several other aircraft and saw machine going down. Broke away left and saw another ME 110 flying east, attacked beam attack, left engine in flames enemy did a stall turn to left and dived to ground. Returned to scene of combat at 1,000 feet, saw first enemy 'plane in field on fire. Enemy machines painted dark green stood out very clearly. Encountered fire from rear gunner on first machine, which ceased quickly. EA made no evasive tactics. Weather hazy. Took off at 1626, landed 1730."

Bland words to describe a violent battle, but understatement had a certain dignity. Longer term the effects of combat could not be disguised so easily:

" I saw Dick the other day and we chatted for sometime he sends his best wishes. He is quite the 'old hand' now having been with for ten weeks. They seem to have been rather busy lately and despite the twinkle in his eye looks a good deal older and tired. He makes light of it, but the boys are obviously earning their pay the hard way and look for some respite...."

CHAPTER SEVEN

"LONDON'S BURNING"

August 31st was another busy day for the Luftwaffe. Raids started at 8 am, with waves of bombers coming in over Kent and the Thames Estuary heading for North Weald, Duxford and Debden. 11 Group were into the air quickly breaking up most of these early attacks.

The assault continued into the afternoon with Eastchurch, Detling, Biggin Hill, Croydon, Hornchurch and Kenley all being bombed. Even though there was plenty happening, 242 saw no action during four patrols. Even so, the RAF lost 39 fighters, with 14 pilots killed, whilst destroying 41 German aircraft. Radar plots had been strong and accurate, but a heat haze allowed many raids to progress unhindered.

Arriving back at Coltishall that evening, Duxford, Dick found a number of letters waiting and quickly scribbled brief replies before sitting down to dinner in the Mess. To a Navy friend he wrote:

> "Well here I am still in the land of the living, though I hear old Pudney and Kestin have gone, whilst we lost Pete Patterson two weeks ago over the sea. Our numbers are beginning to thin out, but you'll be pleased to read that Blakie is still going strong, though wreaking havoc upon his squadron's Mess Account, so I'm told. He doesn't change !
> We are kept fully occupied here and fly south each day to be nearer the action. Yet for every interception we fly it seems we undertake a great many fruitless patrols. It gets very tiring and unsettles the stomach no end, but we have been luckier than most and have kept a solid roof over our heads. No canvas for me so far. Apart from one raid we have been left alone by the Hun, lets hope our luck lasts, though the signs are not good .... "

242 had now settled into a routine, nights at Coltishall and days at Duxford. Yet, despite the critical position in which they found themselves, a routine of rest days and leave still existed, as Jimmy Gardner recalled:

> "The aim was to get a maximum of 12 aircraft available each day, although at any one time we had 20 to 22 on strength and replacements were readily available. Pilots were more of a problem, with accidents and combat taking an increasing toll of numbers, but we were luckier than most and lost only a few pilots throughout the battle.
> If your aircraft was shot up and you were okay, the mechanics just pulled out another Hurricane and off you went again. You might have flown one aircraft more than others and so it became a sort of personal machine, but battle damage and routine servicing would ground it and so you went on to the next one in line.
> Even at the height of battle you would have a regular day off, unless casualties were very heavy, so whilst your comrades were doing battle over London you might be on leave, enjoying yourself. This might seem a little peculiar, but a short break from the intensity of war flying was essential. Though some, particularly Bader, would have flown on every patrol if they could.
> I had my Bugatti and my Matchless motor cycle with me at Coltishall and took them out whenever I could, enjoying the peace and quiet."

19 Squadron was the only unit from 12 Group to make contact with the enemy on the 31st. Flights were scrambled to patrol the skies over Duxford and Debden. They achieved some success, but paid a high price in return. Pilot Officer Aeberhardt was killed when his Spitfire crash landed at Fowlmere, turned over and caught fire. Flying Officer Coward baled out, his leg virtually severed by a cannon shell from an attacking ME 109, and Flying Officer Brinsden had his aircraft shot from under him by enemy fire, parachuting down to safety near Saffron Walden.

Arthur Blake did not fly on these patrols, but watched in horror as Ray Aeberhardt made his approach to land at Fowlmere, then die in agony. Horror and anger at the loss of a comrade were reflected in a letter he wrote a day later to his eldest brother:

"Things are very tense at the moment and our losses continue to mount. The papers seem to be full of 'glorious deeds'
and little about the boys who get shot up or burnt. I suppose
the readers want handsome heroes, not wounded men or
coffins. I don't think a little reality would be out of place,
though I realise how much this knowledge might hurt relatives of those who are dying or facing death. I wouldn't like
Mum and Dad to know how bad things can get, so perhaps it
is best to keep it all quiet until the worst happens and a
telegram arrives.
We were bombed here yesterday and I spent my time sitting
in a trench keeping my head well down. It really does make
you want to hit back and give them a taste of their own med-
icine, but it's a case of catching the blighters. "

Two days later Arthur found himself in a position to do the enemy
some damage. Squadron Leader Pinkham led 8 Spitfires on a standing
patrol over Debden. Listening to the constant stream of messages coming over the R/T, it became apparent that bombers were attacking
North Weald. They were vectored south to intercept them, arriving as
the enemy finished their attack and turned for home. The Spitfires faced
heavy odds, but emerged with some successes, including Blake.

As Yellow 1, with Pilot Officer Cunningham as Yellow 2, Blake
attacked an ME 110 from above on the port quarter. The ME swerved
violently away into a steep dive, with smoke coming from its wing and
engine. Two more ME's appeared and attacked Blakes's aircraft. Gun
trouble forced him to break off after firing only 33 rounds. Meanwhile
Yellow 2's guns also jammed and together they broke away from the
engagement. Arthur claimed an ME 'probably destroyed', though he
made light of this success.

After 2 months in the squadron he had become a well known figure,
aided by his Naval uniform. His nicknames, 'Admiral' and 'Sailor', reflected this uniqueness and the high regard in which he was held:

"Arthur was not a 'Gung Ho' press on fighter boy beloved by
the press of the time. He was quietly spoken, justifiably self
confident and amiable with all ranks in the Squadron without
being patronising. He was a brave and capable pilot."

Frank Brinsden, 19 Squadron.

Others recalled a pleasant, gentle man who seemed, by nature, incapable of an aggressive act. But in the air he fought tenaciously, even recklessly, as Bernard Jennings recalled:

> "Suddenly there were no Germans in the sky, when there'd been a lot of them a minute before, we knew they usually flew down the Thames Estuary on their way home. So when this happened one time, I belted down after them. I caught up with a 110 with a Spitfire on its tail. I flew alongside the Spitfire and saw the pilot was Sailor Blake.
> I said to him, 'What are you doing?' He said 'I'm going to ram that so and so!' I said 'Don't be a fool. We're only about three hundred feet over the sea. You'll go straight into the drink.
> 'He said his cannons were jammed and he wasn't going to let the German get away. I told him I had one cannon still working and to move over so I could take him. He said, 'Only if you give me a half'. I said all right and he moved over to my port side. I said, 'Get over to my starboard side. I've only got my port cannon working and as soon as it fires, I'm going to swing into you.' So he moved there.
> I aimed at the German's wing tip, pressed the button, knocked the top off his starboard engine, and then my remaining cannon jammed too. So Sailor and I flew up alongside the 110. The German pilot was just sitting there, absolutely rigid, as though he was drugged, not looking at either of us. The strange thing was he had no tail gunner, otherwise we never could have done that. Sailor said, 'I'm going to ram him.' I said, 'All right, if that's what you want to do. Cheerio. I'm off back.' I landed at base and five minutes later, in comes Sailor. Of course, he didn't ram the German. "

After his success on August 30th, the days that followed seemed something of an anti-climax for Cork, the squadron spending many fruitless hours patrolling over London and East Anglia. Raids continued elsewhere in the strong September sun, although a thick haze often covered most of southern England and the Midlands.

For staff on duty in Fighter Command's Operation Rooms, the 7th began normally. Attacks against sector airfields were expected, but as the day progressed little developed to trouble the defenders.

All this changed at 4 o'clock when radar began to pick up the trace of a large enemy force forming up over Calais, ready to strike at the airfields again. But this time the 300 bombers, escorted by 600 fighters, made for London in two waves. One group flew up the Thames Estuary, whilst the second flew in a wide circle south of London then headed back towards the city's East End.

Defences were caught 'on the hop' and many bombers managed to drop their loads without challenge. 11 Group tried to divert squadrons away from airfield protection, but only small numbers reached the raiders and were swiftly despatched by swarms of German fighters. The attacking force bombed docks, oil tanks, factories and surrounding areas with great accuracy, wreaking death and destruction on an unwary civilian population. Silvertown was turned into an inferno, burning brightly in the early evening sky, acting as a beacon, as far back as the coast, for fresh waves of bombers.

At Duxford, three squadrons, 242, 19 and 310, had been at readiness since dawn, waiting, with some impatience for something to happen. At 4.55, when the raiders had already crossed the coast, the Wing was scrambled and ordered to patrol North Weald at 10,000ft. With height in combat a necessity, Bader took the formation up to 15,000 feet, but noticed in the distance shells bursting at 20,000 feet betraying the presence of enemy aircraft. He immediately gave a sighting report and obtained ground controllers permission to attack.

The odds were not in their favour. They lacked height and the element of surprise, whilst the enemy were protected by a vast number of fighters stepped up from 20,000 to 30,000 feet. All they could do was open throttles and climb, desperately gaining height before the enemy fell upon them. As they climbed, the formation quickly lost its shape and was strung out in a long line trailing back over the sky towards North Weald.

Bader (RED 1), with Cork (Red 2) as his wingman, pressed ahead and reached the enemy with a clear lead over the rest of 242. Bader described the ensuing combat in fairly unemotional terms later that day:

"Turned left to cut off enemy and arrived on the beam slightly in front with Red 2 only. Gave a short beam squirt at about 100 yards at EA who were flying in sections of 3, line astern in a large rectangle. Turned with Red 2 (who fired with me) and sat under tails of back section at about 100 yards, pulling up the nose and giving short squirts at the middle back aeroplane. This started smoking preparatory to catching fire (an ME 110), but before I could see the result, I noticed in the mirror a yellow nosed ME 109 on my tail slightly above, and as I turned there was a big bang in the cockpit from an exploding (?) bullet, which came in through the right hand side of the fuselage, touched the map case, knocked the corner off the undercarriage selector quadrant and finished up against the petrol priming pump.

Having executed a quick steep diving turn, I found an ME 110 alone just below me. I attacked this from straight and astern and he went into steepish straight dive finishing up in flames in a field just north of a railway line west of Wickford, due north of Thameshaven. P/O Turner confirms the ME 110 which I attacked first, as diving down in flames from the back of the bomber formation."

As Bader and Cork cut through the enemy formation, gunfire converged on them from all directions. Neither turned away even though their Hurricanes were taking many hits. Cork remained glued to Bader's wing tip, then broke away as targets presented themselves:

"I pulled away slightly to the right of my section and fired at a DO 215 on the tail end of their formation a beam attack and the port engine burst into flames after two short bursts and crashed vertically.

Was attacked from the rear by enemy fighter and was hit in the starboard mainplane, so broke away and downwards, nearly colliding with an ME 110. Gave another short burst before pulling away to avoid collision and saw front of cabin break up and machine go into a vertical dive. Two of the crew baled out. Was following enemy machine down, which was stalling and then diving again, when I was attacked from rear by ME 109. One shot from enemy aircraft came through the side of the hood, hit the bottom of the reflector sight and then the bullet proof windscreen. I received a certain number of glass splinters in my eyes from the windscreen. As I could not see very well broke away downwards with a half roll and lost enemy machine.

Before attacking enemy and whilst climbing to meet them received a lot of cross fire from enemy bombers which kept in

"Dick aged 18 months' as the Great War comes to an end - untroubled by the cataclysmic events happening around him (B. Cork).

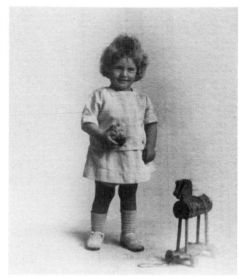

With war a distant memory and the Great Depression receding, Dick arrived at Grammar school - academically not an inspiring period, but a time when his love of sport found an outlet (B. Cork).

1938 - Eton Excelsior at Henley - Arthur Blake as 'stroke' and Dick at No 2 . With war so close the crew would not have a chance to repeat their sucess (B. Cork).

Cornwall 1938 - the last full summer of peace - Arthur, Isabelle and Dick at Looe (I. Nice).

RNC Greenwich - Pilots Course No 6 line up for a group photo - a traditional part of courses passing through the college (Dick sixth from right, front row standing, Arthur on his right) (Authors collection).

Gravesend 1939 - Dick prepares for flight in a Tiger Moth - he had soloed in this machine a few days earlier (Authors collection).

Netheravon - 1939. As training progressed the fledgling pilots moved on to Fairey Battles - one step nearer operational flying (B. Cork).

Harwarden 1940. With the RAF in great need of more pilots, the Navy 'lent' 50 or so men to Fighter Command in June. A brief period at Harwarden followed, giving each man some experience flying Spitfires and Hurricanes before an operational posting (Authors collection).

Navy pilots at Harwarden with their RAF instructors. Back row (L to R) - Jeram, Blake, Cork, Patterson, Paul. Front row (L to R) - Unknown, Bramah, Gardner, unknown. (B. Cork).

Dick and Arthur wait around at Harwarden between flights (B. Cork).

242 Squadron - Summer 1940

Douglas **Bader** and some of his pilots chat between operations - Cork, in his naval overalls, stands out amongst the lighter blue RAF uniforms (Authors collection).

Three of 242's Hurricanes on patrol - a photo taken by B. Cork.

Cork's Hurricane (P 2831, LE-K) with a hand painted naval crown denoting its pilot's origins.

Jimmy Gardner's Hurricane. Like Cork he kept the naval tie open with flags that spelt out Nelson's famous signal before Trafalgar - "England Expects." (Authors collection).

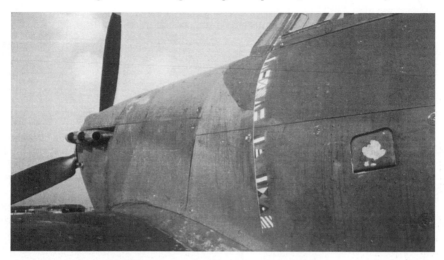

Above - Bader kept up a steady flow of advice to his men, in the air and on the ground. Below - Cork scribbled on the back of this photo - "Me just off on patrol - October 1940."

During the Battle of Britain Dick lost his two closest friends. In August, with 238 Squadron, David Harrison (below left) was killed when his Hurricane crashed into the sea and on 29th October Arthur Blake (bottom) was shot down by German Fighters over Essex. His grave carries the simple, but moving inscription "In loving memory of our precious boy." (Authors collection).

With the battle drawing to a close and training schools making good the losses, Fighter Command released its Navy pilots and in November Cork and Gardner left 242 Squadron. But there was no immediate return to the Fleet Air Arm. Instead they were posted to Coastal Command (252 Squadron) (B. Cork).

These two photographs record their departure from Duxford. Cork's DFC ribbon is clearly visible. Within weeks, at the Admiralty's insistence, it had been replaced by the DSC (Authors collection).

After the rigours of the Battle of Britain a few months with 252 Squadron should have been restful. But Cork found the "inactivity" oppressive and longed for a return to fighters. Above - Cork at the controls of one of 252's Blenheims (B. Cork).

A return to the Navy meant a new posting to a new squadron (880) and a new Commanding Officer, one of the Fleet Air Arm's most unusual characters - the acerbic and unyielding Lt Cdr F (Butch) Judd (Authors collection).

880 spent their early days at Arbroath flying a few ex-RAF Hurricanes, seen here over the Scottish Highands in a good tight formation led by Judd and Cork (Authors collection).

perfect formation and at the same time were attacked by enemy fighters who had the advantage of 3,000 to 4,000 feet in height."

The ME 110 he attacked was flown by Oberleutnant Gerhard Granz from ZG 2. He and his gunner, Feldwedel Willi Schutel, took to their parachutes and spent the rest of the war in captivity. Granz later recalled his memories of this encounter:

"We were escorting bombers on that day in September 1940. I saw a Spitfire, or was it a Hurricane I cannot remember clearly. It was behind one of our planes. I went into a diving turn shooting at the British fighter. Smoke came from its tail as I hit it. It went down in flames.
But another British fighter came towards me. There was a burst of machine gun fire and bullets came right through the cockpit beside me. I told the gunner to bale out. He did. Then I tried to bale out myself. I could not. I was stuck in, trapped. My parachute was caught and so I took the controls again and rolled the plane and just fell out at the last moment.
I was very close to the ground and when I landed in a tree I think it was two steel helmets came up from behind the hedge. My first reaction was to say 'good afternoon' in English. The Home Guard soldiers thought I was English for a while until they made me take off my flying jacket and saw my uniform. They marched me away and I spent the night in Billericay in the police station. Next day I went away for interrogation (Kensington) and then to a prisoner of war camp near Lake Windermere."

The Duxford Squadrons had been caught at a disadvantage and were forced to attack without the benefit of height, surprise and speed. In doing so, they sustained a great deal of damage for the 20 victories claimed. Seven of 242's Hurricanes were badly shot about, whilst Pilot Officer Benzie went down under the guns of a mottled grey, yellow nosed ME 109, crashing vertically into the ground near Chelmsford. But he was the only fatality amongst the three squadrons, so luck seems to have been on their side.

Dick's injuries were slight, but presented him with an immediate problem, as he recalled three years later in a candid interview:

"It was the closest I had come to serious injury when flying
and was rather shocked by the suddenness of it all. My oxygen mask saved most of my face from the slivers of glass that
flew all over the place as the shell hit. But my cheeks were
lacerated and bits were embedded in and around my eyes
they felt terribly 'gritty', when I tried to open and shut them.
Unable to see clearly I broke away downwards and looked
for the machine attacking me, determined to get the so and
so. But we lost each other, so I went down onto the deck and
tried to wipe the blood and muck from my eyes.
The flight back to Duxford was difficult and I was greatly
relieved when the hangers came into view. I put my
Hurricane down as gently as possible. It was rattling and
banging quite badly and I was expecting something to fall off
at any moment, but it didn't and I taxied in, switched off and
took a great gulp of air. Hands reached down, undid my
straps and helped me out, whilst a voice said 'Sir, you have
made a mess of yourself, havn't you!'
Packed off to hospital, much against my wishes by the 'Boss',
a pretty, young nurse set about removing the glass with
tweezers and a steady stream of water. After a clean up I was
allowed back to Duxford, where another Hurricane awaited
me, the other being a 'write off'...."

Overnight German bombers continued to drone in towards London,
drawn like moths to fires in the East End. Long rows of tight knit ter-
raced houses took the worst of the onslaught. Within hours, entire
streets and small communities had disappeared. 306 people did not see
the dawn, whilst 1,337 found treatment for their serious injuries in hospitals ill-prepared for such a large number of casualties.

As the bombs rained down, fighter pilots at airfields around the city
watched the sky redden with the glow of a thousand fires, those with
families in the area growing more and more concerned for their safety.
Attempts to phone home met with failure, as both Arthur and Dick discovered. There was nothing they could do but look on, impotent to
help, their anxiety increasing with each passing hour.

When dawn came, fires burned on, filling the air with thick, acrid
smoke that drifted lazily upwards, the wind from the east carrying soot
and filth across the city into the countryside beyond. As the survivors
crawled from their shelters, most expected the sirens to go at any

moment and fresh waves of bombers to appear over head. But apart from the odd harassing raid the day passed in comparative peace, allowing rescue services to put out fires and search for the living and the dead. The night, when it came, saw a resumption of battle, the defenders unable to provide protection for their people.

Limited to daylight operations, much of Fighter Command spent the the day on standby. By evening, 242 had returned to Norfolk, being vectored onto a suspected raid whilst on route to Coltishall, but saw nothing in the dense cloud that shrouded Eastern England. As they made their way to the Mess for dinner, Luftlotte 3 came to readiness at their airfields in Northern France, for another attack on London. From 7.30 pm to dawn, a steady stream of bombers crept along the Thames Estuary, its shape highlighted through cloud by sudden flashes of moonlight. Fires extinguished during the day were soon alight - beacons relit for successive bombers to mark and follow.

By morning, another 412 people were dead. Although nothing could justify this suffering, the change of tactics had given Fighter Command some respite, tilting the contest in the defender's favour. With Autumn now so close and the weather growing more severe, an invasion in 1940 looked increasingly less likely, but the battle was far from over and Dowding's squadrons were still required to make sacrifices.

CHAPTER EIGHT

EYE OF THE STORM
(15th SEPTEMBER 1940)

"In this crazy world of continuous flying and very little sleep
we exist. I'm not complaining don't think that. In fact I
wouldn't miss all this fighting for anything it really is the
greatest sport.
We had grand fun last saturday (7th September) we ran into
about 200-250 German bombers and fighters. The squadron
got 14 and my share of the bag was one Dornier bomber and
a Messerschmitt 110, which brings my total to five.
Unfortunately or not, I don't know, I was flying in the first
section with the CO and before we knew where we were we
found ourselves in the middle of this mass. Every way you
turned all you could see were German machines, and was
there some lead flying around the sky ! Anyway we stuck
together and got out of it without injury except a few
scratches from glass and odd bits of bullets, but you should
have seen our machines absolutely full of holes and they
couldn't even make one whole aircraft out of what was left."

In these few, understated words Dick described his brush with death
to his parents. One can only guess at the reaction this letter produced
in parents clearly concerned for their son's safety. But it was impossible
to disguise the risks he ran when the battle raged so visibly above their
heads. In any case, bombing had turned the Home Front into the frontline and now civilians shouldered a risk equal to that of airmen, soldiers
and sailors. There was no guarantee of safety and someone sitting inno-
cently at home faced a death as rapid and indiscriminate as any fighter
pilot. So the need to try and minimize the risks he faced could be
muted, though not totally ignored.

On September 8th, Cork flew his battle damaged Hurricane back to Coltishall and the next day accompanied Jimmy Gardner in a Magister to Cosford, in the Midlands. Whilst they were away the Duxford Wing, as it had become known, fought a vicious battle over north London with bombers from Luftflotte 2. Scrambled at 5.00 pm 242, 19 and 310 Squadrons patrolled the skies over North Weald and Hornchurch. Specks appeared from the east at 22,000 feet and gradually two boxes of 60 aircraft each, quarter of a mile apart, became visible, their fighters weaving above. Bader ordered No. 19 to attack the escorts, whilst he led the two Hurricane squadrons down to the bombers. ME 109 dived to intercept the onrushing fighters, three of which turned to face them, throwing their attack into confusion.

In the ensuing fight the Wing claimed 26 enemy aircraft destroyed, but 242 lost Pilot Officer Sclanders and Sgt Lonsdale was forced to bale out. Caught in the crossfire of enemy bombers his aircraft sustained serious damage. Within seconds smoke and glycol were pouring into his cockpit. He took to his parachute at 19,000 feet and drifted down amidst the noise of battle, landing in a pine tree near Caterham, injuring one leg. The tree stood in the grounds of a girls school and for half an hour his presence caused the pupils much amusement until the local police were able to remove him with the help of a ladder.

Only 9 Spitfires from 19 Squadron were involved and these went into line astern, climbing to 23,000 feet. Arthur Blake (Red 2) seemed surprised by the intensity of the battle and did not fire once during this initial onslaught, as he twisted and turned amongst ME 109s and ME 110s. As the fight broke up and bombers and fighters drifted away over Kent, Blake latched on to an HE 111. He expended all his ammunition in several passes and left it dropping towards the sea, flames erupting from its fuselage. But return fire from the HE had hit his Spitfire, rupturing the fuel tank and shattering its toughened windscreen. Despite this, Blake managed to land his aircraft 30 minutes later. 310 Squadron were more unfortunate and lost three Hurricanes.

Although making light of his facial wounds, they clearly caused Dick some discomfort when donning goggles and oxygen mask, as Douglas Bader later recalled:

"He was okay, but the twisting and turning necessary when looking for the enemy would soon have opened these wounds up again. Against his wishes he was rested, flying only very briefly on the 10th when we were hard pressed. Being a

Londoner he was very keen to get home and reassure himself that all was well after several days and nights of heavy bombing. He came to me (on the 11th) for permission to take a Hurricane to an airfield near his home the following day, so that he could spend a few hours with his parents. I had no objections, but it wouldn't have surprised me to discover that he had stooged about on the way over London by himself, looking for some action."

His visit to Burnham had been heralded by phone earlier in the day and his arrival announced by a fly past, recalled by his brother:

"He used to come over and do a few low passes and slow rolls above the house. My mother would ring up Hugh Reid, the local vicar, who was very keen on flying, and say 'Dick's just been over' and he would know that Dick would land at nearby White Waltham. He was one of the few people in the area who had a car and some petrol, a special allowance because of his duties. So he whipped over to White Waltham, where Dick had parked his Hurricane, picked him up and deposited him outside our home, having first taken him to the Five Bells pub in the centre of Burnham for a celebratory drink."

These brief periods of rest allowed those bound up in the day to day battle to relax. Yet it could produce the opposite reaction to that expected, magnifying the ways in which their lives were dictated by operational flying, as Arthur related in a letter written on September 14th, the eve of one of the battle's most crucial days:

"Things are getting much hotter here and there is little time to relax. We spend the daylight hours waiting by our aircraft, trying to keep our minds occupied, but the battle is never far from our thoughts and the telephone ringing makes us jump. It really is most exhausting and makes you long for a day off, though even this cannot disguise the strain for long. I managed to snatch a day in London and found everyone quite unruffled by the bombing, but I couldn't relax and longed to be away from it back with the squadron where everything seems more normal. It is really most strange, despite the pressure, life here seems more tolerable...."

During the summer months misty mornings had been common and September 15th was no exception. It clung to the ground even after sunrise, its chill permeating the air, causing condensation to rise in poorly ventilated buildings. The morning sun gradually heated the earth and by eight the mist had begun to lift.

The night had seen more bombing raids on London; the eighth in succession, but cloud had cloaked much of the city after midnight obscuring aiming points. Bombs fell on Chelsea, Fulham and Westminster in strong concentrations, killing and wounding 50 people. Clapham Junction was brought to a standstill by an unexploded bomb found embedded in the track beside platform 6. The rest of the city emerged virtually unscathed, but 'alerts' had kept large numbers in their shelters, where sleep was almost impossible. The fact that it was Sunday meant little in terms of a 'lie in', when daylight bombing might commence at any moment. So a bleary eyed population concentrated instead on less leisurely activities.

All around London, guncrews stood down, whilst supply officers made good ammunition fired during the night, though expenditure had been the lowest since the 7th. For all their noise, the guns rarely brought anything down, but their impact on morale was tremendous and did force the enemy to fly higher.

Throughout the Home Counties up into East Anglia, Fighter Command brought its squadrons to readiness, controllers registering pilot and aircraft availability. Since July, units had been rotated as losses and exhaustion depleted numbers, but over the last four days, more fresh squadrons than usual had returned, giving 11 and 12 Groups a boost and tired pilots a well earned rest.

An hour before dawn pilots rose from their beds and followed a routine of dressing and eating, reflecting varying degrees of strain. The newcomers might be too nervous to eat, but there again, so could those who had been in the frontline too long.

Arrival on the airfield was greeted by a cacophony of sound as engines were warmed and tested by fitters, who in many cases had spent the night repairing battle damage or completing essential servicing. They did sterling service, but at times the need to grumble was overpowering, as recalled by one young fitter with 242:

> "The pressure could get pretty intense at times and we often
> spilt blood trying to get a particular job done. Covered in
> filth, working under poor lights in stuffy conditions, tired and

decidedly fed up, the only recourse was to moan and groan about officers and NCOs or anything else that took our fancy. It allowed us to let off steam in a harmless way. Occasionally, though, a genuine resentment built up that could cause trouble. The CO in particular was a hard task master and liked his Hurricane to be on top line as though ready for a display at Hendon. He would insist upon it being highly polished. On top of our other duties this got a bit too much and caused some ill-feeling, especially when some of the other pilots demanded the same treatment. Of course we supported the pilots as best we could and admired their courage, but we saw another side to that favourite portrait painted by the press. We saw them when they landed after difficult patrols white faced, hands shaking, sometimes vomit around the cockpit. Yet they would go back up again a few minutes or hours later. Even now I can only marvel at such bravery and realise that all the polishing was not too high a price to pay to keep them happy."

242 had spent the night at Coltishall as usual and at first light, flew to Duxford, joining 302 and 310 Squadrons there. Number 19 remained at Fowlmere, but were now joined by another Spitfire squadron, 611. All five would operate as Wing. In 11 Group, a similar experiment was underway, but here squadrons would fly in pairs. Now that the airfields were safe and the target London, the RAF could afford to concentrate its fighters. Time was still of the essence, but now they had some breathing space to assemble their defences.

For the first few hours, little happened. Various incoming aircraft were registered by radar and interceptions ordered, but these were mostly high flying reconnaissance flights that made off before fighters could attack.

The atmosphere at Duxford grew increasingly more tense, as Stan Turner recalled:

"Everyone was ready to go, but nothing happened and we wondered whether the Luftwaffe might be switching all their efforts to night bombing. We lounged around, some playing cards, others just chatting or resting. But we were all very conscious of the telephone and would jump if it rang, though most calls didn't concern us directly. I often wondered whether the so and so's who rang were just malicious or ignorant of the effect such calls would have on us.

I don't think anyone was immune to the stress these hours of waiting could inflict, though some seemed to cope with it pretty well for a time."

At 11.00 hours, radar began to pick up the first signs of activity over Amiens and Abbeville and within minutes the raid had been confirmed. At first 11 Group responded with two squadrons of Spitfires from Biggin Hill, but quickly increased this when the size of the raid became apparent. At Northolt, Kenley, Debden, Castle Camps, Hornchurch, Hendon and Martlesham Heath squadrons scrambled and climbed quickly away to intercept the raiders. With all its squadrons engaged, 11 Group sought assistance and at 11.25 the Duxford Wing was scrambled.

"Our Hurricanes were dispersed around the perimeter of the airfield. When we were scrambled it took a few seconds for the message to reach all the pilots, though language differences (Czech, Polish and English) thought to be a problem presented no difficulties, 'scramble' having, by that stage, a universal meaning.

242 were airborne first, almost in line abreast, as 310 reached the takeoff point, followed by 302. We wasted little time and once in the air I turned on a southerly course to London and climbed. There was no manoeuvring backwards and forwards over the airfield to allow everyone to form up. We just turned on course, getting into formation as we did so.

At Fowlmere 19 and 611 were scrambled at the same time using their better rate of climb to get above the Hurricanes, taking up station 5000 feet above us, where they could take on the 109s."

Douglas Bader.

By 1200 hrs they had reached the Thames Estuary, just beyond Gravesend, Dick close in on Bader's starboard side, the rest of the wing spread out behind and above. Over their R/Ts came a disjointed flow of talk, marking the progress of the incoming raid over the coast, to Canterbury and Maidstone. Despite the attention of so many squadrons, the bombers pressed on towards London. Two groups of enemy bombers passed right underneath the Wing flying north west. They dived down and attacked the last section of bombers in the group, as Dick later described:

> "Whilst flying as Red 2 the enemy were sited to the south below us. We kept in the sun till we were directly above and behind the enemy formation, when the order was given to attack. Kept in formation and dived on the starboard enemy machine and opened fire at approx 200 yards. Dived to the right after my attack and climbed up again to see the starboard engine of the enemy machine in flames, as it did a steep diving turn to the left towards the ground. The machine was now being attacked by four other Hurricanes and one Spitfire, so I did not follow it down, but saw another enemy machine (ME 109) to the right and attacked it with three other fighters. The machine was seen to dive steeply into the clouds."

By 1245 hrs the attack was over and the last bombers had drifted back towards the coast pursued by fighters determined to inflict still more damage. Amongst them Arthur Blake, who wanted, it seemed, to chase them across the Channel to their own airfields. But finally, even he broke off and turned for home.

At Duxford and Fowlmere, ground crews waited for their fighters to return, unaware of the condition of pilots and machines. Some, they expected, would be in a bad way and 'blood wagons' stood ready to move the injured, whilst a few replacement aircraft had been made ready. But there were no losses and damage was slight.

There followed a brief period of recovery, coloured by thoughts that more scrambles lay ahead:

> "The mission completed, pilots ambled back to the crew room, completed the debrief, in some cases stopping a rocket from the CO or flight commanders for some piece of poor airmanship, and then grabbed something to eat. One by one our aircraft were reported back and turned round with squadron readiness soon confirmed.
> The high tension and excitement generated throughout the squadron, gradually receded. Pilots' sweat-ridden shirts dried

out, and stomachs returned to normal. If it had been a morning show, we all knew that there could be at least two more formidable raids to contest before the day was through. Occasionally the activity called for five scrambles in the hours of daylight, but some were false alarms and not all resulted in combat. A quick visit to our aircraft for the usual cockpit check and we'd settle down with some apprehension to await the next call to action."

Flight Lieutenant R. W. Oxspring,
66 Squadron.

Whilst pilots grabbed some food and tried to relax, Intelligence Officers directed their attention towards Air Ministry Form F's Combat Reports. Some of these were dictated, but for the most part pilots grabbed pens or pencils and quickly scribbled down their first impressions of those recent actions.

In his report, Cork gave only the most cursory description of his part in the battle over south London, but in a most revealing statement ended his account with a testimony to Douglas Bader's leadership:

"The success of the whole attack was definitely due to the good positioning and perfect timing of the CO of 242, who was leading the Wing Formation."

Ground and air defences had little time to recover before radar located a second raid over France, approaching the Channel in three waves. By 1400 hrs Fighter Command had scrambled eight squadrons from Hornchurch, Debden, Kenley and North Weald, each rising swiftly through the cumulous cloud into a brilliantly blue sky, to make contact with the enemy over Romney Marsh. Within ten minutes they were joined by twelve more squadrons as 11 Group committed the bulk of its force. All along the Thames, from the coast to London the battle raged.

With only a small number of squadrons in reserve it soon became apparent that 10 and 12 Groups' assistance would be needed again and at 1415 hrs Duxford's Wing was scrambled and directed to patrol Hornchurch at 25,000 feet. With the raids coming in at 20,000 feet and an escort some 10,000 feet higher, the Wing was at a distinct disadvantage. Bader later recalled the problems this created in a brief, but scathing report:

"12 Group Wing were sent off from Duxford. Clouds 8/10ths at 5,000 feet. Climbed through gap and proceeded south, still climbing. 3 Hurricane Squadrons in line astern and 2 Spitfire Squadrons on the right and slightly below. At 16,000 feet sighted large number of EA through AA bursts. At 20,000 feet endeavoured to climb and catch them, but unfortunately was attacked by ME 109s from above and behind. I told Spitfires to carry on and get the bombers and told Hurricanes to break up and engage fighters.
On being attacked from behind by ME 109 I ordered break up and pulled up and round violently. Coming off my back I partially blacked out, nearly colliding with Yellow 2 (242), spun off his slipstream and straightened out 5,000 feet below without firing a shot.
Climbed up again and saw twin engined EA flying west-wards. Just got in range and fired short burst (3 seconds) in a completely stalled position and then spun off again and lost more height.
Eventually went through clouds near Ashford (Kent) to try and find stragglers, but no good, so came home.
I understand the remaining Squadrons in the Wing managed to get at some EA, but the lead was hopeless for them as we were up sun, too low and I spun out of position, so all they could do was seize whatever opportunities they could, which they did with some success. If we had managed to get off 10 minutes earlier and got our height we could have had a good time."

As 12 Group's squadrons struggled to gain height, a massive battle had developed across Kent. Fighter Command deployed 276 Spitfires and Hurricanes, but faced an enemy force more than twice its size. Yet the Luftwaffe had committed a tactical blunder. Aware of increasing losses amongst its bomber fleet, ME 109s had been ordered to fly close escort. In effect they could not seek out the enemy if it meant leaving the bombers. On their approach to London the British fighters took advantage of this inflexibility and deployed hit and run tactics, return-ing each time ME 109s broke back to protect their lumbering charges.

Over Chatham the raid turned west and headed into London, coming within range of clustered anti-aircraft batteries. Overhead the sky was blanketed in almost continuous cloud, obscuring the gunners aim, but it cleared occasionally to reveal a target and a heavy salvo of shells streaked skywards, bursting all around the bombers, making them skid away to avoid being hit. Some were damaged and dived into cloud cover, others struggled gamely on, waiting for fighters to strike again.

It was these distant bursts of anti-aircraft fire that Douglas Bader spotted as they tried to gain height. Yet their arrival had been observed by a large group of enemy fighters, which swooped down forcing the Wing to break in all directions. As they split up Cork managed to stay alongside Bader for a few seconds only:

> "On the way we were attacked from above and behind by a number of ME 109s. The order was given on R/T to break formation so I broke sharply to the right with an ME 109 on my tail. I was now in a dive and suddenly flew through the second squadron in the wing formation and lost the enemy machine, and at the same time saw a Do 17 to my starboard flying NW. I dived 6,000 feet to attack and fired a long burst at the port engine which started to smoke. I attacked again on the beam large pieces of the enemy machine flew off and his starboard wing burst into flames near the wing tip! He dived straight into the clouds heading for a clear patch so I waited until he came into the open and fired another burst in a head on attack and his machine dived into the ground. I climbed up a thousand feet and was attacked by two yellow nosed ME 109s from above, so I did a steep turn to left and managed to get on the tail of one fired a very short burst and then ran out of ammunition. No damage was seen on enemy machine, but as I was being attacked from behind by a second fighter I went into a vertical dive down to 2,000 feet and returned to base. No damage to my own machine (Hurricane P 3515)."

The final part of Dick's account is a little misleading as his Logbook reveals:

> "Landed Rochford few holes in aircraft, two in cockpit on windscreen, wings, prop."

One of the first people he saw on landing at Rochford was Arthur Blake, who like Dick, had seen some violent action and had put down for some essential repairs at the nearest airfield.

Having noted 'innumerable enemy aircraft' over London, Arthur had dived alone onto six Dorniers that had become separated from the main formation. As he intercepted them, instinct made him look upwards where some ME 109s hovered. He hauled his Spitfire round and upwards, put on full boost and attacked, two brief bursts from his guns catching a 109, which burst into flames. The other aircraft swung round and their fire thudded into Arthur's Spitfire. Spinning away he spotted a lone HE 111 being attacked by four other fighters and made a single pass, registering many hits.

In his report, Arthur played down his part in the encounter, but after his death in October, 19 Squadron's CO, Brian Lane, gave a fuller account:

> "He attacked one enemy aircraft and shot it down, but his own aircraft was badly hit in the engine. The cockpit was filled with smoke and the plane was liable to catch fire at any moment. He opened the hood to clear the smoke and then proceeded to attack another Hun, which he also shot down. I don't think many pilots would have stuck to it as he did under the circumstances.
> He didn't know it, but he had been recommended for a DFC for this feat."

Arthur left the Heinkel to its fate, swiftly dropped away, easing back on the throttle, trying to minimize stress on his damaged engine. Rochford was nearest and within minutes he was overhead in the landing circuit, handling his Spitfire most gingerly until it was safely on the ground, where he and Dick met, much to each others surprise and pleasure, as Arthur later recounted:

> "I had one or two problems and force landed in Kent. There were quite a few of our boys already down, milling about, but one looked remarkably familiar as he ambled over to greet me, though with my face blackened its a wonder he recognised me. His machine had been hit in various places and like me got down as soon as possible, to get things sorted out and was waiting for the all clear.
> Despite the fact that we serve together we see little of each other at the moment, our time being taken up with the old Hun. Of course, we are based on different airfields, which

doesn't help, so it was very pleasant to meet him in a strange place.

Whilst we waited, bombers droned back overhead, but we couldn't see them above the cloud, though the noise of gun-fire occasionally reached our ears.

Old Dick certainly looks worn out and ready for a rest. Old wounds on his face have opened up and so he didn't look quite as handsome as usual."

Despite Fighter Command's best efforts, a substantial number of enemy aircraft reached London and, before 1500 hrs, had bombed West Ham, to the north of the city. But thick cloud had confused many raiders. Unable to find their targets they turned for home, scattering their bombs over a wide area on the way, causing some damage and a number of casualties.

By 1530 hrs, remnants of the bomber force were approaching the Straits of Dover where most of Fighter Command's aircraft left them, though some continued to chase their quarry across the Channel. Despite the onslaught, most bombers held formation boosted by the arrival of fresh squadrons sent up to cover their withdrawal. Damaged aircraft dropped below their groups and landed first, whilst ME 109s tried to shepherd any stragglers, sometimes going deep into enemy ter-ritory to get them.

After so much energy had been expended, the peace that followed seemed false. Squadrons drifted back to their bases short of fuel, ammu-nition and stamina. Many pilots, like Dick and Arthur, had landed away from their bases, so there would be a pause whilst they sorted them-selves out. But sufficient squadrons were down in the right places to reassure Fighter Command that a third daylight raid could be chal-lenged, if it came.

At Duxford, groundcrew again turned their aircraft round, refuelling and rearming. Despite attacking at such a disadvantage, they had lost only one pilot, Fl Lt T. P. Chlopik from 302 Squadron, whilst Sgt Potter from 19 Squadron was missing. He had pursued the enemy too close to France, had been shot down and would spend the rest of the war in captivity. Four other pilots baled out, but were safe, whilst 2 crash land-ed. Others, such as Cork, landed at other airfields for repairs and report-ed in by telephone.

As darkness fell, riggers and fitters set to work patching, servicing and repairing some very battle worn aircraft. The day had been a busy one and most expected the Luftwaffe to continue these massive raids, even with the losses they were taking. But if any reminder was needed of their potency a brief look south towards London provided. it Clouds again glowed brightly that night reflecting a multitude of fires from fresh raids by 180 bombers. Despite this show of strength the tide had turned and daylight raids rapidly reduced as Hitler turned his attention to other, more promising targets.

CHAPTER NINE

LIFE WON'T BE THE SAME

After a busy day on the 15th expectations of more action were high, but for the most part remained unrealised. The battle raged on for a few more weeks as Germany's High Command sought to damage British morale, without incurring serious losses itself. The RAF strongly resisted these raids and so the Luftwaffe's daylight tactics became simply a means of drawing British fighters into the air, where swarms of ME 109s waited to destroy them. As September gave way to October, and the enemy changed tactics, Fighter Command remained on high alert to counter the daytime threat, but could do nothing at night to kerb the activities of bombers, which pounded London and other cities without serious challenge.

Activity at Duxford reflected this change; many patrols over London with no sight of the enemy. A tiring, but necessary business. There were some compensations, however, as Dick recorded in his Logbook, confirmed by a signal from 12 Group:

> September 22nd Awarded the Distinguished Flying Cross
> "Heartiest congratulations on your well earned DFC."
>
> *Leigh Mallory.*

After his gallant showing on September 7th, 12 Group recommended Dick for this decoration, with the briefest of citations. It read: 'For exemplary courage and coolness in successful action against enemy bombers'. Yet this award caused some controversy, as Douglas Bader recalled:

"Towards the end of the battle he was awarded the DFC, the

first naval pilot to be so decorated. We received the usual
telegram from the Air Ministry to the effect that His Majesty
the King, on the recommendation of the Commander-in-
Chief, had been graciously pleased to award the DFC to Sub
Lieutenant R. Cork RN. We celebrated and my wife sewed the
ribbon on his uniform (albeit upside down the first time). A
couple of days later a second telegram arrived, this time from
the Admiralty. It said:'For DFC read Distinguished Service
Cross'. The latter being the Royal Navy's equivalent.
Through the proper channels we firmly expressed non com-
prehension. The King had given him the DFC and only His
Majesty could change it. Corky continued to wear his DFC.
Whilst this exchange continued, we received a visit from the
Air Minister, Sir Archibald Sinclair, to whom we told our tale.
He assured us of his support, declaring that we were
absolutely right. "

Bader was offended by the Navy's reaction, which he considered
mean spirited and promoted this grievance in his usual determined
manner, enlisting support and exerting influence in a number of ways.
For most Squadron Commanders the matter would have rested there,
but Bader was no ordinary man and pursued Dick's case with great
determination. In this he had an unflinching ally in his Adjutant, Peter
MacDonald;a serving officer and a Member of Parliament. At Bader's
insistence he questioned the Navy's attitude towards Cork's DFC and
within days this debate reached the ears of Harold Balfour, Under
Secretary of State for Air. Attitudes soon hardened and opinions became
entrenched. Yet the campaign did not stop until questions had been
asked in the House of Commons and a direct approach made to the
King himself, by Macdonald.

Inevitably such a minor issue had been promoted beyond its true
importance and became an unnecessary distraction at a critical
moment. The Admiralty did not give way and chose to ignore such a
superfluous debate, explaining away any disagreement as a innocent
misinterpretation of Naval Regulations. Nevertheless it was an argument that ran on into 1942, when a letter from the King's Equerry to
MacDonald finally ended the debate, by which time Bader had been
shot down over France and taken prisoner:

"In continuation of my letter of September 12th, the story of

Lieutenant Cork is that he was given an immediate award of the DFC by the Air Officer CommanderinChief Fighter Command on September 23rd,1940. This was due to a misunderstanding on the part of the latter, because Lieutenant Cork was not at that time in the service of the Air Ministry but of the Admiralty. In agreement with the Admiralty, the award of the DFC was cancelled and the DSC substituted, and gazetted on October 18th 1940. Since then the Fleet Air Arm personnel serving with the Royal Air Force have in fact become eligible for the DFC, but it is obvious that Lieutenant Cork could not get both the DFC and DSC for the same action.... "

MacDonald sent Dick a copy of this correspondence and gently chided the younger man about his Navy background:

"I am sorry this letter is not more satisfactory because I am sure you would prefer to have a flying decoration rather than one granted for your own 'inferior Service!' However, there it is. I'm afraid it is another instance of what happens at inspections when a great deal is said and very little is ever heard of it afterwards."

This heated debate had one unexpected and unpleasant outcome. Many Navy pilots served with the RAF during 1940, some with great distinction. Fighter Command recommended the award of DFCs to a number of them. But it seems that Bader's condemnation of the Navy meant that these proposals were held in abeyance, as though debased by the argument. One amongst them was Arthur Blake, whose bravery on September 15th subsequently went unnoticed by officialdom, though acclaimed by his Commanding Officer, Brian Lane.

Dick's reaction to these events is not recorded, but his feelings may be gauged from a story told by Douglas Bader some years later:

"After the Battle of Britain, Dickie Cork and Jimmy Gardner were posted back to the Fleet Air Arm. During his time with us Corky had acquired four buttons from the tunics of fellow pilots in the Duxford Wing. These he wore as the left row of his double breasted naval tunic. From top to bottom they were an RAF button, Royal Canadian Air Force button, a

Czech Air Force button, and a Polish Air Force button. The last
named was in silver and particularly conspicuous, as all the
rest on his tunic were golden.
A week or so after his departure, Corky flew in to see us. As
he walked towards us we noticed with horror that he was
properly dressed, and worse still he was wearing the ribbon
of the DSC, instead of our DFC.
He told us that soon after his arrival, he had encountered an
Admiral whom he saluted, intending to pass on. The Admiral
stopped him, pointed at the purple and white diagonal
stripes of his DFC ribbon and asked 'What's that?
'Respectfully, Sub Lieutenant Cork told him. The Admiral's
gaze shifted to his tunic with its row of exotic buttons. His
face suffused, then became empurpled. There was, Corky
assured us, 'an unparalleled scene'. Since then he had been
correctly dressed as an officer of the Royal Navy."

Whether he consciously involved himself in these efforts to get the
Navy to accept his 'foreign' decoration, is unclear, but the strength of
Bader's character would have quashed any desire on Dick's part to
comply with the Admiralty's wishes. Until, that is, he returned to the
senior service, where a more discreet approach seemed appropriate. In
any case the London Gazette (October 18th) carried confirmation that
the DSC had been awarded and so the matter should have rested, and
would have, except for Bader's uncompromising stance. Small wonder
that Dick should have explained away his DSC ribbon in such a diplomatic way, when next he saw his mentor.

Much to his embarrassment Dick found himself the subject of local
press reports:

"A Burnham man belonging to the Fleet Air Arm, now tem-
porarily attached to the RAF, with seven planes to his credit
has been awarded the Distinguished Flying Cross for his work
in the air fights. He is Sub Lieutenant Richard John Cork, of
'Lurley', Dawes East Road, Burnham.
He was awarded the DFC for shooting down an enemy
bomber and fighter on a single day when Goering's German
Air Force made determined assaults on England. Sub
Lieutenant Cork's Commanding Officer is Squadron Leader
Bader, the legless pilot who has recently been awarded the

DSO, and who has been in the news a lot lately.
Burnham's hero was home last week on 48 hours leave,
before returning once again to his base to repel the Nazi
planes. Though he is intensely proud to be serving his country in this way, he admits that he enjoys every moment when
he is in the air 'straffing the Hun' and has never been shot
down."

When death became a daily ritual to be endured, decorations and
rewards could seem of little importance and as 1940 came to a end the
business of survival continued to exert its sobering influence. Although
the enemy's strategy had changed, it brought little respite and as each
day passed, alerts and scrambles continued to take a heavy toll of men
and machines. The weather was deteriorating, with rain and low temperatures making life miserable. Patrols at 20,000 feet and above, where
arctic temperatures were commonplace, soon sapped the strength of
even the most robust airman. A letter written during October by Cork,
hints at the fatigue he and most others must have felt:

"We are still terribly busy long patrols over London every day.
It really makes you dammed tired this high flying still there
we are, one just has to stick to it.
Oh hell I'm so fed up with this dammed war we keep losing
people and one's best friends all seem to go and what will
happen next. Sorry to write such a gloomy letter. I will write
again when I feel a little less bloody minded."

The days followed a familiar pattern early morning flights from
Coltishall to Duxford, patrols, interspersed with scrambles. Even though
Dick flew on many of these missions they only seemed to encounter
the enemy on his rest days, though bringing some success to his fellow
Navy pilots, Arthur Blake and Jimmy Gardner.

On a windy, but sunny Wednesday (September 18th) Bader led the
Wing into battle against two groups of enemy bombers over
Gravesend. A diving attack, followed by the inevitable confused melee,
saw Gardner taking on a group of stragglers, already being attacked by
a lone Hurricane piloted by Douglas Bader. He selected a Dornier and
attacked from the port quarter, setting wing and engine alight after a
single pass. With its controls shot away, and a wing crumpling, the
stricken bomber dived into the Thames Estuary.

With ammunition and fuel to spare he gained height and saw a small group of bombers in the distance, heading south east, trying to make good their escape. For three minutes he gave chase, using full boost, and gradually caught them over Chatham. One of their number trailed behind the group, clearly struggling to keep up. Gardner attacked from the port side, then moved to starboard, hitting both engines, before pulling away to attack another bomber with his last few rounds of ammunition.

Nine days later, after many fruitless patrols, Duxford's Wing achieved its final large scale interception of 1940. At 23,000 feet over Kent they fell upon a large formation of ME 109s 'aimlessly' circling around some 5,000 feet below, a strange sight to those more used to seeing them sitting up high, waiting to attack. For once they were being hunted and 13 were claimed as destroyed in the brief, but bloody battle that followed.

Flying as Red 2, Arthur Blake followed his comrades down in line astern, but at the last moment looked back and saw a group of of higher flying 109s slipping onto their tails. He broke away in a steep right hand turn, to discourage them, firing at one as he went. Pale white smoke and a fine mist of petrol streamed back, as Arthur fired second and third bursts. It began to turn, but went into a dive that became steeper and steeper before crashing into a cold and choppy English Channel.

Pausing briefly to look around, he saw far below, other 109s streaking for home a few feet above the sea and set off in pursuit. Using height advantage to good effect, he rapidly closed the distance between himself and the rearmost 109. Before he opened fire, the German flew straight into the sea, quickly disappearing into the depths, without trace or chance of survival.

Throughout the summer both Dick and Arthur had corresponded with their old friend David Harrison, teasing him, with a gentle familiarity, about his 'slow' progress towards a squadron. Although joining the RAFVR in January 1939, he had not commenced flying until September, reaching an Operational Training Unit (No 6) in August 1940. After a short, but concentrated spell on Hurricanes his posting came through and on September 12th, as the battle reached its height, he was dropped by RAF car outside 238 Squadron's office at Middle Wallop.

At 29 he was a bit old to be a fighter pilot, but he was very fit and this went in his favour when recruits were being selected, a view reinforced by his 'above average' performance at flight school. Like many, his training was foreshortened by the need to make good losses and he was ill prepared for the sudden switch to combat flying.

Over Padstock on September 25th his machine was so badly knocked about by two ME 109s that he force landed, shaken and bruised. He was quickly back in the air, too soon some said, and during a fight over the Solent, three days later, he was picked off by a 109. This time there was no recovery and he crashed into the sea. His body was washed ashore on October 9th in an advanced state of decay, making identification difficult. A few days later both Dick and Arthur were released by their squadrons to attend David's funeral at St Andrews Church, Tangmere.

In his logbook Dick recorded this gradual erosion of numbers, a few cryptic words recording each loss, but giving no hint at the effect they had upon him. But the worst was yet to come:

"29th October Sub. Lieut A. G. Blake RN. Killed In Action."

On the eve of his death Arthur wrote a last letter to his parents, one that was never delivered:

"It has been a while since I last wrote, so you must think me very remiss. Our lives here are still pretty hectic and there seems to be no let up in sight. Even when the weather is poor we can be up 2 or 3 times a day. As you can imagine our nerves get a bit ragged. So everyone is looking forward to a rest, but no signs of this yet !
On each patrol we get up as high as 30,000 feet and it really gets most bitterly cold. The other day my boots got fairly wet and muddy tramping across to my aircraft before takeoff. The cold was so extreme that I had to thump my feet against the cockpit floor to restore circulation. But my boots were frozen to the controls and it took all of my strength to remove them. We fly patrols over London most days and through the clouds, beyond barrage balloons, I occasionally catch glimpses of the Thames as it meanders westwards. It really makes me most home sick. As they say 'so close, yet so far away'.
In your letters you ask me to take care. You must try not to worry. I've survived since July and come through many

scrapes without a problem. In any case this pace cannot last much longer in the bad weather, so we will fly less and less. So take heart I'll be home before long...."

Late on October 29th, before posting this letter, which remained on his bedside table, Arthur went on patrol over the autumnal fields of Kent and Essex. Acting as 'weaver' above and behind his squadron he carefully searched the sky for enemy fighters. In the far distance, a number of enemy machines were picked out by bursts of anti-aircraft fire, whilst seven 109s were observed hovering above, keeping a 'respectful distance'. Nothing developed and as this mild sparring came to an end, they dipped their wing into the rapidly darkening sky and made for home. The sun's rays deepened in tone throwing up a pale glow in the west, translating the Earth's shades into blackness. As darkness enveloped them, save for the occasional glint of wings, Arthur's life came to an end, unseen by friends, but not foes, who watched him dive vertically from 30,000 feet, until blackness shrouded his descent:

> "We followed a large group of enemy fighters for some minutes, but could not gain any advantage. A single fighter sat above the rest and as we approached he turned to meet us head on. His gunfire hit three of us, doing some damage, but after several minutes our numbers proved too much and he fell to fire from a number of aircraft. During the fight he made no effort to escape, although he could have dived away at any time...."

> *Luftwaffe Intelligence Summary*

At 1715 hours in Chelmsford's London Road, there came the sound of an aircraft hurtling downwards out of control. Several workers on their way home, saw with horror Arthur's Spitfire plunge into the ground and explode in flames. Some looked up hoping to see a parachute, but none appeared and it was realised that pilot and machine had been consumed by the fire.

When he did not return, Squadron Leader Lane expected Arthur to phone from another airfield, but as time passed so concern for his safety grew. There were few casualties that day and by 9 o'clock Arthur's death had been confirmed. Knowing of their close friendship Lane rang Dickie Cork at Coltishall, where he had been relaxing on his day off, and asked him to help Blake's parents with funeral arrangements. Next morning he travelled home, with a heavy heart, to do what he could to ease their suffering. Only in the briefest of letters did he reveal the extent of his own distress:

> "By now, of course, you will have heard about Blakie it was awful the whole business and to make matters worse I had to arrange everything about his affairs and the funeral. He was shot down while on patrol over London at 30,000 feet so I don't suppose he knew much about it thank God.
> Life won't seem the same without him...."

Amongst so much sadness, there were particular moments of terrible poignancy. Packing up and disposing of his friend's kit, the funeral, but the worst came when his parents asked to see their son's body. Gordon Aitken, a later comrade of Dick's, described the impossibility of meeting such a request:

> "Two collided overhead and there were bits all over the place. Just before the funeral one of their mother's came along and asked if we could open the box, so she could see her son for the last time. 'I don't think so' was the response. It was very difficult. You can't tell a woman that their loved one is in little pieces. She couldn't understand, she thought it would be as though he had died in bed, or something. 'Why can't I look at him?' One could only say the coffin had been screwed down...."

> *Lieutenant(A) G. Aitken RNVR.*

Perhaps it is best to let it rest with the strangely impersonal, yet moving account of Arthur's funeral that appeared a week later in the local press, copies of which Dick cut out and kept amongst his personal papers:

> "The funeral took place at St Mary's Church, Langley, last Wednesday and representatives from the RAF acted as under-bearers. A guard of honour was formed by cadets from Slough Grammar School, who also sounded the Last Post and a Rouse, bugle calls which Sub Lieutenant Blake himself

always used to sound at school camps.
Family mourners and others present included his parents,
one brother and sisters, Mr. E. Clarke, Headmaster of Slough
Grammar School, Squadron Leader. B. J. Lane, Sub Lieutenant
R. J. Cork, Mrs. D. Harrison, Mrs. Cork and many others. The
large number of wreaths included tributes from the Grammar
School, the Rowing Club and the Windsor Rugby Club, as
well as two from the squadron to which SubLieutenant Blake
had been attached."

The Gazette.

"His greatest friend at school was Dick Cork and together
they played for Windsor Rugby Club. On Wednesday Sub
Lieutenant Cork, Fleet Air Arm DSC., DFC., was present at the
funeral of his great friend."

The Observer.

In a little over a year, many aspects of Dick's life had changed irrevocably. The war in its relentless, unforgiving way had stripped him of
much that he held dear. But his personality, whilst deeply affected by
these losses, had adapted itself to a changing, hostile world as Douglas
Bader observed:

"When he arrived, Dick was uncertain of himself. Basically
confident, but lacking the self assurance that comes with
experience. As the battle progressed he grew in stature and
showed a toughness in combat that came as a surprise to
some. But it wasn't just as a pilot he flourished. He had an
easy manner, yet it commanded respect and so he had few
problems exerting authority when required. If he had survived he would certainly have become an Admiral - a bloody
good one.
When he came to leave us in December 1940 I wrote in his
confidential report, 'He is one of the finest young officers I
have ever known'. I think that says it all. "

Hugh Popham, who later served with Dick on HMS Indomitable, met
him for the first time in 1941. He later presented a view of Dick out-

wardly reflecting Bader's observation, yet interpreting it in a different way through the eyes of a civilian turned pilot and not a professional soldier, whose values might well be less prosaic:

"Some people, of course, have a talent for war and acquire merit, quite justly, by employing it:Dickie Cork was one of these…. For those of us who have a bent for it war provides such a fulfilment as no other trade can give"

Sub/Lt (A). H. Popham RNVR.

By 1941 Dick had seen a lot of war and so Popham met a man who had been matured by its violence and the sight of many friends dying at its hands. By necessity he presented a face to the world apparently unconcerned by these casualties, though as his letters reveal, he felt these losses keenly. He played the role of committed naval officer, but this was just one way in which he and many others coped as traumas were heaped one on top of the other. It would seem that Popham did not see anything of this and simply portrayed Dick as a cold, unimaginative, professional sailor. His reaction to Arthur Blake's death and determination to carry on, bear witness to his depth of feeling and revealed a personality that remained firmly hidden from all except a small circle of friends.

Dick returned to Coltishall shortly after Arthur's funeral, flying 242's Magister in a long detour around London, over his home and then St. Mary's Church. In the days that followed he sorted through the remainder of Arthur's belongings and flew patrols over Kent and London, in search of an elusive enemy. As November wore on, action grew increasingly rare, but occasionally they did encounter hostile aircraft and combat ensued, as Jimmy Gardner recalled:

"On November 5th I was involved with a bunch of 109s off Sheerness and my Hurricane sustained some damage, so it seemed that I would have to put her down fairly quickly. I was familiar with the area, having lived on the edge of the Thames at Lee-on-Sea near Southend. So directly I was hit and steam coolant from the radiator underneath came up into the cockpit, I realised that I would be a sitting duck. I just went into a tight spiral turn hoping, and having been taught, that it would be very difficult for anybody to get their gunsights on me whilst doing this. I came down through the clouds over the Thames near Shoeburyness and the marshes I had known before the war lay beneath me. I had to make up my mind how long the engine would keep going. Should I land on the marshes or carry on? I thought about the tides and wondered whether it was low or high tide where I proposed to land I didn't want to end up under water later on. Also landing on such a surface might flip me over onto my back and getting out might be quite a problem. But I wasn't keen on jumping out, so as I was close to Southend, where I knew the aerodrome, I throttled everything back to take all power away from the engine. In this way I managed to nurse my machine along, gliding down to land. As my wheels touched the ground the engine stopped dead and that was it. If it had stopped sooner I would have had a few problems, but that's the way it was."

As operational flying diminished, so squadrons resurrected training programmes ignored as the battle raged. With so many newcomers replacing casualties, it was essential to give these inexperienced men as much practice as possible. Veterans led the novices through exercises that might help them survive when the air war revived.

As replacements arrived and numbers from training schools exceeded attrition rates, Fighter Command soon reached a position where they could return pilots 'borrowed' from other services. But the Navy seemed in no hurry to get their men back and for a time their futures remained in limbo. In reality they had little for them to do and placed no pressure on the RAF to hasten their release. On the other hand Coastal Command were in need of pilots and happily absorbed as many Navy men as possible, including Dick and Jimmy Gardner, who went to 252 Squadron at Chivenor, North Devon.

Dick used whatever influence he could muster to stay with 242, but to no avail and on December 8th travelled westwards to join a squadron formed only 17 days earlier. Before leaving Duxford, he flew his Hurricane one last time. Taking it out over the Channel before swinging inland along the Thames towards London, watching the city's eastern reaches emerge occasionally from thick swirling mists.

Before celebrating the departure of his two 'navy blue boys' in Duxford's Mess, Douglas Bader wrote in Cork's logbook:

"Ability as a fighter pilot on Hurricanes 'Exceptional'.
One of the best pilots I have had in my squadron. A good
Section Leader who has displayed courage in the face of the
enemy. Awarded the DFC whilst in this squadron! I am loth to
lose him. Would make a good Flight Commander. "

252 proved to be a meeting place for quite a few Navy pilots, as Ken
'Slim' Holmes recalled:

"I had spent the previous six months in Bomber Command flying Fairey Battles and we were about to convert to Wellingtons
and the future didn't look very bright. I thought long range fighter patrols over the sea (252's role), would lead to a longer life !
252 Squadron was a bit like a flying club. No hard and fast training just getting the hours in and doing more or less what we
wanted. We were equipped with Beauforts, Blenheims and
Beaufighters, all twin engine types of varying standards. I flew
my first Beau on 10.2.41 and 10 days later was giving dual to a
new pilot ! The blind leading the blind. I never did a twin engine
course the CO said I would have to pick it up as I went along.
The other Navy pilots were S/Lt Hopkins, ex Bomber Command
like myself, S/Lt Ian Fraser and S/Lt 'Killer' Crane, both RNVR.
These two had just completed the torpedo course before joining. Fraser was later shot down over the desert, survived, but
was killed in a Navy squadron.
Cork and Gardner were in 'A' Flight, whilst I was in 'B'. They lived
in a separate crew room at the end of the corridor and they
were much more senior to me a very junior Midshipman! But I
can remember them saying they thought 5 hour Atlantic convoy
patrols were not going to be very exciting and wanted to get
back to a real fighter squadron and into the action. A pity a few
months later, after they had left, in the Med it was all there.
Their Flight Commander was F/Lt Lockyer, who called our aircraft 'Beaufrighteners'. Like Cork and Gardner he didn't stay
with us very long and left for a PRU unit, was shot down and
became a POW."

Within days of arrival Cork requested transfer back to a fighter
squadron, making himself unpopular with his easy going CO, Squadron
Leader Yaxley, in the process. His positive approach to this problem bore

all the hallmarks of Douglas Bader, but in Dick's case it was achieved rather more gracefully.

His frustration can be gauged by a letter he wrote to his brother on December 17th:

> "I haven't bought you a Christmas present its practically impossible stuck in this God foresaken spot, so I'll do something about it when I next get to town. I have left my old squadron and am now above all, flying twin engined bombers round the sky and hating it like poison after my Hurricane.
> Apart from this I'm nearly speechless with fear every time I take off with those two awful great propellers and engines whistling in my ears. Needless to say I'm pulling strings and hope to get back before too long into the Navy."

Whether his 'string pulling', or a sudden shiver of activity sweeping through the Admiralty's appointing officers, had any effect is uncertain, but as 1941 dawned, the Navy reached out and began pulling in some of its wandering sons. Within days Cork and Gardner were re-absorbed by their parent service, ending a brief, but exciting period with the RAF.

CHAPTER TEN

EIGHT EIGHTY SQUADRON

After leaving 252 Squadron on January 6th, Dick travelled to Yeovilton, where the Fleet Air Arm began re-educating him in the ways of Naval aviation. In six days, with 759 Squadron, he flew several types of aircraft; the Gladiator, Martlet and Fulmar, the latter giving him some problems when the hydraulics failed. A small drama that could have had very serious consequences, but rated no more than a short, cryptic comment in his logbook.

After this brief 'refresher' course he was posted to 880 Squadron and ordered to proceed to Scotland. Dick had a few days to spare and took leave, staying with his parents in Burnham. There was no war damage, but familiar sights were now translated into a town under siege. Sandbags lay around 'vulnerable points' and gun emplacements seemed to be everywhere. It came as a shock to see how much the town had changed whilst he had been away.

Each night when the weather was fine, London was bombed and for the first time Dick experienced an attack from ground level. As his train approached Waterloo from the West Country, after darkness had fallen on the 12th, alarms sounded all over the city, their haunting wail being heard above engine noises and the clatter of wheels. Passengers peered into the murk wondering how close they would be to the bombers, as the train pulled to a halt in the suburbs around Clapham.

High above the capital, 141 bombers from Luftlotten 3 began their attack in a continuous stream stretching back over Kent. As the first bombs rained down, Dick and his fellow passengers sat and waited for the raid to end, fairly confident that they were too far south to be in any real danger.

The raiders main target had been the docks, but heavy clouds hindered crews in the early stages of this attack and some unloaded their bombs blindly all over the city. As the raid continued a light breeze swept in from the west breaking up the cloud cover, allowing them to see aiming points. By midnight, as Dick finally arrived home, fires raged over the city and hospitals began the unpleasant business of patching up the wounded and laying out the dead.

For the next three nights the city lay untroubled under a blanket of cloud and rain, so the Luftwaffe attacked Plymouth, Derby, Bristol and Swansea instead, returning to the capital on the 19th, in a short, but violent raid. Dick spent part of the afternoon in the Admiralty buildings, Whitehall, leaving as alarms sounded and anti-aircraft guns barked out their response. This time the bombers hit targets around dockland, with Greenwich at its centre. There was some damage, but only 56 enemy aircraft participated and their bombs fell in too wide an area to be of much use.

After this brief period of leave, Dick journeyed northwards on January 22nd. He had hoped to catch a lift from Yeovilton, but there were no aircraft available and he was forced to catch a train, changing at Perth for Arbroath. In total darkness he arrived, to be met by a Naval van that negotiated the narrow, winding lanes to HMS Condor, the Fleet Air Arm's base to the north west of the town.

880 was a fighter squadron in name only, one of many established by the Navy to meet the needs of a rapidly expanding carrier fleet. Although it had no aircraft and few personnel, it could boast a Commanding Officer. Lieutenant Commander F. E. C. Judd RN was a daunting man by anyone's standards, as Hugh Popham discovered when joining the squadron some months later:

> "It was a meeting we had anticipated with some foreboding. 'Wait till you meet the CO.,' Steve had said on more than one occasion, and with an unpleasant relish. 'You won't get get away with that with the Butcher'
> 'The Butcher', known familiarly as Butch was certainly unsettling in appearance. He was tall, perhaps six feet two and wore a reddish beard and moustache. They require separate mention, for while his beard was trimmed somewhat after the fashion of King George V's, his moustaches were allowed to run wild. They sprang out horizontally from his upper lip, stiff, plentiful and coarse, like a couple of tarred rope's ends in need of whipping. He was forever handling them; thrusting them away from his mouth in a pensive way when he was in

good humour; grabbing and tugging at them when, as was more usual, he was angry. His temper was volcanic, and his ferocity a matter of legend."

In some ways Francis Judd was a strange choice to lead a fighter squadron. A South African by birth he transferred to the Navy from the RAF in the mid1930's when the Senior Service began to reclaim its air arm. Overnight he changed from Flight Lieutenant to Lieutenant RN and some wondered, perhaps unkindly, whether his transfer was more a matter of expediency and less the need to place the right man in the right job.

This eccentric man found a niche in the Navy and, in the years before the war, saw service with 716 Squadron, flying Ospreys, Seafox and Walrus aircraft. Switching to 764 Squadron at Lee on Solent, where as CO he oversaw seaplane crew training, before moving on to 771 Squadron at Donibristle, with its Rocs, Skuas and Swordfish. But these second line units held little attraction and as the war progressed he, like Cork, began pressing the Admiralty for a posting to a fighter squadron. The Navy considered him suitable to command 880 and on January 15th his appointment was confirmed.

His selection raised many eyebrows when it was made public. In truth, it reflected the Fleet Air Arm's poor state during the second winter of war. A carrier building programme had survived Britain's prewar cutbacks and as 1941 dawned, the Navy had a substantial fleet in being, or under construction. But it was a fleet without modern aircraft, all resources having been committed to other services.

Nothing existed in the Fleet Air Arm's inventory capable of facing a well equipped enemy. The only option seemed to lie with the RAF and their well tried Spitfires and Hurricanes, neither of which had been designed to withstand the rigours of life on a carrier. Nevertheless the Admiralty began developing both designs for operations afloat, a stop gap measure that would present its pilots with a substantial challenge, later summarized by one Sea Hurricane pilot:

"Short on range, went down like a submarine when ditching, had harsh stalling characteristics, a mediocre view for deck landings and an undercarriage that would bounce so vigorously it would see you right over all arrestor wires into the crash barrier. In addition it was a blighter to man handle on deck, because you couldn't fold its wings. But despite all this it acquitted itself well in the short time it remained at sea. Testimony, perhaps, to the high quality of naval aviators at that time...."

With little or no time on fighters, Judd was clearly at a disadvantage and looked to Cork for help as more pilots arrived. He recognised the important part Dick would play in squadron life and gave him full reign in tutoring the newcomers.

For ten days they had few aircraft to play with, but eventually three dark blue Grumman Martlets arrived. Until February 16th Cork flew these machines regularly, waiting for the moment when the RAF would release some old, surplus Mark 1 Hurricanes.

Judd was impatient to fly a Hurricane and asked Dick to contact Douglas Bader, to arrange a visit and some flying time. Bader was more than pleased to accommodate his protege and in mid February they flew south in two Martlets to Croydon. After a day's leave they journeyed from London to Duxford, where they had two hours flying, at first by themselves and later with elements of 242.

Over lunch Cork was shocked to discover that three old friends, Latta, Cryderman and Willie McNight, had all been killed. In McNight's case it seemed that this hardened veteran may have reached the end of his tether, with exhaustion contributing to his loss. Though serious disciplinary action shortly before his death could also have had played a part. In the final analysis it was impossible to specify any cause, perhaps his luck had just run out.

Back with 880, men and equipment arrived daily, including some well worn Hurricanes; patched, knocked about, leaking oil, with the smell of vomit still lingering in some cockpits. So different from the gleaming new aircraft Dick had flown days earlier at Duxford. But even these battered machines had sufficient life left in them to give 880's new pilots a taste of flying high powered fighters, sometimes with unfortunate results:

> "April 6th
> Lt. B. Fiddes collected Hurricane V 6881 from Silloth. On arrival at Arbroath Lt Fiddes found the duty runway blocked by a Fulmar with collapsed undercarriage and so was forced to land on a crosswind runway. As he was touching down a gust of wind lifted the starboard wing of the aircraft making it crash with considerable damage to itself. The pilot was unhurt. "

The next day Cork flew Brian Fiddes back to Silloth to collect another Hurricane, Judd's biting comments ringing in his ears. Despite this castigation Fiddes was the unhappy victim of another accident a little later, writing off another Hurricane, as recorded by Cork in his Logbook:

> "Camera gun attacks Drunry and Fiddes collided head on. OK. Hurricane and Glad bent. "

Sometimes the victims of these accidents were not so lucky:

> "June 11th
> During night flying training on June 10 to 11 the first fatal accident to occur in the squadron resulted in the death of Sub Lieutenant Bunch. His Hurricane V 7244 collided with a Swordfish during its take-off run. "

Not all squadron training took place in Scotland, and on one trip to the Lee on Solent for catapult trials, Cork and Judd took the opportunity of visiting Bader again at Tangmere, where he was now Wing Commander. It was supposed to be a social call, but developed from there as Bader later recalled:

> "The last time I saw him was in the summer of 1941 at Tangmere. He had flown in with a bearded friend called 'Butch'. The Wing was due over northern France two hours later. We put them each in a Spitfire and took them with us. Like old times Corky flew alongside me."

The operation, codenamed Circus 27, took the fighters in a wide sweep over occupied territory, from Dunkirk to St. Omer, then down the coast to Le Touquet and Boulogne. To the east other squadrons escorted three Stirling bombers inland over Lille, where they attacked the town's power station. As they lumbered back towards the coast, Tangmere's Wing picked them up, providing cover across the Channel. Despite the numbers involved and the clear challenge they presented to the Luftwaffe, there was no response, so the Navy men saw no action during the two hour flight. Just as well, because it was Judd's first flight in a Spitfire and he wallowed around trying to keep his place in formation.

After landing, the familiar pattern of debriefings and report writing got underway. Whilst Bader was engaged, the two naval officers wandered round looking closely at each Spitfire, noting modifications and comparing these latest Marks of fighter with their own aircraft. Dick saw that Bader had his initials painted on either side of his machine:

"Dick asked me about my initials 'emblazoned' along the side of my Spitfire. I explained the difficulty of recognition whilst flying in large formations and he gave me a wry smile, as though saying 'its showing off !' But it wasn't, because this simple identification made me instantly recognisable in the air, when leading a large formation. "

There was no need to return that night and so they stayed at Tangmere, having dinner with Bader and his wife. It had been an interesting day, full of incident, but they marvelled most at the generous resources enjoyed by the Wing. 880 and most other naval squadrons seemed to exist on a shoestring, making do with other peoples' cast-offs. As they climbed into their battered Hurricanes parked amongst rows of gleaming Spitfires, the difference was only too apparent.

From Lee on Solent, 880 flew directly to St Merryn, their new base in Cornwall. The move had been on the cards for some weeks, but had been delayed by St Merryn's lack of accommodation. They finally arrived on July 1st, their appearance proving rather more troublesome than expected, as their Record Book relates:

"The rail party first and later the aircraft arrived. The landing at St Merryn resulted in two minor accidents, SubLieutenant (A) Forrest RNVR, in N 2367, landed with his wheels up, and Sub Lieutenant(A) Davies, in W 9221, overshot, ran off end of downhill runway into barbed wire defences and the Hurricane tipped over onto its nose. From these accidents S/Lt Davies was taken to hospital with a broken nose, S/Lt Forrest received no injury. "

For two weeks, 880 flew exercises over the Cornish Coast and out to sea. Each evening, with work over, they walked or drove the short distance to the beach, climbing down steep paths set into the craggy coastline to bathe. After the chill air of Scotland it was a delight and few missed the opportunity of enjoying the warm weather; more so because word had been received that the squadron might soon be operational.

On June 22nd Hitler launched his long awaited attack against the USSR. With Nazi ambitions now set firmly in the east, the British could breathe more easily, but it was politically expedient to demonstrate support for a new found ally. So when the Soviets requested assistance, the British deployed their forces to help. A land invasion was out of the question, but the Navy could disrupt the flow of German seaborne reinforcements transitting from Kirkenes and Petsamo.

The Admiralty began assembling a task group capable of striking the enemy and deployed the two carriers Furious and Victorious. Albacore, Swordfish and Fulmar squadrons would provide the main thrust of the attack, but a few modern fighters were needed to protect the fleet itself. Yet only four could be accommodated in the limited space left on the carriers' decks and these came from 880:

> "Lt Cdr Judd, S/Lts Cork, Haworth, and Forrest proceeded to Yeovilton to collect new aircraft (Sea Hurricanes). They then proceeded to Twatt via Dumfries on 20th, embarking in HMS Furious on 21st."

> *Squadron Record Book.*

All these movements were carried out in the strictest secrecy and no one in 880 had any idea of their destination:

> "One evening four crews, of which I was one, were told to pack their bags and hammocks and be ready to leave at dawn the next day to destination 'x' this turned out to be RNAS Twatt in the Orkneys. We then went aboard HMS Furious and our four Hurricanes flew in after we had left for sea (July 23rd)."

> *R. A. Picken, CPO(AME)*
> *880 Squadron.*

As the Hurricanes flew out, personal possessions crammed into cockpits, each pilot had only the vaguest idea what to expect. They had been briefed, of course, by an elderly Commander at Twatt, but words were insufficient when you were about to make your first decklanding in an aircraft still largely untried in this role. Ten miles out they saw two carriers steaming north west, with other, smaller ships in attendance. As they approached the Fleet turned into the wind ready to receive them. Judd did not want to hurry his men and circled over the fleet for some minutes as they eyed the carriers 'tiny decks', lost in the sea's grey vastness.

HMS Furious was their destination and her swept back, slightly rakish look, with a small island perched on one side, provided identification. She looked a bit weather beaten and old fashioned, when set against Victorious, steaming along on her port quarter, but she was warlike for all that, with camouflage patterns on each flank and guns swinging around following the path of the Hurricanes.

The moment could not delayed any longer, and one by one the fighters came down, Judd first, leading by example. Wheels and hook, watch the batsman, over the round down, 'CUT', take the wire and snap forward against the straps. Let the wind push her back, hook released and taxi forward over the crash barrier, gun the engine and switch off. Remarkably all four landed safely, cheered by their arrival on board a carrier for the first time. It had been a long journey, as Cork remarked in a letter written that evening:

> "It's funny to think that I joined the Navy over two years ago.
> So its taken me all this time just to reach a carrier. Must be
> some sort of record! We landed on without incident, though
> it would have been nice if we could have completed our full
> decklanding training before reaching an operational ship,
> under the eyes of the Fleet, so to speak."

Judd reported to Commander (Flying) then the Captain, whilst the other three were taken below to their cabins, through a maze of gangways and ladders. As they passed through the ship, unfamiliar smells and noises bombarded their senses. Hugh Popham, who experienced the same feeling of disorientation some months later, described the feelings that swamped a newcomer to a big ship:

> "At first it was utterly baffling. The ship is so huge, and her
> geography so complex. One is continually losing oneself,
> drifting into seaman's messdecks, or the galley, full of shining
> ovens and sweating cooks in soiled white aprons, or reaching
> deadends, chilly metal corners smelling of potatoes, and lob-

bies smelling of hundred octane......Any fantasy can sweat
coldly to birth, like a mushroom, in those long, lit, empty,
echoing corridors. And the roaring air is electric with half-
heard orders and shrill with bosun's pipes, and brassy with
bells and bugles. "

Having settled into their cabins, the four newcomers briefly toured
the ship ending up on the flight deck, where their Sea Hurricanes had
been secured to the deck. The two carriers were now in line astern,
with escorts, two cruisers and six destroyers, moving freely around
them. Flying ended as dusk fell, although the Hurricanes on Furious and
several Fulmars and an Albacore on Victorious could be scrambled
quickly if needed, but the night remained quiet.

Early next morning, aircrew were briefed more fully about the operation. The force consisted of seven squadrons 812(9 Swordfish), 813 (9
Albacores), 800 (9 Fulmars) and 880 on Furious, whilst Victorious carried 827 and 828, with 18 Albacores, and 809 (12 Fulmars). In theory
the Albacores and Swordfish would bomb or torpedo shipping, reported 'massing' in the area, whilst the Fulmar squadrons would provide a
'top cover defensive screen' to deal with any fighter opposition.

As the Fleet sailed northwards Rear Admiral WakeWalker,
Commanding the First Cruiser Squadron began keeping a daily record
of events:

> "24th July.
> At 0856, Devonshire detected an Aircraft approaching. A
> fighter patrol was flown off from Furious, but it quickly
> became obvious that Devonshire had detected the A/S
> patrol. One Fulmar landed on when Furious was stern to
> wind and crashed.
> The weather was overcast all day, with visibility from 1
> mile to five. I regarded this as something of a blessing as it
> reduced the possibility of our being sighted by the enemy.
>
> 25th July.
> At O258 Achates struck a mine.
> It had been my original intention to send Victorious and
> Suffolk into Reydarfiord, but decided that it was unwise to
> leave them to make this difficult entrance in the fog.
> Glettinganes Light was sighted and it was possible to fix

our position. The force then proceeded to Seidisfiord,
Devonshire and Furious anchoring above the mine field and
Victorious and Suffolk joining Adventure near the entrance to
the fiord.

26th July.
A/S air patrol was arranged using Suffolk's and Devonshire's
Walruses.
Force 'P' sailed from Seidisfiord at 2300 at 20 knots. An A/S air
patrol had been asked for by Admiral Commanding, Iceland,
and on leaving Seidisfiord this was provided by a Northrop.
The patrol was later taken over by a Catalina, but as the
weather closed down the Catalina was not seen.

27th July
At 0345 the force ran into fog. This continued until the afternoon, when the visibility varied from two miles to ten miles,
with low cloud overhead.

28th July.
Oiling took place. During this time Furious and Victorious
acted independently and maintained an A/S patrol.

29th July.
At 0058 Furious reported fog ahead. At this time the force
was spread about, Devonshire was close to Black Ranger (an
RFA), and Adventure, Suffolk seven or eight miles away to the
southwestward, Furious and Victorious with two aircraft up
were fives miles to the south. Nothing more seen of the
Squadron until 0900 on the 29th when the aircraft carriers
formed up, followed by Suffolk and six destroyers at 1047. I
was glad to hear that Victorious had succeeded in landing on
her aircraft. "

After two patrols on the 22nd, during which Cork circled the fleet
for twenty minutes, 880's Hurricanes stayed on Furious's deck for seven
days. Whilst poor weather was chiefly responsible for this, the need to
preserve the force's small fighter screen proved decisive. So the four
pilots kicked their heels, remaining on alert in case intruders appeared
on radar. It was just as well that little happened, because three of their

number were suffering from seasickness. Finally on the 29th Dick flew two long patrols as the fleet closed the enemy coast and the threat of attack grew larger. Both flights passed without incident, the first ending on Victorious' deck, Furious being too busy to receive him.

"30th July
The weather continued overcast. I realised that there was a possibility that fog might come down in the middle of flying off. So I ordered one carrier to operate on a line parallel to wind through the flying off position and the other carrier on the far side. I arranged that, so far as possible, Devonshire and Victorious should operate on the inshore side of this line, thus giving Furious a clear run to seaward.
At 1200 the clouds thinned and cleared away with good visibility. Still the force had not been sighted and there appeared every reason to hope that the attack would be launched without being detected. But these hopes were doomed from the start. At 1346 just as Furious was flying off two Hurricanes, which had to be launched before her TSRs (Torpedo, Spotter, Reconnaissance aircraft) could fly off, an HE 111 was sighted. An enemy report was made by this aircraft and from that moment the German forces operating off Tana Fiord ceased to transmit. I considered it was too late to call off the attack and it was launched as planned.
Victorious flew off 20 TSRs, in one range, followed by 12 Fulmars eighteen minutes later. Furious commenced ten minutes before Victorious, by flying off 4 Hurricanes and 9 TSRs. These were followed by a second range of 9 TSRs and finally by 6 Fulmars. The Striking Force went into the attack as planned at 1429 followed 7 minutes later by the fighters. Three Fulmars from Victorious and the four Hurricanes from Furious were kept for protection of the force. During the attack the Hurricanes refuelled on Victorious. Two of them would not start after refuelling and had to be kept on deck. The resulting congestion caused a delay in the landing on programme just at the time when (but for lack of initiative)a German bombing attack should have developed. This delay might have had serious consequences."

Rear Admiral Wake Walker.

Capatin. A. G. Talbot on Furious, with direct access to the returning
aircrew, later provided a more detailed account of the raid:

"At 1349 one enemy aircraft was sighted right ahead. The
Hurricanes of the first range, which was at that time being
flown off, endeavoured to locate it without success.
On passage Furious's squadrons passed 12 miles West of
Majakkaniemi, flying low over the water in an effort to avoid
visual and radar detection. They climbed whilst proceeding to
the entrance to the Gulf of Petsamo. 812 Squadron led, followed by 827, at 2000 feet, with 800 Squadron above and
astern of them.
At approximately 1450, single engined monoplanes were
observed, but it is thought that they were Fulmars from
Victorious. If this was the case, presumably they had lost
their way. By flying above the agreed height and over the
land, they frustrated all efforts to evade detection.
One Fulmar from 800 Squadron forced landed in position
260 degrees, six miles from Heinasaari Island light with
smoke pouring from its engine. The crew were seen to get
into their dinghy.
There were no suitable ship targets for torpedoes at either
Trifona or Liinahamari. One small ship off Paksuniemi was
unsuccessfully attacked and a photograph revealed that
another small ship, unseen by aircraft was actually berthed
alongside Number 1 pier. One torpedo was fired at this pier
and was seen to run. A second observer saw an explosion,
but he also failed to see this ship. Other than these vessels,
there were only small craft present at Liinahamari. One
Albacore was shot down by enemy fighters after making his
attack, and one Fulmar which is missing is thought to have
met the same fate. One other Fulmar engaged an ME 109,
which was driven off by means of a 'Tommy' gun from the
back seat. Returning aircraft were landed on from 1615 to
1658.
During the retirement heavy fighter opposition continued
and one JU 87 was shot down for certain by a front gun and
a probable ME 109 with a rear gun. 827 Squadron lost six
Albacores. The air gunner for whom the probable ME 109 is
claimed, died in the aircraft and was later buried at sea. 809

Squadron shot down two ME 110s and one ME 109 and claimed another ME 110 as a possible. Two Fulmars were missing, but the pilot of one was seen to escape by parachute...."

Facing such intense opposition, torpedo and bomb attacks were severely hampered. Only 828 Squadron managed to avoid German fighters long enough to hit targets and left two ships on fire at the northern end of Bokkfjord, losing five of their Albacores in the process.

As remnants of this battered force made their way back out towards the carriers, two serviceable Hurricanes, flown by Judd and Cork, plus three Fulmars, rose above the fleet and watched their return. From over their radios they were told to expect an enemy attack, but as time passed radar screens revealed nothing and only friendly aircraft approached. With petrol running low they eventually joined the landing pattern and put down on Furious, the scene of much activity as serviceable aircraft were prepared for a second strike if needed:

> "At 1900 the force withdrew to the north. No attempt was made by the enemy to locate or attack fleet. I had previously arranged for a Walrus from Suffolk to pick up any survivors, but the only reports of aircraft down were from Furious. Two of her crews were known to be in the water in position 260 degrees Heinasaari 6 miles, but as this was only 5 miles off shore and a long way from my position it would have entailed fighter protection and remaining for several hours longer near the flying off position. I did not think it justifiable to send the Walrus in. "

The scene on board the two carriers in the hours after the raid differed considerably. Victorious's squadrons had been hit hard. From 20 Albacores that had left her deck 11 failed to return, and 8 more were damaged. 2 Fulmars had also gone down. By comparison Furious's losses had been slight 2 Fulmars and 1 Albacore.

880's two Hurricanes remained on Victorious over night, its hard pressed fitters trying to get them going. Steve Forrest and Dickie Haworth paced back and forth, anxious to be back with Furious. The atmosphere amongst surviving aircrews on 'Vic' was very sombre and there were many expressions of anger in 'Ready Rooms'and wardroom that night. They had little time for 'strangers', particularly those whose

aircraft littered their deck, making landing even more difficult. The two
Hurricane pilots wisely kept a low profile, whilst more senior officers
tried to analyze and justify the attack. Whichever they looked at it, there
was little to show for these losses:

> "The material results of this operation were small and the
> losses heavy. This had been expected. The heaviest losses
> occurred in the squadrons from Victorious and there is no
> doubt that some survivors felt that an attack on such poor
> targets against heavy opposition was not justified and their
> morale was rather shaken until they appreciated the political
> necessity of the operation.
> The gallantry of the aircraft crews, who knew before leaving
> that their chances of survival had gone and they were certain
> to face heavy odds is beyond praise.... I trust that the encour-
> agement to the morale of our Allies was proportionately
> great."

Despatch submitted by Admiral Sir John Tovey, C in C.

Despite these heavy losses there was no let up for aircrew. Admiral
Wake Walker, on board Devonshire, planned further strikes against
German shipping:

> "July 31st.
> Destroyer activity off Tana Fiord had made me suspicious that
> they might be using Smalfiord as an anchorage for supply
> ships or other such vessels. As this might form a target for a
> second attack I arranged for a Fulmar with its distinguishing
> marks erased, as far as possible, to reconnoitre this fiord dur-
> ing the night. At 0316 one Fulmar was flown off from
> Victorious. This returned at 0455 and reported that she had
> found four twin engined aircraft patrolling off the entrance
> and had not been able to reconnoitre the fiord. Five minutes
> after this Fulmar returned the squadron ran into thick fog.
> Furious's fuel situation made it necessary for her to return
> immediately as she would have little more than 500 tons on
> arrival at Seidifiord and had no margin for possible loss due
> to damage. I accordingly arranged to complete Victorious as
> far as possible with aircraft from Furious. Owing to fog this

could not be started until 1215 when it cleared sufficiently to allow the operation to begin.

Whilst this transfer was in progress the force was sighted by a Dornier 18. At about 1300 Furious flew off two Hurricanes (Judd and Haworth) which shot it down, but not before it had time to make a report on our presence. As the whole force was then steering west in company I was not unduly disturbed as I wanted the enemy to think that the force was returning together.

Transfer of aircraft was completed at 1530 and course was then altered to 305 degrees, ie to the north, in order to avoid observation by the enemy. At 1633 a report of another aircraft was received, and fighters were again flown off, but saw nothing and returned.

August 31st

We held this course until 0001 when Furious was detached, with escort, in a position 40 miles northeast of Bear Island. Hurricanes flew defensive patrols, searching briefly for a shadower, but none was intercepted. "

Now stripped of her strike aircraft with only sufficient numbers of Hurricanes and Fulmars for her own protection, Furious' part in the operation came to an end. Meanwhile Victorious continued to patrol, but found little of note to attack and broke away on the 6th, arriving at Scapa Flow late on the 7th.

As Furious reached home waters, supply boats came out, bringing fresh food, papers and, most importantly to men returning from operations, sacks full of mail. As 1941 passed, correspondence with Isabelle in Canada had dwindled; long term separation inevitably having a cooling effect on their relationship. After two weeks at sea he, like his comrades on board, keenly anticipated the arrival of letters and parcels, but there were none from Canada. Concerned to discover what might be happening to Isabelle, Dick wrote to her mother in Slough:

"HMS Furious,
5th August 1941.
Dear Mrs Trudgett,
I was wondering if you had any further news of Isabelle.
Actually I havn't heard from her for six weeks now, but of

course perhaps the letters havn't caught up with me yet. As I told you in my last letter the only thing I have heard is the cable a friend of mine had from his firm in Toronto saying Isabelle had decided to stay in Canada. Of course I had the cable given to me just as we sailed some time ago and since then I have been unable to get ashore to fix anything up. However if I do get some leave, as I hope to shortly I will come over to see you and perhaps you will be able to tell me something in the meantime I wonder if you could just write me a line about all this, because honestly I don't know what to think about things now everything has just gone flat and any plans I did have all seemed to be washed up.

I hope that Mr Trudgett and yourself are keeping well and perhaps the old German does not trouble you so much at nights now. Will you please excuse this very short note, but we get so little time to do anything nowadays I hope to see you all soon,

My love to you,
Dickie. "

Their relationship had changed, but it would be several months before the reasons for this became clear. For the moment, work on board Furious kept him fully occupied and within days they sailed to join Convoy WS ('Winston Special') 11, forming up at Liverpool.

By chance, Dick's brother, Brian, now a commissioned officer with the Royal Horse Artillery, was sailing on one of the troopship being escorted by Furious; destination Suez and the Desert Army. Neither was aware of the other's presence, as Brian Cork recalled:

"We went out of Liverpool, north of Ireland right out into the Atlantic and as we progressed the escorts increased all the time another two destroyer, a battleship (Repulse on her way out to Singapore). Second day out I saw an aircraft carrier coming up behind us, which was unmistakable with its flat top. There were one or two naval chaps on board and I asked them which carrier it was and one said, 'Its the Furious'. I replied, 'Oh my brother's on it' and wondered if we might get in somewhere to refuel and meet. But it didn't happen because after about a week out in the Atlantic the Furious turned east and went into Gibraltar. So I didn't meet him. Just one of those things.

We had in fact met during June when our home leave over-lapped and as things turned out this was to be the last time. When he was at home I was abroad and vice versa. It was unfortunate; at an age when I would have liked to know my brother better we had split up he had gone his way and I mine and because of the war our paths did not cross, which I regret.

A little later Dick wrote home saying something to the effect of, 'You'll be interested to know he (Brian) is safely on his way and while he's sitting down in the bar knocking back Pink Gins I'm having to fly round this damn convoy guarding it!' which happened to be true.

After Furious left we made our way down to the Cape, Repulse staying in close escort and she remained with us until Mombassa where she peeled off. Its strange how you get very attached to a ship when she is close to for such a long period providing protection, moreso than a carrier because she looks so big and solid. Each morning she was there sailing serenely by. Of course we had no idea of her destination or the fate that would soon befall her. "

Each day Furious' fighters circled around the convoy, watching for the enemy. Occasionally anti-submarine patrols took off, quickly disappearing into the distance. These flights reminded Cork of life with 242 Squadron in 1940, when he had spent so much time over the Channel guarding convoys. Now a hard, unpredictably mobile metal deck awaited his return, not a sedate green field and for the first and last time he experienced the embarrassment of a bad landing at sea:

"Squadron Record Book
S/Lieut Cork in P 3056 aboard HMS Furious crashed into island during deck landing, damaging starboard wing and engine. Aircraft was virtual write off. Pilot unhurt. "

As the troopships continued their voyage to South Africa then onwards, round Cape Horn to Egypt, Furious was detached a single operation in the Mediterranean flying off RAF fighters to reinforce Malta; a role growing increasingly more important as Axis forces continued to attack the troublesome island. Once complete Furious was bound for a much needed refit in the States and called into Gibraltar on the way:

> "Squadron Record Book.
> 880 Squadron detachment aboard HMS Furious disembarked at Gibraltar to await passage to United Kingdom, aircraft being left in storage at Gibraltar. The personnel returned in three groups in escort vessel Fowey and destroyers Nestor and Laforey. "

Despite the heavy losses inflicted by the enemy on air crew during the Petsamo raids, 880's four pilots had escaped unscathed, learning a great deal in the process about carrier life and the Hurricane's performance at sea. More importantly they had seen the deadly side of seaborne operations and the forbearance displayed by squadrons taking crippling losses. It was a lesson that would serve them well in the year ahead.

CHAPTER ELEVEN

HMS INDOMITABLE

In the last few months of 1941, Britain's carrier fleet was over-stretched. Victorious, Ark Royal, Eagle and Hermes were operational, but the remainder were in dockyard hands. Formidable and Illustrious had been badly damaged by enemy bombs and Furious was in refit; all three would be out of commission until 1942. Meanwhile the Fleet's newest carrier, Indomitable, faced months of trials before becoming operational.

As Indomitable exercised in the sheltered waters off the west coast of Scotland, Judd, Cork, Haworth and Forrest, fresh from operations on Furious, landed at Devonport. In their absence, the rest of 880 Squadron had continued training, some even managing deck landing practice on board the light carrier, HMS Argus. Others arrived too late for this and faced their first landings on Indomitable herself, which they all safely accomplished during October.

Having collected four new Sea Hurricanes, the 'Furious detachment' flew out to join Indomitable near Ailsa Craig on the 10th, displaying a confidence born of recent experience; landing without difficulty or fuss, much to the relief of the unseasoned flight deck party.

Many new faces had appeared in the squadron since St Merryn and the process of getting to know each other started afresh:

> "It was sometime before the two halves knitted in our
> minds. Moose (Lt W. H. Martin) we knew with his flat,
> bony face; in the air he was first rate; in the wardroom,
> laconic; and with Butch he used a kind of self-contained
> cussedness that was near contempt.... Brian Fiddes, we

knew too;a tall, flexible, rather foppish-looking chap, with strawy hair and protuberant, pale blue eyes. His voice matched his appearance;it was affected, blase, the instrument of an amused indifference…. Steve Harris we knew, a flashy pilot for all his bloodhoundlook and almost imperturbable good humour; and the 'Boy'(S/Lt H. L. Cunliffe Owen), rich spoilt, slovenly and usually late, a sheaf of unimportant vices carried with disarming and ruthless charm. We shared a cabin; and on the rare occasions that he used a toothbrush or a hairbrush, he used mine, yet one suffered even this.

And now there were the others; first amongst them, Dickie Cork, with a DFC and seven or eight confirmed, gained while flying on loan to the RAF with Bader at Duxford during the Battle of Britain. Dickie, the only one of us with fighter experience, had the quality men follow. An immaculate pilot, with the workings of the squadron on the deck or in the air at his fingertips, he moved with the radiance of the Head Prefect about him, taking the worship of the lesser fry for granted and joining in their sport with a certain well-disguised condescension. He treated Butch as if he were a woolly, temperamental housemaster;and no one ever saw him drunk. Johnnie Forrest, a rugger player of note, shared some thing of the same indestructible boyishness, the same inbred ability. He would be Head Prefect one day…. Jack Smith and Dickie Haworth, RNVR to the bone, were of a different stamp. Jack, a geologist by inclination, regarded life and his fellow men with mature irony, almost as if they would one day be good for classification in a textbook of tolerable fossils; and Dickie, short and saturnine, was the squadron's licensed clown. He had Butch's indulgence, which he abused, and capered as he pleased.

These eight, with Butch, were the squadron's more or less seasoned core, with Bungy Williams, our own PO pilot, who lived a shadow life outside the precincts of the wardroom… And bringing up the rear were Crooky (S/Lt J. Cruickshank) myself, and a serious-minded two ringer RN, new to flying, named Lowe…."

Hugh Popham.

Many years later, when asked to describe Cork, Popham added a brief postscript:

> "I remember him as one of those people who were natural pilots, professionally super competent, whom one would always be glad to know was present if there was anything doing. You could not imagine him rattled or caught out in the air which makes his death, later in the war, all the more incomprehensible. On the ground he was equally efficient and off duty, delightful company. In short, he had absolute integrity, both as a pilot and man."

After losing his closest friends in 1940, Dick seemed to foster a casual approach to relationships, choosing to maintain some distance. It was a defence mechanism, but it tended to set him apart from his comrades, who treated him with a certain deference. As Popham observed, the mantle of 'Head Prefect' fitted him perfectly and it was an act that gave him a shield, behind which he could disguise his feelings on board ship; a world where there was little privacy to be had at the best of times.

Once her squadrons were safely on board, Indomitable spent several days in the Clyde waiting to join an eastbound convoy. With the threat of U Boat attack so great around Britain's coast, the Admiralty decreed that this new capital ship would spend two months exercising in the safer waters of the Caribbean.

Although she had not worked up to full efficiency, there was sufficient experience amongst her aircrew to provide the convoy with fighter and anti-submarine protection. But as soon as they rounded Ireland and headed out into the Atlantic they met the full force of a south westerly gale and thoughts of attack soon evaporated. Within hours of leaving the grey calmness of home waters, towering green waves were crashing over Indomitable's bows, cascading down her flight deck and sweeping anything away that was not secured. Below decks the scene was equally as violent and few escaped the worst effects of seasickness; groaning masses confined to bunks and hammocks; unsecured personal possessions crashing around their ears; the sound of breaking crockery, and sliding furniture echoing in the distance.

Four days out, the weather improved. Though the skies remained grey and overcast, the ship rolling in a deep swell. Radar threw up a number of ghosts and a Fulmar from 800 Squadron was sent off to intercept an enemy aircraft, thought to be a long range Focke Wulf 'Condor'. The crew found nothing, lost contact with Indomitable and, as darkness fell, went down into the cold, inhospitable Atlantic, where their chances of survival were slim. The carrier reduced speed and turned about, waiting for dawn when Albacores and Fulmars could be flown off to search the vast, empty sea for a tiny dinghy, being tossed, then hidden by the waves. Against all odds, an Albacore spotted the two survivors and radioed the ship. Within an hour she had picked up a cold, but thankful, pilot and observer.

During the voyage 880's aircraft stayed in the ship's hangars, any fighter protection being provided by Fulmars. By the time Indomitable had detached herself from the convoy and was heading south to the West Indies, Judd's pilots were impatient to fly their Hurricanes again. After a brief stay in Bermuda, to replenish, their opportunity came and for two days the squadron undertook air firings and formation flying. Pilots and aircraft responded well and these exercises passed off uneventfully, until Moose Martin missed the wires and flew straight into the barrier.

In Bermuda, Butch Judd spotted several Walrus seaplanes floating in Hamilton Sound. Keen to rekindle his association with this aircraft, he borrowed one from the Naval Base and flew it quite contentedly around the islands. But, in his own uncompromising way, he wanted the rest of his squadron to fly the type as well, press ganging a number of unwilling junior officers in the process. Only Dick and Petty Officer Williams were exempt, having flown the type with Judd before, the latter being hit most ungallantly over the head with its joystick, by the short tempered Judd, when things went wrong. But on this occasion each flight passed without incident and Indomitable proceeded to Kingston, Jamaica, with 880 still intact.

Kingston Harbour, being virtually land locked by a ring of coral reefs, required great care when entering port. Buoys marked the route, but even with these in place navigation, through many sharp turns to port and starboard, could prove a nightmare, particularly for a ship the size of Indomitable:

> "My mind, or simply my body, perhaps, recorded the heel of
> the ship as she swung into the outer channel, the sudden
> drop in engine revs. That was normal.... Even after an
> uneventful day of exercises in sight of land, there was the

unmistakable feeling of ease and relaxation that comes with
the end of any voyage, however short.
I changed quickly. I should be just in time to watch our
arrival off the town. There was a crash and shudder, and my
chair shot along the floor and fetched up, with me still in it,
against the washbasin.... I dashed out of the cabin and
joined them, and we scrambled up on the flight deck by the
shortest route, a sick feeling of apprehension working in
the pits of our stomachs.
After a time, Dickie Cork joined us.
'Well, we're on the rocks chaps. Thank God I'm not the
pilot!'
'But how? What happened?'
'Lord knows. But it looks as though we've been trying to
pass the port side of a porthand buoy. I always heard there
was no future in it.' He was perfectly right of course, as
always...."

Hugh Popham.

Within minutes, damage control parties had inspected
Indomitable's injuries. She was not taking in much water and her
Captain ordered 'hard astern', to see if she could be pulled clear from
the coral, now seen clearly beneath her bows . They were unsuccessful and by nightfall a signal was despatched to the Admiralty:

"3rd November
Regret to report ship grounded at 16.21 r/3 with stem in
position 174 degrees 600 feet from Rackum Cay Beacon.
Way was nearly off but ship is fast from stem for about 100
feet. Am lightening ship. No tug available here. Weather and
sea calm. No wind."

Meanwhile efforts to move her continued, some appearing ridicu-
lous in their execution:

"The ship went aground and all attempts to free her failed.
The next high tide was at midnight so everyone was
ordered not to turn in. At 2359 'clear lower decks' was
piped and everyone assembled on the after end of the flight

deck and to the tune 'Pop Goes The Weasel', played by the Royal Marine Band, everyone jumped in unison, with engines going full astern. Finally we managed to free the ship."

Rex Picken.

By morning Indomitable had completed her voyage and was swinging gently around her anchor, as though nothing had happened. But her hull had been damaged and divers were over the side at first light to assess her condition. In the meantime signals flashed back and forth across the Atlantic, demanding information; notes of censure barely hidden in advance of a Court of Enquiry. As the day progressed it became clear that Indomitable would have to dock for repair and the Navy would be deprived of a 'valuable asset' at a time when they could least afford it.

For forty eight hours little happened; thought being given to Indomitable's future. She was seaworthy, but there was no yard capable of taking her in the West Indies and a long perilous trip across the Atlantic was not considered a sensible option. So the Admiralty turned to the US Government for help and permission was given for her to enter Norfolk Navy Yard.

Whilst her crew seemed happy to be 'in the States' on an impromptu holiday, the carrier would be sorely missed. Two days after docking, word came through that Ark Royal had been sunk in the Mediterranean; a major blow to the Navy's carrier strength and a blow to national morale. Yet worse was to come.

With Japan threatening friendly countries in the Far East, the War Cabinet decided to strengthen Empire Forces in the region. Strained to breaking point, the Admiralty could only release two capital ships, the new battleship, Prince of Wales, and the First War veteran, Repulse. With the experience of Taranto in mind, a carrier was assigned to provide air cover for the operation. Indomitable was destined to fill this role until her accident.

If Japan had not attacked Pearl Harbour on December 7th this might have gone unpunished. But the loss of so many American battleships made reinforcement an overriding priority and Prince of Wales and Repulse were the only ships available to support the depleted Pacific Fleet. Like lambs to the slaughter, they sailed from Singapore, without adequate air cover, and were duly attacked and sunk, by Japanese aircraft in the China Sea.

In the days that followed, the Admiralty came to see Indomitable's absence as a major cause of this disaster, even though her Air Group, with its ageing and outdated aircraft, could hardly have tackled such a large force. Yet despite this the carrier became something of a scapegoat for this ill-conceived, poorly prepared mission. Whilst remaining with his ship for several months more, Indomitable's Captain would eventually be replaced and face a court martial for his part in a chain of events that began on the coral reef around Jamaica.

On November 10th, Indomitable reached Norfolk, where 880 flew off all serviceable aircraft, leaving two on board. They wished to make a show of their arrival and landed in formation at the Naval Air Station nearby, two and three abreast. The two Hurricanes left on Indomitable arrived a little later, in equally impressive style:

> "Two Hurricanes remained on board to have their 120 hours inspections. Once completed Judd wanted them at the airfield, so they held up all the traffic from the docks to the airfield and made them taxi all the way on public roads. The Yanks thought this was a great event."

> *Richard Brooke*

Having grown used to life in a country under seige and the austerity of shipborne existence, their sudden and unexpected release in America seemed to some like Alice entering Wonderland:

> "After years of rationing, where all your favourite foods and sweets just couldn't be found and everything was in short supply, arriving in the States was akin to arriving in Mecca. As the convoy approached its eastern coast late at night the glow of lights, in buildings and streets, came as a great surprise. After years of living with the 'blackout' you felt quite exposed and wanted to pull curtains and turn lights off from force of habit. But the feeling soon passed.
> Being a youngster with a sweet tooth, my first port of call, after we'd landed, was a candy store, where I gorged myself on chocolate, making myself sick in the process. But most of us did something silly like that making up for lost time I suppose. Anyway it was a marvellous experience until you

grew accustomed to it all and then you remembered everyone at home and the shortages…"

Bernard Graves.

For Cork, being in the States had one other advantage, he was suddenly much closer to Isabelle and soon after landing he sent a telegram to
her:

"Wire telephone number to HAS BOQ Breezy Point most
important.

Dickie Cork."

Dick wanted to speak to Isabelle and suggest a quick journey south
so they could be married. But in the two years since they last met much
had changed and this moment of elation soon turned to disappointment. Unable to return home and separated from friends and family,
Isabelle had struggled to survive in a foreign land. She could not transmit her feelings of isolation to Dick by letter and so their relationship
had grown more distant and less intense. Whilst the war lasted, it
seemed that their friendship stood little chance of renewal and she was
forced to make some sort of life for herself in Canada. So in an increasingly hostile world she had met and married a young Canadian.

Telephones are no medium for bad news, their remoteness height-
ening the power to injure, yet at the same time allowing each party to
disguise their feelings under a veneer of politeness or forced under-
standing. Kept short by restrictions on cost, their phone call was very
brief, allowing little time for explanation or recrimination. But it left a
soreness of spirit that lingered in the months ahead, though the closeness of war proved a distraction.

Three days later Indomitable, her repairs complete, slipped out of
Norfolk. As dawn broke she set course for Jamaica and within hours her
Air Group had landed. All 880's Hurricanes were struck down below
deck, where they remained until the 29th, being made ready for the
final part of the ship's work up. The resumption of flying bought with
it the usual spate of accidents, as recalled by Richard Brooke:

"After we left Palisadoes the aircraft came back on board
with their guns covered in fine dust, so we had to strip them

down and clean them. This we started to do on the flight deck, but after a short time the wings got so hot that we could not climb on them to get the guns out; all the guns being loaded when the aircraft came back. We had to unload them first and take out the ammo tanks. I unloaded seven guns, then the flight deck party came and pushed my aircraft on to the forward lift to go down into the upper hanger.

We followed a safety drill by lifting all breech block covers, just in case you fired the gun with a round up the spout. If the covers were open it would only fire one round, because the guides in the cover would not be able to feed a round into the breech block. In my case seven covers stood open, but the last one was closed. Down in the hangar I inadvertently pressed the firing button! I only fired three rounds, but it seemed much more to me.

I was marched off by a burly marine to the cells (in case I had gone mad with sunstroke), where I spent the night. The padre came to see me, and the Duty Officer of the squadron called to ask if I wanted anything. No one was allowed to talk to me about this incident. Last of all the doctor looked me over and passed his verdict as 'finger trouble', adding I was as sane as he was.

Unknown to me Lt Cdr Judd had been busy and when I saw the Duty Officer I was placed on Commander's Report, then Captain's Report and saw him later in the day. He said as the ship had not been damaged and no person hurt, he would give me a caution, but it would not go on my record, so promotion would not be at risk. He also said in a low voice for my ears only, 'We all make mistakes, some larger than others'. I know how he felt, he left the ship soon after, for a Court Martial, and I never heard about him again.

Judd had been to see the Captain and put in a good word for me. He always looked after his men in the squadron, even though he worked us night and day."

In the way he supported his men, Judd displayed a trait that few thought existed and many respected. It came as a surprise that such a belligerent, uncompromising personality could develop this ability. Though for the most part his sharp tongue caused resentment, where

a diplomatic word would have proved more productive. Some resolutely managed to fall foul of his temper, becoming personal 'whip-
ping boys' in the process:

> "Hugh Popham was duty officer and during the dogwatches
> was on the flight deck, so were plenty more playing deck
> hockey etc. Our CO saw Popham way down aft and called
> him. Popham started walking up the deck. 'Double man dou-
> ble', shouted Judd. Every one looked as poor old Popham ran
> up and stood before Judd and saluted. He never forgave him
> for that, because some time later, when we were back at
> Stretton, my mate Turner and I were in a local pub. Sitting at
> the next table was Popham and some other pilots. One of
> them said that they had been pushed around by someone at
> the station, adding that it wouldn't have happened had Judd
> still been alive. Popham banged his fist on the table, all the
> glasses jumping about, saying in a loud voice, 'No ! I'm glad
> he's dead and if he was buried ashore I'd go and dance on his
> grave every 12 months.
> It's true Judd was a bad boy at times, in as much as every-
> thing had to be just right; nobody got away with anything.
> But on the good side, nobody put upon us, he knew his
> squadron was the best and no matter where we went he got
> the best out of us...."

Rex Picken

In contrast, Judd's reaction to Cork was benign, even friendly. Though
only a Sub Lieutenant, his experience and professionalism commanded
respect, a fact that Judd recognised and used to good effect. He was also
RN, not RNVR, and in Judd's eyes this counted for a lot; he was a 'club
member', not a hostilities only man.

By mid December Indomitable was finally declared operational and
on the 18th put to sea, with three destroyers in attendance, her future
uncertain now that the Eastern Fleet had lost Repulse and Prince of
Wales. Strategists in London saw the threat posed by the Japanese to
British interests in the Indian Ocean and began marshalling the few
ships available to counter this threat. Indomitable was seen as a part of
this reinforcement and, as the New Year dawned, she crossed to
Capetown to await further orders.

During her passage officers and NCOs continued to push the crew, sharpening performance for the campaigns that lay ahead. It was also a time in which the customs and routine of life were firmly established and naval authority exercised:

"The ship's Commander took an instant dislike to all Fleet Air Arm ratings. To him we were scruffy, never dressed in the rig of the day and worked all hours of the day and night, disregarding normal watch keeping four hours on, four hours off. Our dress did seem odd to the rest of the ship's company, because we always wore overalls, and, heaven forbid, plimsolls, instead of issue boots! So when the Commander wasn't shouting at us, his 'Jimmy the One' was.

Lt Cdr Judd used to have it broadcast over the tannoy for all hands to muster in the forward hanger at the double. If the Commander was in the vicinity he used to stop us, and tell us to walk; as we could only run at the sound of 'Action Stations'. That did not go down well with Judd and after a few weeks, when the aircraft did not get onto the flight deck at the time prescribed and Commander Flying was pulling his hair out, Judd sent him to see the ship's Commander. As a result it was decided to allow us to proceed 'at the rush', which meant the same thing.

When not working, our main interest was food. We had a fixed menu in the Navy, which was probably the same in any ship in any part of the world, at any time. One slight exception was local fruit, which was bought in the ports we happened to visit.

On Sundays it was always bacon and eggs for breakfast, roast pork, apple sauce, roast potatoes, apple pie and custard. At tea we always had bread and jam, and a slab cake. I used to make a sandwich by putting the cake between two slices of bread. At other times I filled them with salt and pepper and a thin smear of mustard. With a good imagination you could think it was an egg sandwich.

The ship was built to hold a crew of 1800, but always seemed to carry about 2400. A large overspill. So we were always short of fresh water. We were allowed so much for drinking and washing, and the only way to ration it, was to cut the supply to the bathrooms. It was usually on for 30 minutes at breakfast

time, and again at evening. They also staggered the times for
different bathrooms. If we had been working late into the
night they would turn on our bathrooms for a limited period.
Our only drink on board was a 'Goffer', it was served in the
canteen flat after working hours, and it was a fruit cordial
mixed with fizzy water. We also had a two in one tot of rum.
This was to stop you building up a stock, and getting tiddly,
as rum will not keep with a mixture of water. It had to be
drunk on the spot. We all craved for the day when promotion
made us Petty Officers, because they had their rum served
neat, and it could be put in a bottle and swapped at a later
date for money or favours...."

Richard Brooke.

As Indomitable crossed the Atlantic, her Air Group flew whenever
conditions allowed; anti-submarine patrols, practice scrambles, formation flying and fleet defence against torpedo bombers; in this case
Albacores in disguise. A busy schedule, but in these quiet southern
waters undetected and undisturbed by enemy action, though their
defensive guard remained firmly in place. Yet even in these 'peaceful'
conditions accidents still happened with appalling regularity. Steve
Forrest flew into the barrier on December 22nd, then 800 Squadron hit
a patch of bad luck and managed to damage all of their Fulmars in a single stroke; each clipping the tail of the one in front as they taxied forward and skidded on a sheen of night time dew, after landing. 880's
pilots and Judd, in particular, looked on in amusement, enjoying the
other squadrons embarrassment:

"Even Commander Flying, at whose instigation the original
exercise had been organised, was rendered speechless by
such a holocaust. Only Butch, submitting his squadron's state
of aircraft that evening (Serviceable 12, U/S 0) seemed in an
exceptionally benign humour, and bought the 'Boy' a drink."

Hugh Popham.

However, 880 experienced its share of accidents, some amusing and
others near fatal:

"One day our kites were ranged aft on the flight deck and the gunners in the after turrets were having a practice. Upon elevating their guns the barrels came up under the mainplane of one of our Hurricanes and lifted the whole aircraft on that side. S/Lt Forrest, who was a great cartoonist, seized upon this incident and quickly drew a picture of the incident, which he stuck on a board in 880's hangar."

Rex Picken.

"We had one of our aircraft stationary on the forward lift and a couple of hands ready to pull the wheels chocks out of the way. These were whipped back and one knocked the key that operated the lift, which started to descend into the hangar. One of the men didn't get clear quickly enough and was crushed between the Hurricane's wing and the deck."

Stan Elmes.

The arrival of any big warship was a matter of some importance to the population of Capetown. To traders, it meant sailors with money and to the city's elite socialites, a ready made audience of officers to be entertained. For their part, Indomitable's crew did their best to meet all calls on their services. But before this could happen there was one more serious issue to be addressed and this could only be answered by her Captain, who left Capetown for London, during the first few days of 1942, to face a Court Martial. His replacement, Captain Troubridge, slipped on board without fuss or ceremony and, by the time Indomitable left Capetown, had firmly and unobtrusively established his control over the ship.

Whilst every opportunity was taken for leave in South Africa, some unlucky souls had to remain on board:

"New Year's Eve I, curiously enough, was duty boy; and so, more curiously, was Jock. Moreover, there was work to be done. More than one Albacore had come to grief during the past two months, and it was Jock's job to unload these carcases on to the dock. It was mine, similarly, to preside over the funeral rites of our Hurricane, including, as a measure of justice my own.

880 Squadron in flight on the eve of joining HMS Indomitable (Authors collection).

Having flown ashore Cork poses with officers and men from 880 whilst Indomitable is anchored at nearby China Bay, Ceylon. Two years later Cork would be killed on the runway that can just be seen in the background (Authors collection).

On the eve of Operation Pedestal, as Indomitable sailed from South Africa to the Med.

Victorious, Indomitable and Eagle steam into the Med at the beginning of Pedestal. Within days one would be sunk and another crippled, limping back to Britain (H. Popham).

Wtih her deck damp from sea spray an 880 Squadron Sea Hurricane takes off on patrol (H. Popham).

August 11th 1942 - Indomitable passes the convoy under her protection

The RAF pilots faced the coming operation and their first carrier take-off with a certain amount of pessimism. Yet they took some heart from the appearance of Sea Hurricanes on deck, clearly demonstrating that it could be done without undue problems. To help them on their, way 880's pilots provided encouragement and Butch Judd, with Dickie Cork, briefed them at some length:

> "The RAF pilots had not flown off a ship before, but they all managed it okay, except one. A Sergeant Pilot took off without a problem, but had a bad glycol leak so had to land. Now these were not Sea Hurricanes and had no arrestor hooks, so all three barriers were raised and after a couple of dummy runs he came in and landed, slithering to a stop without hitting anything. We had just had a tropical storm and the deck being wet caused him to slide when he applied the brakes, otherwise he would surely have tipped onto his nose.
> Our CO, Lt Cdr Judd, was the first to congratulate him, and after the leak was fixed he took off again...."

> *Rex Picken.*

Sadly the fighters arrived too late to be of much use and within 48 hours all had been destroyed, mainly on the ground, as the Japanese captured more and more territory. As the last of the fighters left Indomitable the hopelessness of their task seemed only too apparent to some observers, Dick amongst them, as he related in a letter two days later:

> "Wherever we go we seem to have our backs to the wall. Its the Germans in Europe and Africa and now the Japs out here. It really is quite desperate.
> Our deck has been crowded with lots of RAF Hurricanes for the last few days making it difficult to get our own fighters in the air on routine patrols. However, as we approached Java they flew off to face Lord knows what. I must admit I don't envy them one little bit. At least in 1940 we knew what was coming and could fight back on fairly even terms, returning to something like a normal life each evening, but here things are so different.
> We hear that the Japanese Navy is prowling around and after

Pearl Harbour and Prince of Wales we stay on full alert waiting for enemy aircraft to appear. So far we have been lucky
and they don't seem to have come this far west, but this cannot last and we are all expecting a battle soon...."

Once the RAF fighters had departed Indomitable set course for
Ceylon arriving without incident a few days later. 880 flew ashore to
the Naval Air Station, Ratmalana, near Colombo, transferring north to
Trincomalee, to be nearer their carrier;now berthed in the naval base
there cleaning her boilers. In normal circumstances they would have
stayed on board, but with the Japanese so close the threat from enemy
aircraft grew and the Hurricanes would be a useful addition to Ceylon's
defences.

On the 15th enemy submarines were reported near Trincomalee and
Cork was scrambled, with his Flight, to investigate. They found nothing
during a two hour patrol and landed believing the sighting to be false.
However, a later patrol found some evidence of enemy activity, as Dick
recorded in his logbook:

"Patrol A/S. Found cutter and wreckage of torpedoed ship."

When off duty life ashore was rather dull, with little to do but rest,
though the intense heat made this difficult:

"....no clubs, hotels, cinemas and whatnot. The little town
had a native bazaar which fairly reeked of the mysterious
east, and there was the harbour to bathe and sail in.... On
board there was the occasional film, shown to the officers on
the quarterdeck; and of course deck hockey matches, fought
to the death between squadron officers and ratings, and
between teams from every department on the ship, played
five a side, with walking sticks and a rope puck and with virtually no rules."

Hugh Popham.

There was some relief from the boredom when Indomitable undertook a second ferrying operation, described very briefly in the
Squadron's Record Book:

"One of the RAF Hurricanes Mk 11 which was left U/S and had been converted into a Sea Hurricane was air tested by Lt Cdr Judd. This aircraft was taken over by the squadron (20th Feb).
Lieutenant Martyn in Z 7055 struck the barrier, the aircraft incurring minor damage. The pilot was unhurt (3rd March).
Squadron personnel were again predominant in assisting RAF Squadrons taking passage to erect their aircraft for flying off to Colombo and Trincomalee. 880 Squadron pilots acted as guides when the 60 aircraft were flown off in four batches at 0740, 1140 and two further batches the following day (7th March). Lieut Cork (O/C 'B' Flight) led largest group and gave them a guided tour of the island.
880 pilots remained ashore as fighter protection for the ship. Squadron 'scramble'. No enemy sighted (9th March).
'Scramble' enemy planes reported off the stern of ship. Lt Cdr Judd and three pilots took off to intercept. No enemy encountered (10th March).
The ship put to sea hurriedly, information being received about the Japanese Fleet. The squadron was at 1st degree readiness for the Eastern Fleet (29th March). "

Events were moving with ever increasing speed and Indomitable sailed to Addu Atoll, the Fleet anchorage in the Maldive Islands to join the Eastern Fleet. In over three years of war the Navy had lost many ships, but could still create a large task group when the need arose. At Addu Atoll the results of this effort were only too apparent; three carriers Indomitable, Formidable, and Hermes supported by five battleships, all veteran of the Great War, cruisers and destroyers. On paper a strong force, but its strength was illusionary. The Fleet's cutting edge was blunted by inadequate aircraft and ageing, outclassed battleships. The Japanese, in contrast, entered the battle with five large carriers and three hundred modern strike aircraft;all veterans of Pearl Harbour. A hopelessly one-sided battle seemed unavoidable.

CHAPTER TWELVE

ANOTHER DAY, ANOTHER ENEMY

"Everything has been rushed in recent days and by the time you read this we will probably have seen action. It seems that the war has become seasonal. As May arrives so the action starts, and in October we 'draw stumps' for the winter. Perhaps it is a poor simile, because we are playing a much more deadly game, but at the moment, before we know the worst, it is adequate.

We face the next few weeks with a mixture of anticipation and apprehension. The 'old hands' take it all with a quiet resignation; very professional, but giving little away, beyond, that is, a meticulous attention to detail. They check their aircraft over and chase mechanics around, to ensure their machines are on top line. One can see in this, experience driving their actions and one, of course, tries to follow suit, but in many ways it is a poor copy.

One of our Flight Commander has something of a reputation, having seen service with the RAF over London in 1940. So we have tremendous confidence in his abilities, though he won't be drawn into discussing his part in that battle, except in an oblique way when advising us on how to avoid being shot down. He's a charming character, whose good nature absorbs the CO's more extreme bouts of aggression, but he does it in such a way that neither side feels offended or rebuffed. Beneath it all the two clearly respect each other and have the squadron's well being at heart.

As you probably realise from this, my mind is beginning to wander and I'm finding it difficult to express myself clearly.

I can't say its strain, but I would gladly have the next few
days pass as quickly as possible...."

SubLt. J. Cruickshank, 880 Squadron.
(Letter written on March 31st 1942).

All of a sudden their training seemed more relevant and briefings
were followed with greater attention to detail, every inflection of
speech being scrutinized for double meaning or understatement.
Before they had seemed trivial, but now the need for reassurance, in
a world growing daily more uncertain, was paramount.

The Japanese Strike Group, with the carriers Akagi, Hiryu, Soryu,
Shokaku and Zuikaku at its centre, was capable of destroying any
fleet it might meet and thrust westwards without due concern for
safety. Admiral Somerville, C in C Eastern Fleet on HMS Warspite,
could not afford such a luxury and made plans for a night strike
Intelligence was all important and for this he relied upon a handful
of RAF Catalina flying boats operating from Ceylon.

To counter the Japanese threat, Somerville deployed his ships in
two groups; Fast Force A, including Indomitable and Formidable,
and Force B made up of slower warships commanded by
ViceAdmiral Algernon Willis. Force A would attempt the strike,
unhindered by the need to protect Force B, which would stay in
reserve, where its four cumbersome battleships would not be a liability.

The two fleets searched for each other on April 1st and 2nd,
without success, breaking away to refuel, leaving their long range
aircraft to establish contact. With little information to go on,
Somerville led his force towards Addu Atoll, believing that the
Japanese had abandoned the operation. On the way he detached
Hermes and the cruisers Dorsetshire and Cornwall, not realising
that a Catalina had found the enemy perilously close to Ceylon,
preparing to attack Colombo. Force A immediately turned about
with the intention of delivering its night strike, but again failed to
find the enemy and, with dawn fast approaching, withdrew to the
southeast, leaving RAF Hurricanes to protect the island.

In the early morning of the 4th,127 Japanese aircraft attacked
inflicting minor damage, losing seven of their number in the
process.13 RAF fighters and six unsuspecting Swordfish, en route
from Trincomalee to Minneriya, were destroyed, but this was a

small return for the size of force committed. Nevertheless other targets presented themselves as the day progressed.

A seaplane from the cruiser Tone, searching well to the west of its parent ship, sighted two enemy vessels heading south at 25 knots. Dorsetshire and Cornwall were steaming at full speed to rejoin Force A. Devoid of cover, they now faced a merciless onslaught by enemy bombers and torpedo planes. At 1340 the enemy's strike group found them and within 20 minutes they had been sunk. In the distance, Indomitable wallowed in a mild swell, her fighter pilots anxious to intervene, as they had been since first light, growing increasingly more impatient as the battle developed over the horizon:

> "We were at Action Stations before dawn, hurrying up and down the flightdeck almost as if the enemy might be hull-up ahead, almost as if we might be missing something. There was no news and nothing to be seen. We rushed down to break-fast in ones and twos, lifebelts and anti-flash gear near at hand and hurried back on deck. All was still and expectant. Pilots, observers, air gunners, with their Mae Wests unbuttoned and their helmets hanging round their necks, moving restlessly about the deck.
> What are we waiting for? Instead of driving northwards at full speed, we were dawdling about on the leisurely swells. We began to get edgy with impatience.
> At 1030 the fighters on deck were put at readiness, pilots strapped in. We sat there sweltering, fingers on the starter button, muscles aching with the effort of waiting. There were enemy aircraft on the radar screen. A W/T message had just been received from Dorsetshire and Cornwall....'We are being attacked by enemy dive-bombers.'
> Then why weren't we airborne and on our way? For Christ's sake why?
> A last message from the two cruisers as they went down, and we raged and blasphemed with frustration. Commander Flying was bombarded with the demand, and could only answer: the Admiral says no.
> All day it was the same: the sour anger of enforced inaction, of a sapping impotence."

Hugh Popham.

It was indeed a hard lesson to learn. Yet whilst these young men-cursed their senior officers for 'lack of fight', they had no way of knowing that a more aggressive stance would undoubtedly have seen the British Fleet decimated. Somerville could not commit his ships to such a one sided daylight battle, but in preserving it, he became the butt of much ill-feeling amongst his men.

On the 5th Indomitable and Formidable flew off regular patrols in ever widening arcs, searching for any sign of the enemy, but found nothing. At the same time Japanese reconnaissance aircraft fanned out over the ocean, noting oil patches on the surface, with wreckage and survivors from Dorsetshire and Cornwall. Yet in the rush to find the enemy's fleet they failed to answer one obvious question: where were these two southward rushing cruisers heading when they were attacked? By extending their search along this line they would surely have found Force A and struck before night fell.

To counter this threat Indomitable launched two Sea Hurricanes late in the afternoon, one of which was flown by Cork. They flew northwards ahead of the group, chasing shadows thrown up by radar, but found no sign of the enemy and landed back as their fuel ran out.

Frustrated by such a fruitless search and in need of fuel again, Nagumo altered course to the south east and a rendezvous with supply ships. Replenished, he planned to strike again at Ceylon and continued hunting for the illusive Eastern Fleet. Meanwhile four Albacores from 827 Squadron, on Indomitable, plodded northwards still looking for any sign of enemy carriers. At 1541 one of them spotted the main Japanese force, but was shot down by a Zero before transmitting a sighting report. Within minutes, a second Albacore appeared on the scene and reported 'five unknowns' to Somerville, just as a Zero dived to attack. The British pilot, Sub Lt Grant Sturgis, threw his machine around, diving to sea level, where he made good his escape, having been damaged by enemy fire.

His brief report did not reach Somerville until 1655 and then it provided the haziest of pictures. Only when Grant Sturgis landed could a more thorough account be given; a delay of another hour. Yet there still remained some doubt over the size of the enemy fleet and its heading. Somerville again altered course, to the north west, as darkness fell, unaware that Nagumo was only 150 miles away on a parallel course going in the opposite direction.

Somerville needed more information before committing his two Albacore squadrons (831 on Indomitable and 820 on Formidable) to an attack and launched more reconnaissance flights during the night. They flew in a wide arc, but found nothing. At dawn he considered withdrawing westwards to avoid a daylight attack, but, after much discussion, he turned the fleet south east instead, to search for the enemy. Albacores from both carriers scanned the ocean ahead, finding nothing but wreckage and survivors from Dorsetshire and Cornwall. On another day his fighting spirit might have been rewarded, but the moment when battle could be joined had passed and would not occur again.

At sunset, the British Fleet retired westwards and steamed in a wide arc to Addu Atoll, arriving on the 8th. Continuous air searches were flown, but they found no sign of Nagumo's force, which, after replenishment, was now some distance away preparing to strike Ceylon again. It was here that a lone Catalina spotted the Japanese Fleet and warned the island's defences of their approach.

Before first light, all shipping had put to sea, scattering in all directions, including Hermes, which had only just arrived in port after being detached by Somerville. RAF Hurricanes again rose to meet the bombers, suffering heavy losses in the process. But the raid caused little damage and proved a frustrating distraction to a fleet grown use to spectacular successes. However, there was to be one compensation.

As the Japanese aircraft withdrew Hermes was sighted and her presence reported to Nagumo, who mistakenly believed that the remainder of the Eastern Fleet must be close. He ordered a second strike and, within 30 minutes, 50 'Vals', escorted by 20 Zeros had been despatched, altering course southwards once the first strike had been recovered and fresh fighter patrols flown off to protect the carriers. The only danger they faced came from Blenheims of 11 Squadron, which spotted the Japanese fleet and dropped their bombs from 11,000 feet, doing little damage and losing five of their number.

Meanwhile, Hermes, in company with several smaller ships, was heading back towards Ceylon, hoping for protection from shore based fighters. Her crew had seen Japanese aircraft passing to the north and few believed their presence would go unnoticed. By chance the second strike did miss her and reached Ceylon before realising their mistake. Turning south east they soon found her and dived to attack, quickly overwhelming the carrier's defences.

Eight Fulmars, from 803 and 806 Squadrons, appeared on the scene, but only in time to witness a huge fireball hurtling skywards from the carrier moments before she sank. Though outnumbered, the Fulmars waded into the enemy formation and claimed four 'Vals' destroyed and two damaged, for the loss of two Fulmars. A small return for a carrier and the three hundred men who died with her.

As the hours passed the two Fleets still jockeyed for position, but nothing happened, as 880 Squadron's Record Book relates:

> "Easter Sunday (April 5th)
> Japanese Fleet sighted by searching aircraft, which reported being attacked by enemy fighters. The Squadron were ready the pilots eagerly awaiting for the 'Tally Ho'.
> A torpedo attack was scheduled for sunset, and later for 2200 approx, but the Japanese unfortunately gave us the slip and were not sighted again. It is presumed they headed eastwards to their base as fast as possible. Consequently we could do nothing but return to our base (Ceylon).
>
> April 11th
> Sub.Lt. Cunliffe Owen in Z 7057 struck barrier. The machine had to be written off."

After days of waiting for a battle that never came, it was strange that Indomitable's withdrawal should witness the squadron's first casualty. However, it allowed Butch Judd to release some of his pent up anger, though on this occasion the victim responded in kind:

> "Cunliffe Owen came from a very wealthy family and had obviously been to Public School. One day as we headed for India, he crash-landed a Hurricane on deck. Lt. Cdr. Judd raced down the deck and really tore him off a strip, to which the 'Boy' replied, 'If that's all you're worried about I'll buy you a b****y plane,' and stalked off…"

Stan Elmes, Flight Deck Party.

For all the pilots this operation had been a deeply unhappy experience, made worse when news of the Fleet's losses became known, as Cork described in a letter:

> "Having got so close to the Jap Fleet we failed to engage them and in the chase around the Indian Ocean missed each other completely.

You will probably have heard by now that some ships in the
area were hit pretty hard. We knew what was happening, but
were too far away to be of much use. But it was very difficult to
stay calmly on deck when our own people were suffering just
over the horizon. A few old Hurricanes could have made all the
difference and given these ships a fighting chance. As it was, the
enemy attacked at will, without worrying about their tails.
Let's hope we have a chance to hit back as soon as possible...."

The chance came sooner than expected. Two days after Hermes'
destruction, Indomitable was detached by Somerville and proceeded to
Bombay, en route to Madagascar, where she would form part of an
amphibious assault force. It was feared that this Vichy French controlled
island would let the Japanese establish bases from which it could attack
vital supply lines along the east coast of Africa. To remove this risk an
invasion was planned, with Indomitable and Illustrious providing air
support.

Illustrious arrived in late April and, whilst waiting, 880 were based
ashore at Juhu aerodrome near Bombay, ostensibly to 'act as fighter
cover for the ship', but in reality enjoying a short break, when not on
standby.

Bombay lay a short train journey away and each evening groups of
officers, dressed in their 'whites', made for the city, most congregating
in the Taj Mahal Hotel or the Yacht Club. After the heat and dust of Juhu
the pilots enjoyed the luxury of these expensive establishments.
Invitations to dine with local dignitaries also arrived, though Butch
Judd's inability to keep his temper, or control his energetic language
always made these affairs interesting. The contrast between CO and
Senior Pilot was very pronounced on these occasions. Cork as always
was self possessed, polite and debonair, whilst Judd was irascible, bul-
lying and unrefined.

By day they flew their Hurricanes over Bombay and surrounding
countryside, keeping their flying hours to a minimum, allowing ground-
crew to undertake servicing in the comparative luxury of tents and not
Indomitable's baking hot hangars. Not much of an advantage, but the
city's nightlife and cheap drink was a compensation few ignored.

Before rejoining their ship, 880 repaid some of the city's hospitality
by 'shooting up Bombay for H. E. the Governor'. For an hour and twenty minutes they flew in formation, breaking off into smaller groups to
buzz the local population, then flashing through loops and roles, before

reforming and returning to Juhu. It was a fitting finale to their stay.

On the 20th they returned to Indomitable, as she left Bombay and sailed for Colombo; now in company with Illustrious. With few aircraft to spare and driven by a need to conserve flying hours, fighters on both carriers stayed on deck until May 5th, when the operation, codenamed 'Ironclad', began. Dick managed two brief flights one to air test a Hurricane with a new engine, the other to tow a high speed target drogue.

Briefings for the operation commenced once the fleet had sailed from the Seychelles on April 29th. At first sight, the task seemed a simple one, with a straightforward plan of action. The attack had the natural harbour of Diego Suarez at its centre. Once secured it would provide a jumping off point for the main invasion. To achieve this Army units would land on the west coast at dawn on May 5th and move inland taking the enemy from the rear. Albacores would attack the island's airfield and harbour installations, whilst Hurricanes, Fulmars and Martlets would provide cover for the army.

The landings around Diego Suarez began as planned. Illustrious's aircraft dealing with shipping, whilst Indomitable's squadrons swept inland, shooting up and bombing any 'hot spots' reported by the army. 880 were up in the air early, as the Squadron Record Book relates:

> "The operations against Diego Suarez Harbour and aerodrome began at 0430, an hour before dawn. A striking force of Albacores of 831 Squadron launched a dive-bombing attack on the aerodrome to coincide with the landing of the Commandos on beaches to the west of the town.
> Half an hour later, at 0500, eight of our aircraft took off in two sections Black Section consisting of Lt Cdr Judd, Lt Smith, S/Lt Forrest and S/Lt Harris, and Blue Section, Lt Cork, and S/Lts Haworth, CunliffeOwen and Cruickshank. Their mission was to complete the work of 831 Squadron and destroy by machine gun fire anything and everything of military importance left on the aerodrome. They arrived over the target as dawn was breaking and attacked in two waves of four aircraft, Black Section leading. Some damage had already been done, but the Hurricanes went in and completed the destruction as best they could, leaving the hangar and eight aircraft on fire. Light flak but no fighter opposition was encountered and all our aircraft returned undamaged.

At 0620 Lt Martyn and PO Williams took off to carry out a
patrol over the town. They encountered no opposition
except light flak, and landed on at 0750.
0905 Further town patrol carried out by Lt Fiddes and S/Lt
Popham. They met with light flak and destroyed a light aeroplane on the aerodrome.
1300 Lt Cork and S/Lt Cruickshank took over the town patrol
and restarted the fire in the hangar, leaving four aircraft on
fire. All aircraft returned from the patrols undamaged."

After six months of waiting, 880 had finally flown their first operation as a squadron, yet the description, written so dispassionately in the
Record Book, played down their contribution. Cork's logbook is even
more concise:

"May 5th
Hurricane Z 4642 Dawn attack on Diego Suarez aerodrome.
Hangar set on fire.
Hurricane Z 4039 Attack on aerodrome. Set hangar on fire.
Destroyed 3 Morane Fighters and 4 Potez bombers in hangar."

Beyond official reports, few had the opportunity to record their
thoughts in any detail. In Cork's case prowess in combat and the need
to portray successes to an increasingly war weary nation brought him
into contact with two journalists during 1943. In an exercise sponsored
by the Admiralty, he was encouraged to describe his flying experiences
for publication in the press and, later, in a book entitled, "So Few". Very
reticently he agreed to participate, finding these encounters both
embarrassing and intrusive:

"Our briefings stressed the lack of enemy aircraft and it is
true to say that they hardly threatened us during the first few
hours of the attack. But an early morning reconnaissance
flight, followed by the Albacores attack, revealed a number of
machines scattered around the aerodrome at Antsirane.
Sitting in the Ready Room we tried to work out what they
might be, because they clearly weren't types we had come
across before. After much discussion with our CO and
Commander 'F', we concluded they were old French
machines and so of little danger to us, though they might

trouble the Albacores, if their pilots could be bothered to get out of bed.

Eight of our Hurricanes were ranged on deck ready to go in behind the bombers to mop up any resistance, whilst others circled over the carriers just in case any enemy aircraft appeared. Our engines were warmed up and a cooling breeze swept over the deck as we steamed into wind. At that moment you can't wait to start and your eyes scan the controls and dials, checking and rechecking, until finally the signal for take-off is given.

The CO went first and one by one we followed, forming up in a series of circles around our ship, eventually settling on a course that would take us straight over the aerodrome, east to west, at a fairly low altitude, so we could see our target and have the sun behind us as we made our passes.

As expected, there was little opposition, though tracer rounds from light flak guns did come whistling up, harmlessly passing either side of my section. Ahead of us Black Section, in accordance with our pre-arranged plan, swept across the aerodrome whilst we circled watching the fun, working out where the best targets might be when our turn came. All the while, voices crackled over the R/T and above the din the CO could be heard cursing and swearing as he always did.

A large hangar dominated the aerodrome and we could see a number of aircraft inside. So we flew on a course that would take us through its doors, if we held it, and raked the building and its contents with our gunfire. Pulling away, I spotted two monoplanes to one side, banked to bring them into my sights and fired a three second burst, hitting both 'midships'.

There were now a number of fires around the aerodrome and the hangar was well alight, with eight aircraft clearly being seen amongst the wreckage. All in all a job well done and a good raid in which to 'blood' some of the newer men, who, up to then, hadn't fired their guns in anger.

Back on board we tried to work out who had destroyed what, but with so many aircraft firing at the same targets it proved impossible and so Commander Ops gave credit for eight machines destroyed to the squadron as a whole.

Later that day I led another Hurricane over the town on patrol and decided to have a look at the damage. Imagine my surprise when I saw the tail of an aircraft in the burned out hangar that wasn't there in the morning and dropped down to inspect it more closely. There were seven machines inside, four bombers and three fighters all appearing to be fully operational, with a large petrol tanker in the process of refuelling them. It was clear the French thought we would pay no more attention to the burned out hangar and concluded that it would be the safest place to hide their aircraft.

Whilst Blue Two circled the airfield, drawing off some of the flak and watching for any other enemy aircraft, I turned my guns on the hangar and made three passes. The tanker exploded on my first run, blowing burning fuel over the seven aircraft and my second and third runs completed the destruction. Tired of waiting for me to finish, Blue Two then came down and fired at two machine gun posts on the edge of the aerodrome.

As we flew out to our ship we looked back and saw smoke rising high into the sky from the fires we had started. I can't say there was any feeling of elation, just a desire to get back on deck and change into some dry clothes my kit now being drenched in sweat...."

Elsewhere the attack had gone well. Thirteen thousand soldiers had landed at two points along the coast, before moving swiftly inland towards Diego Suarez. Ahead of them Swordfish and Albacores softened up the defences. On all fronts casualties were light and by nightfall a firm base had been established from which these gains could be exploited on the 6th:

"Squadron Record Book 6th May 1942.
At 0530 Lt Martyn and PO Williams opened the second day's operations with a dawn patrol nothing to report.
0700 Lt Cdr Judd, Lt Fiddes and S/Lts Harris and Popham took off on a 'Scramble' to attack the French Colonial Sloop D'Entrecasteaux, which was holding up the advance of our troops. Light flak was encountered but no damage was done to our aircraft, all of which returned safely. The sloop

was left on fire.
0920 Six Hurricanes, piloted by Lt Cdr Judd leading, and Lt Smith and S/Lts Haworth, Harris, Forrest and CunliffeOwen were scrambled in order to strafe a mined battery of 3.5"s and .5"s which were holding up our troops to the south of the town. Lt Cdr Judd was compelled to return with a severe Glycol leak, but he arrived just as four more Hurricanes were scrambled to reinforce the other five and so was in time to lead these off, the other machines being piloted by Lt Cork, S/Lt Cruickshank and PO Williams. The sortie was successful, the Directors being hit and the guns silenced, enemy troops were strafed and the grass and undergrowth around them was set on fire;S/Lt Haworth received a shrapnel wound in the hip and force landed on board with the starboard fuel tank damaged. S/Lt Harris also force landed successfully on the deck with a bullet through his radiator. During the afternoon negotiations for surrender were started."

"7th May
Patrols over the beaches were maintained throughout the day and no opposition was encountered. Diego Suarez surrendered."

After the initial onslaught, the enemy rapidly lost heart. Resistance on Day 2 was muted, but in places efforts were made to claw back some lost ground. In the air a squadron of Vichy French Morane Saulnier MS 406Cs and some Potez 63.11s tried to disrupt carrier operations, but Martlets from Illustrious quickly broke up the enemy group, shooting down 4 Moranes and two Potezs in the process. By Day 3 local resistance had all but collapsed and surrender seemed the only realistic option, the troops around Diego Suarez laying down their arms on the 7th. Not so the Vichy Governor, Armand Annet, who, from a position further south, refused to capitulate, believing himself protected by the dense jungle.

The carrier group stayed at sea until the 8th, but with the harbour secure, Vice Admiral Syfret brought his fleet in, for a brief period of rest and recuperation. But as Indomitable approached the harbour's narrow entrance, two torpedoes, fired from an unseen submarine, passed across her stern, running harmlessly aground on the distant shore.

With all resistance crushed, men from the ships went ashore for a look around. 880's officers toured the area. It was something of a novelty and they laughed and joked as though on a bank holiday jaunt, but behind the facade there lay a much more sombre purpose to see the reality of life on a battlefield at ground level:

> "Not that the trip ashore had been uninstructive, offering it might be said, a whiff of realism to the romantic and isolated exponent of flying. Removed from everyday brutalities of the infantryman, even a dead horse or a ransacked barrack-room had a novelty for us, though it still left unresolved that closest and most terrible relation of all, the relation between killer and victim. One could imagine the casual violence of war weaving these complex patterns in the humming air, making every minute more of these desperate relationships. Suddenly there seemed something utterly coldblooded and inexcusable in not knowing whom your bullets would strike.... a sense of taint and loss."

> *Hugh Popham.*

For 12 days Indomitable swung round her anchor ready to put to sea if trouble arose, but it remained quiet and on the 20th she sailed for Kilindini, the Naval Base at Mombassa, for maintenance and repairs. As soon as she docked leave commenced and the pilots took advantage of this sudden freedom. Some journeyed to Nairobi, to spend their days relaxing with a drink in hand, whilst the more adventurous travelled further afield exploring more remote corners of Africa.

Everyone was ordered back on board when it seemed that trouble was brewing in the Indian Ocean. Indomitable immediately put to sea on the 15th, but it was a false alarm and within hours she was slipping back into harbour to continue her maintenance programme. As she approached Kilindini, 880 flew in land to provide a 'standby fighter patrol' at Port Reitz aerodrome. Two Hurricanes remained on duty throughout the day ready to scramble. False alarms were frequent and Dick found himself racing across the aerodrome, raising clouds of dust, chasing shadows on two occasions. It was a frustrating business, but at least there was a cooling breeze when flying with the canopy open.

Their stay at Mombassa proved a pleasant interlude, but the war could not be ignored for long and on July 9th Indomitable sailed from Mombassa her future uncertain. In the absence of a definite plan rumours were rife, 'we're going home, we're going into the Atlantic, perhaps it's the Arctic again, the Tirpitz's out'. The hardest option, all agreed, would be to join a Malta convoy, but, as their Captain informed them, it was here she would go.

CHAPTER THIRTEEN

PEDESTAL

By June 1942 Malta and its defences were hanging on by the thinnest of threads. Heavy casualties, lack of food, fuel and ammunition had gradually eroded resistance and only massive replenishment would see the island survive in Allied hands. But to achieve this the Royal Navy had run a gauntlet from Gibraltar along sea lanes dominated by enemy ships and aircraft. As summer approached only a few submarines and fast minelayers had got through, but they could only carry small quantities of stores.

In a bid to break the enemy's stranglehold, the Admiralty planned a two pronged assault with convoys from Gibraltar and Alexandria. The west bound group would be the stronger with two carriers Eagle and Argus, as escort, whilst the eastbound convoy would only have cruisers and destroyers for cover. Within hours of leaving Egypt these terribly exposed ships were spotted and four were sunk in short order. Worse still an intelligence report confirmed that the Italian Battle Fleet had put to sea. With only light escort at their disposal, no air cover and ammunition running low, the convoy was forced to turn back or face annihilation.

The other group had more luck and managed to force a passage through hostile waters, losing only 4 merchantmen and a destroyer before reaching Malta. But the pace of Axis attacks did not slow and by early July another convoy was needed to stem the fast disappearing reserves of men and material.

Experience had shown that only a powerful force of ships could break through and if this were to be achieved all other fronts had to be stripped. A desperate measure, but one the War Cabinet thought essential and during July ordered all available warships to converge on Gibraltar and await the arrival of supply ships from Britain. The Home and Eastern Fleets would provide the bulk of the escort, strengthening the 'Mediterranean Force' to an unprecedented level with four carriers Victorious, Indomitable, Eagle and Furious, two battleships Nelson and Rodney and a host of cruisers and destroyers. On land, the RAF assembled some 250 aircraft to provide protection, though only 100 of these were single seater fighters.

Furious' sole purpose was to ferry 38 RAF Spitfires to Malta, detaching herself when this task was complete. To achieve this she was stripped of Navy squadrons and so had no means of supporting the convoy itself. The other three carriers would provide this defence, with 70 Sea Hurricanes, Fulmars and Martlets. A strong force on paper, but one barely strong enough for the task at hand.

As the freighters left Gourock, to begin their voyage south to Gibraltar, Indomitable, with her cruiser and destroyer escort sailed from South Africa and ploughed through a gentle swell into the Atlantic. Under blue skies and bright sunshine, men not watchkeeping or working in kitchens, engine rooms or hangars, lounged on deck, making the most of the good weather. Every now and then their peace was disturbed by Albacores taking off on anti-submarine patrols. As they neared the 'war' zone the atmosphere grew noticeably more tense:

> "We had about three separate buzzes going about the mess decks, the strongest being a Malta Convoy. On our way up to Gibraltar Captain Troubridge came on the ship's broadcast system and confirmed our worst fears. He told us we would be part of the largest convoy ever to sail to Malta and it was a case of do or die, as Malta could not hang on until the end of August, owing to fuel, ammo and food being in short supply. He also said (after referring to the Ark Royal's 'premature departure') that he would not give the order to abandon ship until she was lying at 90 degrees. Until then we had to stay put!"

> *Richard Brooke.*

On August 5th Indomitable, Victorious and Eagle rendezvoused east of Gibraltar to rehearse battle tactics before joining the main convoy. For two days their squadrons practised patrols, scrambles and interceptions at all heights and weaknesses soon appeared. The two big carriers carried different radar systems, neither having the capacity to monitor activity at all altitudes. To overcome this, each ship was assigned specific tasks. Indomitable, with her Type 281 radar, concentrated on the low level threat, whilst Victorious, and her Type 79B system, scanned the heights. Similarly each type of aircraft was also given particular tasks. Fulmars operated below 5,000 feet, where their sluggish performance would be a match for low level bombers. From 5,000 feet up to 20,000 feet Martlets would ply their trade, whilst above them the higher climbing Sea Hurricanes would wait.

Cork only flew once during these rehearsals; a high exercise lasting one hour and twenty minutes, during which 880 Squadron were vectored onto imaginary intruders approaching the fleet at heights over 20,000 feet. After many months at sea, their coordination was effortless and even Judd seemed reasonably content with their efforts.

As their aircraft roared back and forth overhead, other elements of the convoy began to arrive. HMS Furious attached herself to the rear of the formation late on the 7th, her presence noted by Dick, who recognised her familiar shape. Like most on board he was unaware of her role in the coming operation, but the sight of RAF Spitfires on her deck confirmed her purpose. Later that evening he remarked to his fitter, "it's a shame we can't swop our Hurricanes for the fighters over yonder", echoing the sentiments of many young men who flew from carriers at that time. They saw themselves as poor relations and longed to fly aircraft that gave them an even chance in battle.

As dawn broke on the 8th, the main convoy came into view:

> "It opened with a scene on the scale of a Hollywood epic the rendezvous with the all important freighters of the convoy; fourteen, including the large tanker Ohio escorted by those wonderfully impressive 16 inch battleships, Nelson and Rodney and another group of cruisers and destroyers. There seemed to be ships in every direction as far as the eye could see. I counted sixty seven a magnificent sight, but what a target. I had gone down to the lower hangar on some errand when an ear shattering series of explosions echoed from all directions. My stomach turned over and thinking the worst had happened I climbed as fast as I could up to the flight deck. There I found the whole fleet was firing all its guns in a practise anti-aircraft barrage a Brock's benefit we called it. Up to that time I had never heard the fearsome sound made by our sixteen 4.5 inch guns. It was a taste of things to come.

In the afternoon all three carriers flew off fighters from all
their squadrons for a 'Balbo' over the fleet. It was a stirring
sight to see over fifty aircraft overhead and it was hoped that
this display would stiffen the morale of the merchant ship
crews.... We Albacore types felt a special sense of pride in
our fighter pilots, many of them larger than life characters
like Butch Judd and Dickie Cork. And, of course, we envied
them."

Sub Lt. G. Wallace RNVR,
Observer with 831 Squadron,
HMS Indomitable.

With all ships in place and with fuel replenishment complete, the
convoy, codenamed 'Pedestal', sailed at night through the Straits of
Gibraltar, then hugged the coast of Algeria all through the 10th. Fighters
were kept at readiness and regular patrols were flown throughout the
day. But nothing happened, until 5 pm that is, when the calm was broken by a French passenger aircraft flying overhead, its crew broadcast-
ing details to shore based radio stations. Within hours news of their
position had reached enemy ears, though night fell before an attack
could be mounted.

Within the close confines of 880 Squadron, these developments
were observed with increasing concern. Darkness brought some
respite, but few believed this peace could last for long. Sleep, when it
came, was fitful and few bothered to undress and retire to their cabins.
Many pulled mattresses into passageways aware that they could
respond more quickly should the ship come under attack whilst they
slept.

By 4 am everyone was awake on Indomitable, with aircrew, dressed
ready for action, occupying the Ready Room and Wardroom. Major Pym,
Officer Commanding the ship's Royal Marines, took up his post in the
Fighter Direction Room ready to broadcast events as they happened to
the ship's crew. His clear, matter of fact voice would relay descriptions
of the days activities to the hundreds of men toiling below decks,
unable to see what was happening for themselves.

As his commentary started, Judd and Cork were seen to exchange
wry glances and joke briefly about ' the absurdity of a pongo directing
operations!'. To RNVR officers the sight of two career officers slipping
back into the normal strictures and antipathies of peacetime life was

itself a cause of some amusement. Despite the closeness, there was a cultural difference between those who played at being officers, 'for the duration', and those who chose it as a vocation. There might easily have been friction, but for the most part each side treated the other with tolerance and good humour.

At first light the fleet came to full alert and fighters took off, on standing patrols, into a brilliantly blue sky:

> "Squadron Record Book.
> 0630 Lt Fiddes, Lt Smith, S/Lt Popham and S/Lt Brownlee, as Yellow Section, took off and patrolled for one and a half hours.
> 0745 Relieved by Lt Cdr Judd, S/Lt Harris and Lts Forrest and Lowe, as Black Section. Neither of these sections reported anything."

At 0900 it was Cork's turn to lead Blue Section on patrol. With his engine ticking over he waited for the green light, canopy locked back and hand on throttle. Behind him Cruickshank, Haworth and Cunliffe Owen sat watching their leader, scanning controls. Finally Cork was away, tail lifting, banking gently away to port and within a minute the other three were also airborne; wheels up, engines revving hard as they gained height over the convoy:

> "Taking off I saw below me the merchantmen steaming along, with destroyers nosing round on the outskirts. In the far distance I could see a Coastal Command aircraft patrolling ahead of the convoy looking for U boats. At the briefing earlier that morning Commander Ops told us about these flights and warned us to be careful who we attacked, so we gave it a wide berth, having first made sure it was a 'friendly'. There had been one or two alarms already that morning enemy reconnaissance flights trying to creep in over the fleet, but our fighters had failed to intercept them. Ten minutes into our patrol, having seen Lt Cdr Judd and Black Section dive away for home, we were vectored onto an incoming raid at 22,000 feet. We gave our engines full boost and climbed to 24,000 feet, where I saw a Junker 88 approaching. He spotted us and dived and for a time it looked as though he might escape, but gradually we caught

up and at 15,000 feet I fired, causing him to twist and lose forward speed. Blue Two blocked his way as he tried to escape and forced him back into my sights, though too far away to open fire.

There was no quick end, because the JU was able to pull away from me in a steep dive. I just managed to stay in contact and for half an hour gave chase, gradually closing the distance between us as he levelled off two hundred feet above the sea. By this time the fleet was lost to sight and the rest of Blue Section had followed my orders and resumed their patrol over the convoy. Pulling out to one side I fired a two second burst, which struck the starboard engine. Smoke and flame erupted from it as I fired a second time hitting the fuselage. Bits flew off, including the rear gunner's hatch, but his return fire struck my machine and I broke away before he could do more damage. As I turned I fired once more and this entered the JU's port engine, which seemed to stutter.

As I flew back I watched the enemy machine slowly slip towards the water, but could not hang around long enough to see it crash."

Dickie Cork (interviewed in early 1943).

Suspecting his Hurricane might be badly damaged, and being some distance from Indomitable, he decided that discretion was the better part of valour and left the damaged bomber to its fate.

Thirty five minutes later he landed, having picked up the remainder of Blue Section on the way, but he was far from happy as Gordon Wallace reported:

"Dickie Cork leading the next patrol, had more success, making an attack on another JU 88 at 15,000 feet and setting fire to its starboard engine before he had to break off. When he came into the Ops Room (where Wallace was Duty Officer) he was complaining bitterly about the poor performance of the Sea Hurricane above 20,000 feet."

Although the enemy aircraft continued to probe the fleet's defences throughout the day, with a series of small bombing raids, the real threat came from submarines. There had been many alarms since they left Gibraltar, but these had proved false. All this changed, without warning and with great violence.

U73, commanded by Helmut Rosenbaum, slipped through the convoy's destroyer screen and stalked the three carriers for several hours. Dodging the continuous flow of ships above him, Rosenbaum brought his U-boat up to periscope depth and found HMS Eagle in his sights. He fired a spread of torpedoes and at 1.15pm observers on board Indomitable and Victorious saw four explosions along her port side. Within minutes she had capsized and sunk, taking with her a hundred or so men and all but four of her fighters, which were flying at the time.

Her sudden loss left an indelible mark on the minds of those who saw her passing. She seemed to go so easily, without fuss or fury. Cork, who had just taken off with his section, saw her sink and briefly circled the area watching. There was nothing they could do and within minutes they had risen to their patrol height, to await the enemy. As they climbed away destroyers scampered across to where the Eagle had been and dropped boats and lines to pick up the survivors, now struggling for life in the warm, but oil covered sea. Unaware of the tragedy, Eagle's surviving fighters were ordered to land on the other carriers.

At 1.30 Indomitable's radar identified aircraft approaching from the south and vectored Blue Section out to investigate. From some distance they recognised the intruder as a another 'Vichy French airliner' and radioed back to Fighter Direction for instructions. Whilst waiting Cork brought the section round in a wide arc, so that they were all lined up to attack from port and starboard quarters. For a couple of minutes 'Ops' considered how best to react, eventually deciding to let the aircraft go. The enemy already had the fleet's position, so little would be served by destroying an unarmed aircraft. As the Hurricanes broke away, Dick buzzed the airliner, forcing it take evasive action and change course away from the ships he defended.

880 Squadron saw more action during the afternoon:

"Squadron Record Book.
1435 Black Section took off to patrol at 24,000 feet. Lt Lowe returned with low oil pressure. Intercepted a JU 88 which Lt Forrest attacked, securing hits on port engine, and received a hit in his oil tank and forced landed in the sea unhurt. S/Lt Harris then attacked and finished off the JU 88. Lt Forrest and S/Lt Harris credited with half the aircraft each confirmed.

> 1535 Blue Section patrolled but nothing sighted.
> 1915 Yellow Section patrolled at 10,000 feet, attacked a JU 88
> and credited with a probable for the section.
> 1955 Black Section patrolled from 25,000 to 10,000 feet.
> Nothing sighted. Both Yellow and Black Sections compelled
> to make night landings. Lt Smith (Z.7055) hit the barrier. S/Lt
> Popham landed on HMS Victorious."

As the day drew to a close the mood on Indomitable relaxed, but radar suddenly picked up the distant echoes of approaching bombers. Four Hurricanes were quickly scrambled, adding their strength to standing patrols already aloft. 30 JU 88s came diving down from 8,000 feet towards the convoy and six HE 111's swept in at sea level, torpedoes slung beneath their mottled grey bodies. Martlets and Hurricanes quickly intercepted them, whilst the fleet unleashed a tremendous barrage of fire from its guns.

With this daunting display of tracer rounds floating passed, the Heinkels lost heart and aimlessly dropped their torpedoes, all of which missed their targets. The JU's pressed home their attack with more determination and two approached Victorious from astern, their bombs going close, before gunfire brought them down.

On the periphery of this frantic action 880's aircraft struggled to make their presence felt. Brian Fiddes and Hugh Popham caught a JU 88 at extreme range, but lost it as a burst of speed carried it to safety. By the time they gave up pursuit the fleet was many miles away. Doubling back, collecting Paddy Brownlee and Steve Haworth on the way, they circled the carriers in darkness waiting for instructions to land:

> "Then we saw the tracer coming morsing up towards us,
> and one or two black puffs of smoke burst uncomfort-
> ably close. We moved round the fleet, and the bursts fol-
> lowed us; and the truth could no longer be disregarded.
> They were firing at anything that flew.
> We pulled away out of range, and called up the ship and
> asked for instructions.... 'Stand, by Yellow Flight. Will pan-
> cake you as soon as possible'.... We closed the convoy
> again, to test their mood and provoked another hail of
> gunfire . We tried switching on navigation lights, which

merely encouraged them to improve on their earlier efforts. Disheartened we withdrew."

Hugh Popham.

Even with wheels and hooks down, each approach was met by fire from nervous, 'trigger happy' gunners, unable to identify friend from foe. To make matters worse the pilots could not identify the carriers in darkness and circled around. Despite the dangers, Captain Troubridge turned Indomitable's deck lights on and continued steaming into wind, although outside the destroyer screen and at the mercy of submarines. His courage was rewarded and all but one of 880's aircraft managed to land. The last, flown by Hugh Popham, missed this golden opportunity, but found Victorious instead and crash landed on her deck. After such an ordeal Judd was in no mood to forgive and forget:

> "Butch had returned to the ship with his flight in the thick of twilight and flown slowly up the starboard side, wheels down, looking as much like Hurricanes as was possible, and had received a short burst from the starboard after pom-poms. Incensed, he had landed-on, flung out of his aircraft almost before it had come to rest, and storming across to the offending guns, grabbed the wretched Lieutenant in charge by the throat and nearly throttled him.
> 'You bloody useless bastard,' he had roared at him, shaking him like a door-mat. 'You brainless oaf! Don't you know a Hurricane when you see one?"

Hugh Popham.

Troubridge was criticised by some for endangering his ship, but at such a crucial stage of the battle the fleet could not afford to lose these fighters, having already lost HMS Eagle, so the risk had to be taken. It was a practical judgement, but those who knew him, realised that compassion also played a part in his decision.

On Indomitable the day had passed in feverish activity. Aircraft had been turned round, refuelled, repaired and rearmed; a task made more difficult as the ship took violent evasive action. By evening, confusion reigned as riggers and fitters sweated over their wards, struggling to get as many ready as possible for the next day's operations:

"We worked in a team throughout the day re-arming and re-fuelling the aircraft. We took violent turns to port then starboard and petrol began swirling on the hangar deck. When it came to the side of the hangar, it was ankle deep. It should have gone down the scuppers and then into the sea, but didn't so the fire risk was tremendous.
A Petty Officer we called 'Tanky' came and opened up the scuppers with tools made of nonsparking metal and let the gash petrol out. Such caution was necessary, yet, for some reason, our working tools weren't of a similar sort and could cause a spark if dropped, but we never gave this a thought. Until we got three direct hits, life on board was one long hectic rush, our only contact with the outside world was a Royal Marine Officer (Major Pym), who kept blurting out how many tinfish had just missed us, how many dive bombers were attacking us, and the amount of bombs reigning down. The latter we did know about, as the ship gave an almighty lurch when she had a near miss."

Richard Brooke.

Although darkness shrouded their movements, all ships kept their crews at action stations. Sleep proved virtually impossible and pilots could be found on Indomitable's hangar decks eager to help, but holding back because they might get in the way. Judd paced around cajoling everyone, with Cork not far behind, smoothing 'ruffled feathers' with words of encouragement.

Even though he went without sleep, Dick tried to maintain some semblance of routine and showered and changed before dawn, snatching breakfast before returning to the Ready Room. Despite the previous day's activities 880 could still muster ten aircraft and pilots, though these had been supplemented by the addition of Lt Cdr Brabner and Sub Lt Macdonald, both stranded when HMS Eagle had sunk.

At 0907 the first raid of the day began and 19 JU 88's soon appeared on radar screens. Ops quickly interpreted this information and waited for a few minutes before committing their fighters gauging, whether this might be a feint, designed to pull them away from the main attacking force. But nothing else appeared and the fighters were scrambled:

"The sky at first sight seemed filled with aircraft. The enemy kept in tight formation and our fighters 'snapped at their heels', forcing them to break in all directions, though most continued to press on in the direction of the convoy. We were in the narrowest of corridors between Sicily and Tunis, and couldn't afford the luxury of biding our time. So we hit them as hard as we could.

One Junker turned away from the main group and I led my section down towards it. I was well ahead and fired when it filled my sights. Smoke poured from its wings and it disappeared below me into the sea. A few minutes later I saw another JU 88 out of the corner of my eye heading along the coast of North Africa and set off in pursuit by myself. At a 1000 feet I came within range and fired. It seemed to stagger in the air, then dropped into the sea with a big splash."

Dickie Cork (interviewed in early 1943).

Sixteen British fighters intercepted the bombers and 8 were claimed as destroyed in the melee that followed. Despite this a number of Junkers broke through the fleet's defensive screen and began their bombing runs, though turned away when fierce anti-aircraft fire came out to greet them.

As the battle subsided, standing patrols began again, relieving those so recently engaged in battle. All 880's pilots landed safely on Indomitable and within minutes were being debriefed.

There was much excited chatter in the Ready Room, sponsored by a relief born of survival. Yet there was little time to record every detail before their aircraft were ready and their presence on deck required.

There was an uneasy lull as the morning wore on. Shadowing aircraft were spotted, but these stayed out of range, intent on reporting ship movements. Occasionally they strayed too close and fighters pounced one Italian Savoai Marchetti SM 79 was destroyed, but a second put up such strong resistance that it escaped, badly damaging two Fulmars from 884 Squadron in the process.

Suddenly from over Sardinia, another large raid was observed forming up. With only 70 miles of sea to cover, the bombers would be on the ships within minutes and little time was lost in getting more fighters into the air:

"Squadron Record Book
1225 Lt Cork took Blue Section on patrol at 5,000 feet.
Attacked and destroyed a JU 88 and ME 110 with several other
possibles. S/Lt Cruickshank shot down by enemy aircraft and
killed.
1315 Lt Cdr Judd took Black Section up. S/Lt Harris was late
taking off. Lt Cdr Judd dived to attack a squadron of Heinkel
111s, which shot him down and he was killed. S/Lt Harris
returned with low oil pressure. Nothing further was sighted."

"Dickie Cork's section was scrambled at 1225 and there was
gunfire up ahead, then a massive barrage began low down to
port in the middle of which I caught glimpses of threeengined
SM 79 torpedo bombers approaching head on and low down
on the water. The battleship Rodney was on our port quarter
firing her 16 inch guns to produce an awesome wall of water
ahead of the incoming planes into which they disappeared. It
seemed impossible for any to survive this hail of gunfire but I
saw only one banking away trailing a plume of fire and smoke.
The Italians seemed to press home their attack most bravely,
even after being harried by our fighters, but not one of the 43
which took part scored a hit even though they each carried
two torpedoes."

Gordon Wallace.

"We were boosted off the deck and were trying to gain height
when we sighted the enemy. Wave after wave of torpedo
bombers came flying over the sea trying to launch their torpedoes. They were 50 feet above the surface, going all out when
my section dived into the attack. But they kept so low that any
attempt to dive underneath would have seen us crash into the
sea. So they managed to evade our attack and we turned away
as our own guns opened up looking for new targets.
There were many enemy fighters milling around. And as we
climbed up to intercept them and the next wave of bombers, a
flock of ME 110s descended on us in 'Vic' formation from out
of the sun. There followed a terrific dog fight not more than a
hundred feet above the surface and as I twisted and turned I
saw Blue Two (S/Lt Cruickshank) picked off by an ME. I got

him in my sights and chased him up to a 1000 feet firing several bursts as we went. Smoke came trailing back and the pilot baled out, leaving his machine to crash beside Indomitable. I chased several more enemy aircraft, putting bullets into several of them without result.

Over the R/T we received a very blunt order to 'push off' because we were too close to our ships and risked being shot down by their gunfire. So I climbed away by myself, my section having been scattered to the wind or shot down. For several minutes nothing happened, but finally our radar had spotted more raiders and our fighters were ordered to intercept this new attack. I counted ten following their usual tactic of flying close to the sea in a tight group, but one lagged behind and I picked him off and he crashed beside a group of destroyers, which then opened fire on me. Without ammunition there was little I could do, so headed back towards my carrier, being shot at by everyone on the way."

Dickie Cork (interviewed in 1943).

As Cork's section tackled the first waves of bombers and fighters, each carrier scrambled more aircraft. Black Section from 880, with Judd in the lead, was the next to go and within seconds three had left Indomitable's deck. The fourth lost revs as it waited in line and S/Lt Harris cut his engine, whilst fitters rushed out and jumped on its wings to open inspection panels and investigate the fault. With Commander Flying staring down, anxious to clear the deck for other aircraft to fly off and land, Harris's engine was kicked back into life and he roared off to join the bitter fighting now spreading over the fleet.

Judd tore into the enemy formations with little regard for his own safety. To those that followed his mood seemed desperate and they watched in horror as he drove his aircraft straight onto the tail of a bomber, without avoiding its return fire. But with the convoy so close he had to hack down the enemy before they could drop their torpedoes and so had to attack whatever the cost. The German gunner had an easy target and Judd's Hurricane dropped straight into the sea, taking its brave pilot to his death.

"Cork's Hurricane landed with the rudder fabric in shreds. My ears were blasted by the sharp cracking sound from our

4.5 inch guns turrets as a stream of JU 88s dived across the convoy ahead of us. This time I was close enough to see their bombs slanting down and many of the ships were obscured by the huge black and white fountains. But only the freighter Deucalion was hit and forced to fall behind the convoy....
I think it fair to say we won the second round.
The price we paid was the loss of the COs of both 806 (Lt Cdr J. N. Garnett) and 880 Squadrons. As the last sounds were dying away, and from a sky smeared with the dispersing gunfire smoke, a lone Martlet came in low and too fast, its hook caught a wire but was torn out of the fuselage and the plane slewed out over the catwalk a few feet in front of me. As though in slow motion I watched the pilot, Lt Johnson, try to climb out of the cockpit but the plane turned on its back and fell into the sea. He had been wounded in one of the many air battles. I felt numb. Later I heard that fiery 'old Butch' had been shot down and killed by return fire.... we had thought him indestructible."

Gordon Wallace.

As Johnson made his approach, Dick was on the bridge with Captain Troubridge. They watched the Martlet topple over the side, whilst beside them a camera clicked, freezing forever this tragic moment in time. There was little to be done and their conversation about Butch Judd's demise continued:

"My Squadron Commander was either dead or missing so I was given command. I actually had about 6 Hurricanes serviceable."

By now most of 880's aircraft had been damaged and it took all the best efforts of riggers and fitters, aided by a host of other bodies from departments around the ship, to keep a few airworthy. Attrition rates were beginning to overhaul the fleet's ability to meet incoming raids and now the narrowest of margins separated the convoy from annihilation.

Once more that day radar played a crucial part in the battle. Taking advantage of the evening sun, a last, massive raid was seen approaching from airfields in Sicily and Sardinia, their primary targets being the carriers and battleships. With these out of action supply ships could be picked off with impunity.

Most of the fleet's remaining fighters were quickly vectored out to meet the incoming force, but the bombers and fighters quickly swamped their resistance:

> "Circling over the fleet I saw a flight of Fulmars being harried by waves of enemy fighters and went to their rescue. There were German and Italian aircraft everywhere, diving in from all directions. In the confusion it was almost impossible to catch anything and my section soon split up, twisting and turning to avoid being shot down. After several minutes I found myself on the edge of the combat area and saw a lone SM 79 preparing to attack one of our ships. Diving on it unawares my gunfire hit wings and engines and it went down towards the sea, one member of the crew jumping out when it was still more than 50 feet up. As I turned away I saw the Savoia's crew take to their rubber dinghy and push off, before the aircraft sank.
> From above and behind four Reggiane 2002s came down and started to knock lumps off my Hurricane. I had run out of ammunition so there was little I could do, except skim over the sea, making myself a difficult target and head back towards the fleet. More by luck than judgement I escaped, but my engine had been hit and began to cough and splutter and lose power, so I had to get down very smartly."
>
> *Dickie Cork (interviewed in 1943).*

Whilst Cork had been engaged away from the convoy, enemy bombers and fighters had pressed home their attack with some venom. Twelve JU 87s appeared in the sky above Indomitable and peeled off at two second intervals to begin their near vertical dive towards the carrier's deck. She opened up with all guns, but her escorts were fully engaged with low flying torpedo planes and so could not come to her help.

From 1,000 feet they released their bombs and within seconds Indomitable was obscured by three explosions along her flight deck. Staggering she slowly turned away from the wind, in the hope that this would give her fire fighters a chance to control the flames now sweeping through the ship. From a distance she looked all but lost, but on board her crew swung into action dousing fires and repairing damage. Below decks the carnage was dreadful:

"I was at my action station (adjacent to the hangar) when I felt the direct hit aft. The ship shuddered and I knew we had been hit. Then a few seconds later I felt another shudder, but this time a lot nearer. It was at this moment that a fitter called Freeman, who was with me, decided he had enough and opened the door leading to the passage and weather deck. That was the last thing he ever did, because at that precise moment the third bomb hit us, it came through the ship's side, about 30 feet in front of us, but a deck above. It killed all the forward gun crew, but by a stroke of luck did not penetrate the torpedo room, which had some live tinfish on racks, they were next to me just forward of the lift shaft.

I had my back to Freeman, as I was facing the bulkhead with the sprinkler wheel on it, when there was a roaring noise, followed by intense heat and I found myself falling to the deck in slow motion. As I fell I could clearly see spots on the rivet heads that the painter had missed, and I thought to myself 'just like a dockyard matey to miss painting something'.

Apart from the intense heat, and brilliant flash I couldn't remember a thing as I wandered about the ship for about an hour. I received second degree burns to face and hands. It took many days for my sight to return to anything near normal and my eardrums were damaged.

When I got to the sick bay I found out that all the people in the hangar had been killed."

Richard Brooke.

"After the attack we began listing to port, but we righted ourselves again fairly quickly, but everywhere was chaos. The forward lift had been blown up two feet above the flight deck and was badly buckled and fires raged fore and aft. In the hangar devastation reigned. I saw my rigger, Sainsbury, lying dead."

Rex Picken.

"The bomb hit abaft the after lift and had made it impossible to use the cabins in that area and another bomb had exploded near to the port side of the ship, completely destroying the wardroom. There was an all pervading smell of smoke and burnt flesh....All six aircrew in the wardroom had been killed including my cabin mate 'Willy Protheroe and 'Boy' Cunliffe Owen. There were many other missing faces..."

Gordon Wallace

"From every ship men watched her anxiously; isolated from the disaster, yet sharing it, impotent to help yet suffering the wound as if it were their own ship and their own friends. For twenty minutes she dragged in a slow circle, her deck heeling and the smoke pouring from her. Then she began to right, and the smoke that seemed to issue from her lifts lost its density and thinned to a wisp; a signal lamp blinked: 'Situation in hand', and she steadied on course."

Hugh Popham.

Dick struggled to keep his aircraft flying, its engine failing fast, and headed back towards Indomitable in the hope of landing without delay, but the smoke that shrouded her deck told its own story. He asked for instructions and was ordered to 'pancake' on Victorious, joining the queue of waiting fighters. On her deck everything was confused, the Flight Deck Party swamped by the weight of her own aircraft and those from Indomitable:

"Out of necessity I had to get down on her deck as quickly as possible and virtually barged into the other aircraft waiting to land. My motor was just about stopped and as I got my nose over the round-down it actually conked out. Luckily my hook took a wire and pulled me up. The handlers pushed me backwards to release the hook, then forward, beyond the barrier, where, after a brief examination, they unceremoniously pushed it over the side, it being a total write off."

Dickie Cork (interviewed in 1943).

With nightfall still an hour away the mess on Victorious had to be sorted out so that standing patrols could be flown off to intercept any more raids. Some aircraft were struck down below deck, but Sea Hurricanes were too large for Vic's lifts. Some were slipped onto outriggers, aft of the island and others joined Dick's aircraft over the side. With her deck finally sorted out four Hurricanes were ranged for take off, with Cork in the lead.

As he waited in the Ready Room, Dick came across Hugh Popham, who had spent the day gloomily watching events on Indomitable:

> "Several members of 880 were now on board, Dickie Cork
> with six enemy aircraft shot down among them, and I heard
> the day's tidings. Butch was dead…. Crooky was dead too….
> Brian (Fiddes) had been shot down by the fleet's ack ack, but
> had ditched successfully….
> 'The first thing Butch had said this morning,'Dickie told me
> was 'Where the devils that man Popham?' They hadn't heard
> till later that I was kicking my heels in Victorious;the rumour
> was that I'd bought it.'You'd better fly now anyway,' Dickie
> said. After the ceaseless strains of the day he was still cool
> and calm as if he had merely been doing half an hour's cam-
> era gun exercises.
> I looked at the day.The sun was already well down;within an
> hour it would be growing dark.
> I nodded.'More night landings?'I said as I lightly as I could.
> The thought of approaching the deck in the dark again in the
> face of the fleet's assembled anti-aircraft armament chilled
> my blood.
> Dickie grinned.'No night landings.You'll be all right.'
> The aircraft was strange and lacked a hood amongst other
> things, and I watched the sun drop below the horizon with
> sheer cold terror on me. It only needs a raid to come in now,
> I thought, and it'll be the same caper over again."

Hugh Popham.

As the Hurricanes split into two groups, Dick partnered by Sub Lt. Peter Hutton, a survivor from 801 Squadron, intercepted a mixed Italian bomber and fighter force, approaching from the north east. Hutton shot one down, but was then killed by gunfire from an Re 2002. Seeing his predicament, Cork broke off his attack on an SM 79 and climbed to help. He was too late and only succeeded in knocking lumps off the fighter's tail, which dived away trailing smoke and flames. He was tempted to follow, but turned about to pursue and harry several other bombers still circling the fleet. After 45 minutes, and in near darkness, the threat had disappeared and the survivors touched down on Victorious' deck.

During the day Cork had flown for five hours, each filled with an intensity of action few fighter pilots ever experienced, or survived. After a meal he was allocated a cabin and fell asleep in strange surroundings, unaware that his part in 'Pedestal' had come to an end. With one carrier sunk, a second badly damaged and a third struggling to find sufficient fighters to mount a worthwhile defence, ViceAdmiral Syfret had little option but to detach the convoy's heavy escort. It had been part of the original plan, but, if his carrier force had been intact, he could have remained with the merchant ships until Malta's fighters could provide cover. As it was, his depleted fleet turned about and headed due west for Gibraltar.

Indomitable arrived on the 15th, having paused briefly to bury her dead:

> "We suffered 44 men killed and 59 wounded.
> Later that morning all the ship's company, apart from those on duty, attended the burial at sea which took place on the port side for'd of the island. By the end of the service and with the playing of the 'Last Post' I could hardly swallow for the lump in my throat. The words 'Burial at Sea' were words until this moment, the reality was harrowing. I was only a few feet away from the incongruous wooden chute canted down over the side. The first few white canvas covered parcels, Willy's no bigger than a small case, slid down the bleached wood to disappear with a distant splash. On and on until I could no longer see for tears. All that was left of my shy, gentle Willy was a pipe and a few photographs in my album."

> *Gordon Wallace.*

As the dead slipped beneath the waves, Dick, now part of Victorious' Air Group, continued the unrelenting business of combat flying, patrolling out over the sea, waiting for an enemy now happy to leave this battered fleet alone. Far to the east, in the narrow waters between Sicily and Tunisia, the convoy ploughed on under constant attack from submarines, E-Boats and aircraft. Only five ships made it to Malta, some so badly damaged they were virtually submerged, but their cargoes proved sufficient to guarantee the islands future, for a few months more.

In Gibraltar, Cork returned to command what was left of 880 Squadron. For a year they had been together on Indomitable and now it seemed all familiarity had disappeared, to be filled by a nagging void. One always expected to lose pilots, but when riggers and fitters were killed and wounded in such numbers the squadron's central core seemed to evaporate with them. The survivors carried on as best they could, hiding their feelings behind a self protecting show of nonchalance:

> "I met Dickie Cork and also Bill Bruen, now COs of 880 and 800. They both seemed entirely unconcerned at the chaos around them, the shattered wardroom and the smell of entrails everywhere."
>
> *S/Lt(A). R. M. Crosley RNVR.*

For a week Indomitable remained in dry dock, her wounds being patched. She would need a refit to restore her fully and the dockyard at Norfolk, Virginia, beckoned once more, after a brief visit to Britain to return the bulk of her crew.

On her voyage home a wooden ramp was constructed over the forward lift and as the carrier closed land she flew off her remaining aircraft. By nightfall she had berthed in Liverpool docks and began decanting her men, the wounded to hospital and the others on leave.

When 880 reformed, on September 7th, at Stretton, Cork would not be with them. Whilst on leave, with his parents in Burnham, he received orders to proceed to RNAS Yeovilton, to begin training duties with 759 and 760 Squadrons. After all the excitement, instructing 'sprog pilots' held few attractions and he began canvassing the Admiralty for a front line posting. But his efforts were unsuccessful and to Yeovilton he went, smarting at the 'injustice' of his appointment, fearing he might not see action again.

CHAPTER FOURTEEN

CHIEF FLYING INSTRUCTOR

After such a prolonged period on board a carrier, life ashore seemed dull and uninteresting. Cork balked at the inactivity and pestered his appointing officer for a swift return to an operational squadron. His pleas were treated sympathetically, but rejected and to the Naval Fighter Pilot School at Yeovilton he went as an instructor. Though frustrated by this 'relegation', he set too with great enthusiasm, soothed by the promise of a return to active service within a year, as he described in a letter to a friend:

"My days are spent leading small groups of pilots around the sky over Somerset or giving some dual instruction on Proctors or Masters. But there's an old Gladiator here which no one wants and which now seems to be mine. Its seen better days, but is still great fun to throw around.
Most of the pilots we see are quite proficient, but lack any idea about fighter tactics, which is why I am here. After a few hours they begin to get the idea and practice attacks as though their lives depended on it. It seems such a long time since we were at this stage and its thanks to DB (Douglas Bader) that we survived. As I lecture these youngsters I can still hear his voice, driving home the do's and don'ts.
There seems little chance of getting back to a squadron in the foreseeable future. I'm told I need a rest, though, of course, I don't agree. It would have been nice to have carried on for a bit longer, particularly as my old bunch now have Seafires. After flying the old Hurricane for so long it would have been fun to fly something with the power to catch the enemy and have some advantage for a change. Still it seems

that I will be allowed back towards the end of next year, so
here's hoping...."

Although he still felt fresh, it was recognised in medical circles that,
after a prolonged period of frontline service, a pilot's general condition
could deteriorate rapidly;although the signs of weariness might be kept
at bay for sometime. Despite his protestations he was getting increasingly tired and needed a rest. Of course, the Navy's decision may have
been coloured by the need to preserve its' best men, so they could
return at some future date, but whatever their motive, service require-
ments and personal need coincided to provide belated relief for a
weary pilot.

For the most part, Dick flew Sea Hurricanes with 759 and 760
Squadrons at Yeovilton, his efforts being absorbed by the process of creating fighter pilots from raw material provided by training schools. This
proved a great success, though, in the early days, its achievements were
diluted by a lack of experienced instructors. But there was a willingness
to learn, and close liaison with the RAF meant that the latest tactics
could be studied at first hand. Instructors were also encouraged to join
nearby Wings and participate in 'sweeps' across the Channel to enemy
occupied France. Cork took advantage of this arrangement and occasionally flew with the RAF.

During November his gallantry during Pedestal received official
recognition when he was awarded the Distinguished Service Order.
Once made public, and much to his embarrassment, local and national
papers carried accounts of his deeds under the heading, "MALTA CON-
VOY DSO":

> "Lieutenant Richard John Cork is front page news again. This
> 25 year old pilot of the Fleet Air Arm, who was decorated
> with the DSC for his courageous flying in defence of London
> during the Battle of Britain, has now been awarded the DSO
> for conspicuous gallantry in repelling attacks during the pas-
> sage through the Mediterranean of a Malta Convoy. He is now
> employed on instructional duties and was spending a week-
> end at home when the announcement of the award was
> made in the London Gazette on 14th November. His younger
> brother Brian is serving as an artillery lieutenant with the
> Eighth Army in Libya."

With their eldest son safe at home, the Cork family had good reason to celebrate and this award increased their pleasure. The war was always in the background, but for a few hours it could be forgotten, though Brian's presence in Libya acted as a constant reminder of the dangers their sons continued to face.

On December 8th, the family made the short journey from Burnham to Buckingham Palace to see Dick receive his DSO from King George VI. Several days' leave followed. In the days before Christmas he returned to Yeovilton to complete his busy training schedule, leading fledgling fighter pilots over the frost covered fields of Somerset, Wiltshire and Dorset, making the most of the good weather whilst it lasted.

Although this recognition was enjoyable, Cork disliked the outside interest it created. He guarded his privacy and made light of his achievements and so resented unwarranted attention. Yet, in naval circles, he was something of a celebrity and this status brought with it certain penalties. As the war progressed, newspapers clamoured for stories of individual gallantry. At first the three services preferred to keep its 'stars' cloaked in anonymity and kept a tight reign on any press releases. But after so many setbacks, with defeat still a possibility, individual bravery remained a fruitful area for propaganda to exploit, in a bid to encourage a population growing increasingly weary of war.

Some press reports were mildly amusing and photographers from periodicals often appeared at establishments to record recruits under training. With London fairly close, Yeovilton became a favourite spot for these exercises. On one occasion, Dick and a group of young pilots posed in front of their aircraft and squadron huts in flying gear, trying to hide their laughter behind a semblance of serious instruction.

On other occasions this attention proved harder to stomach. In 1941 the Air Ministry commissioned an author, David Masters, to write a book describing the lives and deeds of a handful of airmen. "So Few", appeared soon after, its tone suitably heroic. Selling out within weeks, a second edition was rushed into print, but increased in size to keep pace with the demand for more stories. The Admiralty were keen to participate and selected Cork as someone who could promote the Navy's achievements. Later, when interviews had been completed, and a draft passed through his hands, Dick described his reaction to this unwanted attention in a letter to Masters:

"Finally you will notice that I have completely crossed out one or two short lines I cannot honestly feel that anything

> connected with my personal appearance has the slightest
> bearing on the Malta Convoy or in furthering the aims men-
> tioned in your letter.
> I still cannot agree with you that anything I have done, will
> be of any help in the ultimate aim of this war my personal
> view, whether it is selfish or not, is that the Chapter will not
> help my career at all, and candidly even without the above
> lines I shall probably be the laughing stock of the whole
> Service.
> However, I am persuaded by other people that it will do no
> harm, I only hope that people will be inspired by the other
> chapters in your new edition of "So Few."

Despite these brief distractions, 1943 seemed to offer little beyond the day to day routine of instructing. Even with the promise of a transfer some time in the future, he continued to send numerous letters to the Admiralty and canvassed visiting officers in an attempt to speed up the process. With spring came a rush of postings and pilots, with far less experience than Cork, began making their way to America to join Hellcat and Corsair squadrons. In the hope of making this journey westwards, he redoubled his effort, but his requests received scant attention and rapid refusal. However, there were some compensations.

Whilst Yeovilton could cope with all Hurricane training courses, it could not absorb the increasing amount of work generated by the arrival of Seafires, so a second Air Fighting School was commissioned at Henstridge. Now established as an training officer, Cork was an obvious choice as Chief Flying Instructor. It may not have been the posting he had sought, but it was promotion and gave him the responsibility he craved.

Having survived three and a half years of war without loss, the Cork family were suddenly struck a tragic blow. Michael Wayman, Pauline's husband and a fellow member of Eton Excelsior Rowing Club before the war, now flew Mosquitoes with 139 Squadron from Marham. They specialized in the highly dangerous business of low level bombing raids. His skill at this work was undoubted and the award of a DFC gave voice to his gallantry, but the risks were high and life expectancy low, with a high proportion of tours ending prematurely.

On March 20th, six of 139's aircraft flew across the Channel to attack marshalling yards at Malines. Arriving over the coast as dusk fell, the twin engined light bombers were silhouetted against the sun, now low in the west. Flak was heavier than expected and Wayman's aircraft was crippled by a burst of fire. With smoke and flames streaming back behind him, there was little he could do but turn for home and hope to reach land before his engines failed. Arriving over Martlesham, 40 minutes later, he circled once, to warn them of his predicament, then made a wheels up landing on the grass strip alongside Martlesham's main runway. With bombs still hung up in the Mosquito's bay, a safe landing proved impossible and Wayman and his navigator, Flying Officer Clear DFC, were killed in the resulting explosion. In early April, his funeral took place in Sunderland, where his father was Lord Mayor.

Whilst Dick's family absorbed this terrible news, his posting to Henstridge came through, but any pleasure he might have felt was muted by this tragedy.

His natural reaction, when faced with sorrow or a setback, was to press on and throw himself into the task at hand, disguising his feelings behind a mask of professionalism. In this, he was helped by a brief posting to an RAF Wing, operating from Biggin Hill. In the two years since visiting Douglas Bader at Tangmere, the RAF had made a massive commitment to its fighter force, and Wing attacks now dominated aerial activity over Northern France and Belgium.

Dick joined 611 Squadron and spent several days familiarising himself with their new Spitfire MK IX's; taking part in a patrol high over Beachy Head, on April 1st. He saw nothing of note, except the distant flash of anti aircraft fire as a Focke Wulf 190 darted inland to drop a bomb and skip back over the Channel at sea level, before it could be caught. But despite this lack of activity, he enjoyed his brief visit and marvelled at the lavish benefits enjoyed by his opposite numbers in the RAF. In this he was not alone:

> "It was interesting to be part of a big organisation, entirely geared for flying and nothing else. The RAF were complete professionals.
> The most impressive part of the RAF was not its flying, which was barely average by Fleet Air Arm standards, but its back up organisation. Aircrews were briefed an hour before each flight, not a haphazard 5 or 10 minutes as in Dasher. Every aspect of an operation were given in detail; R/T frequencies, call signs, air/sea rescue details, position of rescue aircraft and ships, likelihood of French agents to contact if shot down and weather in every detail. In addition we had extra 'air-

borne' rations; raisons, sweets, chewing gum for the nervous, soft drinks for those with dry mouths. Back at the Mess we would have extra eggs, fruit, nuts, orange juice and chocolate. There was special transport runs into the local town and to the local pubs.

Entertainers visited the station regularly. Flying clothing was of luxurious standard. We normally flew in battledress uniform at Henstridge as there was nothing else. The RAF flying clothing had pockets for everything and each pilot had a magnificent pair of black leather flying boots which, if we were shot down, would readily convert into tough, unobtrusive walking shoes. The Mae West was of a more recent pattern and had a dye marker, torch and whistle, and could be automatically inflated by pulling a toggle. Besides all this, the runways at Church Stanton were double the width and nearly half as long again as the longest Henstridge runway, making formation landings and take-offs safe and easy and with no strain on the aircraft brakes. Life was very easy and relaxed compared with life aboard ship.

However, for some reason, we in the Fleet Air Arm, struggling with last year's model, were not in the least jealous of the RAF. We seemed to take it for granted that we should be the poor relation. In fact we thought ourselves rather special, being able to cope without it."

Mike Crosley.

Dick went straight from Biggin Hill to his new posting, pausing briefly to spend a couple of nights at home, offering any consolation he could, to his sister and parents. But, in the circumstances, there was little he could do and he motored down, across Salisbury Plain, to Yeovilton, where all his kit was awaiting him, packed up and ready for transfer to Henstridge, just across the border in Dorset.

HMS Dipper was commissioned on April 1st 1943, after a laborious two year construction programme, during which builders had sought to dry out a waterlogged valley to the south of the village. It had a five runway layout, specifically designed for deck landing training, surrounded by huts, hangars and accommodation blocks. To the casual observer it was a standard wartime airfield, but Dipper had some features that made it most distinctive. When acquiring land, in this remote corner of Dorset, the War Ministry gained some elegant farmhouses and their outbuildings, most of which were several hundred years old, but still habitable. Those along the course of new runways were soon demolished, but others survived and were soon occupied;their new tenants converting them into Squadron offices.

Dick was one of the first to arrive and found Dipper virtually deserted and quickly set to, busying himself with domestic arrangements, so that 761 Squadron could be established. With little equipment and few personnel to help, it was an uphill task, but his efforts soon bore fruit and by April 12th the first aircraft arrived a mixture of well worn ex RAF Spitfires, a few Seafires, Masters and Proctors, Dick bringing the first in from Yeovilton.

As the posting system sprang into life, a steady stream of men began to arrive and two Flights were established;'A' under Lt(A) David Carlisle RN and 'B' with Lt(A)'Ben' Lyon DSC RNVR in command, backed up by six instructors. Mike Crosley, late of HMS Eagle and Pedestal, arrived during the summer to replace one of the first batch of instructors. Years later he recorded how the CFI initiated him into this new world:

"The day I arrived, Dickie Cork saw me in the wardroom at lunch time. He said:'Hallo Crosley. You've flown Spits before I suppose. Get hold of one and meet me over the airfield at 1600 for a bit of formation flying. OK?'
I re-read Pilot's Note for the Spitfire 1b. I tried to cast my mind back to a Christmas, eight months ago. I had flown it in in a careful straight line and had learned nothing about it.
'Ben' Lyon showed me the 'taps' and I strapped in, started up and, pretending to know what I was doing, taxied out and took off. After a few private loops and rolls and a bit of slow flying, I came over Henstridge to meet Dickie. He flashed by me out of the sun and I spent the next five minutes catching up and trying to formate on his port wing. I could not have been making a very good impression for I found the stick forces so light in the pitching plane that I was continually over correcting. My Spitfire was prancing up and down alongside him like a mustang. I found that the aircraft I was flying was not a Spitfire 1b, but a hooked Seafire 1b. The latter had almost zero stick forces on the elevator control, a phenomenon that I had not expected and which was totally different from the Hurricane. I described the flight in the

'Duty' column of my flying log as: 'Trying to formate with the CFI'.

I had heard that the Seafire, like the Spitfire was a delight to fly. I would have to get used to the much lighter stick forces."

Mike Crosley.

Whilst most at Henstridge saw the professional side of Dick's character, others were privileged to see other features of his personality. Rhys Chamen, an instructor with 761, was one of these:

"I first met Dickie Cork when he was CFI at Henstridge. He was greatly respected by all who knew him and was an exceptional fighter pilot. He never spoke of his past or future, enjoyed a practical joke and was intensely devoted to fighter tactics.

We soon became friends and often played squash on a neighbouring estate. He was an outstanding sportsman and his reflexes and anticipation were extremely sharp and with his rapid move ment around the court a most difficult man to beat.

He didn't spend much time in the wardroom, several drinks before dinner, then he would retire to his cabin to read. Being a serious individual he never gave vent to his feelings, not even on the squash court.

Dickie was, in my opinion, very frustrated at Henstridge because he wanted to be in action again and the news of his appointment as Group Leader in the Pacific was great news to him. There was no doubt in my mind that he was an exceptional fighter pilot and in every respect an outstanding gentleman.

Whilst he craved a return to operations he didn't allow this to deflect him from the job at hand and many of those stationed at Henstridge benefitted from his personal assistance in guiding them along the proper way of handling a fighter in action."

Lt(A) Rhys Chamen RNVR.

Each day, when the weather allowed, the sky above Henstridge echoed to the sound of Merlin engines wailing and purring, as their pilots progressed through various exercises towards graduation. Cork, and his instructors, left nothing to chance and training took on an intensity of purpose reflecting how close their pupils were to front line service. Most of these young men responded well, but occasionally someone failed to make the grade and was 'scrubbed' from the course. Perhaps their reactions were too slow, or the basic lessons of air fighting were beyond their comprehension; either way they could be a liability to a squadron. When this happened instructors made every effort to encourage the pilot and develop his skill. But when it became clear that improvement was unlikely, it fell to Cork, as CFI, to undertake a final assessment and then break the bad news, as one trainee fighter pilot later recalled:

> "I desperately wanted to fly fighters and arrived at
> Henstridge full of hope. I was rather nervous, but soon settled in to the routine of exercises and found the Seafire a bit of a handful. By myself I had no real problems, though bounced it a bit on landing, but in formation I couldn't get it right and caused confusion to all those around me. No matter how hard I tried I just couldn't get it right and began to flounder. So I soon found myself in the CFI's hands, after other instructors had tried to iron out the problems. He quickly put me through my paces and gave me every chance to show him what I was capable of.
> I suppose I was a little overawed by a chap who had seen so much action, but he soon put me at my ease and explained the situation to me. He was forthright, but fair and left me with my confidence bruised, but intact, as I moved on to less glamorous flying duties.
> Fifty years on I can look back and laugh, but at the time it seemed as though my world had caved in and the CFI's parting words, 'We want you to live to see your grandchildren....', seemed of little worth. However, as time passed I realised the wisdom of his actions and these words took on greater meaning."

Life on an air station centred on flying, but many other trades came together to achieve this primary role. As CFI, Dick saw the need for good relations with all these branches and went out of his way to 'smooth the path', to ensure the best possible service. To his own men he was a good leader, but also someone with whom they could relate, as Mark Busby, 1st Class AMO (Air Mechanic Ordnance) recalled:

> "I trained at Kirkham Armoury School and moved to HMS Dipper, Henstridge, in 1943 where I joined Lt Cdr Cork's squadron and became part of the team working on his aircraft.
> Lt Cdr Cork was a jovial and easy going person, who was well liked and respected by the men working under him. As a side line they maintained his Austin car and filled the tank with high octane aviation fuel it went across the runway like a rocket.
> I personally came in contact with him when a Seafire flown by a young rookie pilot landed on a ploughed field a mile or so off the runway. Lt Cdr Cork took men to check it over and found it up to its hubs in mud impossible to get a truck and crane near to lift it out. To save time and to avoid a lot of 'red tape', he asked me if I would strip down the eight Browning 303s and ammo realising it would be about 5 hundred weight less on the aircraft. He climbed in, got the Seafire's engine running and told us men to get on the tail. He gave it full revs with brakes applied released them and at a signal from him we all jumped off and the aircraft sailed into the air and landed on the airfield. On inspection the aircraft was found to be in perfect order and no more was said about the incident. No doubt Lt Cdr Cork gave the pilot a 'dressing down'.
> The atmosphere on the station was generally good, especially with the pilots, who were a great bunch of fellows, but a few officers were stand-offish and followed the book rigidly. Lt Cdr Cork knew when to be flexible and achieved a great deal more because of it.
> On one occasion he was supervising dummy deck landings with five or six trainee fliers. An American Liberator bomber flew over and requested permission to land. Lt Cdr Cork fired several red flares, but the Liberator had been damaged by Ack Ack over France and needed to land at once. Unfortunately its bomb doors were jammed and so it hadn't ditched its load over the Channel and landed fully laden. The Seafires were waved off' and the Liberator came down, burning out its

tyres on the short runway.

My Petty Officer, known as 'Taffy', and I were with Lt Cdr Cork who was furious with the Americans, because he couldn't get his young pilots down with the bomb laden Liberator blocking the way. But 'Taffy' and I came up with an idea with plenty of palliasses we could do something about it and relayed our plan to Lt Cdr Cork. He immediately sent for a truck load, which we placed under the Liberator. We then forced open the bomb doors.

The American crew wanted to know what was going to happen and on being told, jumped onto a jeep and left the area. Lt Cdr Cork wished us 'Good luck' and also left the area. I then climbed into the aircraft, switched to salvo and at the count of 3 dropped the bombs on to the palliasses safely. There were about 10 tons of high explosives and neither 'Taffy' or I really knew what would happen, as we had no knowledge of American bomb detonators. Lt Cdr Cork came back and said a big 'Thank you' to us.

Working closely under him we soon became aware of his ability to get the best out of people and his fine sense of humour. In particular I remember two white painted footprints painted on the dashboard of his car; left and right, pointing upwards. On another occasion he had the radio removed from his Seafire, to make space for his grip, so he could fly off on a spot of leave. On his return, a few days later, it was replaced quickly and quietly.

Towards the end of his time at Henstridge Lt Cdr Cork was supervising a group on target practice over the Bristol Channel, aiming at a target sleeve. My pilot was Dutch and in broken English he told me how disappointed he was at not being able to hit the target. I tried to assist him by explaining the gun sights in the cockpit, but still he couldn't hit the target.

Not long before this, a Wellington bomber had made a forced landing and crashed on the airfield. I had disarmed its guns, so had access to some tracer and incendiary rounds, all the same calibre as the Dutchman's Brownings, which I proceeded to load with a mixture allowing him to see where he was shooting.

When he returned from his next target practice over the

Bristol Channel his smile said it all he hadn't just hit the target, but demolished it. Lt Cdr Cork had sent him in first and so no target remained for the rest to shoot at. When he got back Lt Cdr C came up to me and said, 'Don't do that too often', with a smile on his face. No more was said normally I would have been in deep trouble for doing such a thing."

Whilst most trainee pilots and instructors were RNVR, there remained a central core of regular officers at Henstridge, who treated 'reservists' with mild condescension. Dick was aware of this and struggled to maintain some balance between the two sides, but inevitably he was caught with a foot in each camp:

"He (Dick) was a valuable buffer between us 'branchmen' and the authorities. The Captain was a kind benevolent man in his dealings with his RNVR aviators, but the Commander was not quite so patient. He was a destroyer man, and Dickie and he did not see eye to eye, 'remarkable man though he is in many ways', the Commander was heard to say. The Commander was equally brave in his own way, verging on the intrepid. He was determined to learn to fly. He came past our Nissen hut at 'B' one morning in a Tiger Moth, with the 'orrible 'otchkiss in the back as his instructor....A flurry of yellow and blue, they zigzagged past us at about 20 mph and the Commander could be heard above the noise of his revving engine shouting, 'Handsomely there, Handsomely', to each rating in turn (one on each wingtip).
The whole lot disappeared past our hangar, in a series of groundloops....
We had no doubt the Commander had seen our merriment as he went by. So next morning we expected and received one of his most meticulous inspections. He descended on us very early indeed and from a great height. There was a long list of matters to attend to in his report. The Commander told 'Ben' Lyon to make sure, next time, to have all ratings with hats on and chin stays down. They should be standing to attention by their aircraft. Drip trays were to be cleaned out, fire buckets were to be full of water or sand and not yesterday's halfeaten Tiddy Oggies or fag ends. All aircraft were to have their cowlings on, even if they had no engines, and all pointed the same

way. There was to be 'clean blotting paper on the desks and pens arranged in order of size'. Ben then told Dickie that our flying would, henceforth, be nil on all inspection mornings, as the finding of clean blotting paper and pens would take time. We had no further trouble from inspections of this sort.

It was inevitable, however, that one of us would eventually fall foul of the Commander. Norman Goodfellow was the unlucky man. In Dicky's absence he had gone to the Captain to complain when one of his best pilots had been thrown off the Course for landing his Seafire in what was judged by authority to have been a carefree manner. Norman had reported that the cause of the accident had been because the pupil concerned was suffering from anoxia following an oxygen climb. When he landed, he, like Barker in 804 Squadron could not remember a thing about it; but Norman's mistake of protocol, in going over the Commander's head to plead for his pupil, was frowned upon even more than the accident. The Captain sent Norman back to see the Commander and he rounded upon Norman and gave him a fortnight's Duty Boy."

Mike Crosley.

In these minor skirmishes Dick was destined to play the role of peacemaker, which he did with an abundance of tact. He even volunteered to give Commander Poe RN, the object of his pilots amusement, flying lessons. Yet these mild distractions served a worthwhile purpose, because they were brief diversions from the serious business at hand:

"I was A Flight Commander and served from July to October 1943 under Dick's command and direction. We all worked and flew long hours to complete our task of training fledgling students to fly and fight. With his experience as a Battle of Britain pilot he was a superb leader to us all. He was an excellent pilot who could ably lead and demonstrate the latest skills in air combat. Training the students came uppermost in his priorities and he would go to any necessary lengths to support us all in carrying out this task. His character and experience were such that he discouraged others to make much of his achievements in the Battle of

Britain. Physically he was a tall, very handsome officer with wavy brown hair, yet his manner was always modest and he went to great pains to play down any 'hero worship'. He had a splendid sense of humour and inspired confidence and trust in all of us who served with him at the Fighter School."

Lt(A) P. Chilton RN.

Despite his determination to succeed as CFI, Cork still longed for an operational posting and for months had pursued his case with the Admiralty. But men of his experience were few and far between and had to be used to best advantage. The coming offensive against the Japanese would see the Fleet Air Arm adopt Wing formations two or three squadrons acting as one and it was men of his calibre who would make this change of tactic work. The Navy had recognised this in February 1943 and marked him down as a future Leader, though kept him in ignorance of their decision until the Summer.

On July 17th, as he landed after a 'wing drill', a phonecall to 761 Squadron's office brought him hurrying across to see Dipper's Captain. In a few, short words the CO announced his posting as Wing Leader, solemnly underlined its importance to the Navy, then provided brief details of his new command, at that moment working up in America. 1830, 1831 and 1833 Corsair Squadrons would embark on HMS Illustrious towards the end of 1943, to form the first fighter wing in the Eastern Fleet - a prestigious role, requiring a maximum effort from all involved. When they returned to Britain, Cork would become their first operational Wing Leader. Until then he remained at Henstridge, taking advantage of any opportunity that might arise to familiarize himself with the Corsair and wing tactics.

Unfortunately there was little expertise in the Navy to draw upon, so he turned towards his old friends in the Air Force for advice. Since 1940, as Cork well knew, the RAF had experimented with wing formations and, by 1943, used them where the enemy was most vulnerable. To train pilots in these tactics they set up the Fighter Leaders School, at Charmy Down, overlooking Bath, and, in August, Dick joined a three week course there. Squadron Leader Jim Hallowes, a Sergeant 'Ace' from the Battle of Britain, was a fellow student:

"It really was quite a surprise to find a 'boy in blue' attached to the course. I hadn't come across Dick before, but knew a little about him from friends in the RAF.

The course was all about tactics and Wings and for three
weeks we rehearsed various drills, with bombers and fighters from neighbouring airfields, using towns and cities
through the west of England, into Wales, as our targets. It
was all good fun, but had some serious undertones.
However, with so many 'old hands' involved, everything
went fairly smoothly too such an extent we began to wonder who knew most, us or the instructors.
We took it in turn to lead and I seemed to be Dick's wingman, whenever his turn came. He was very sharp and easily kept us in order, without any bother. His voice and
instructions, over the R/T were clear and measured and no
one was left in any doubt who was boss. I wasn't surprised to find out later on that he had flown with Douglas
Bader and had probably learned a lot from him. But unlike
Bader, was most unassuming, yet had the ability to lead
and get the best out of those around him."

During the course Dick flew Spitfire MK IXs, delighting in their
performance, finding the Seafire sluggish by comparison. Each day
they practised different exercises, a 'Circus' to Neath, a 'Ramrod' on
Aston Down, a 'Rhubarb' over Devon, followed by close escort to
bombers and fighter interceptions. The pace did not slacken, but
these dress rehearsals lacked the feel of combat. Nevertheless it
allowed them the opportunity to handle large formations and for
Cork it was an invaluable lesson.

The course broke up on August 25th and he flew his Seafire to
White Waltham, to enjoy a couple of days home leave, before returning to Henstridge. In his absence life had gone on much as before
and he found that his pilots and Commander Poe had once again
'fallen out'. In his impervious way he listened to the complaints and
tried to smooth ruffled feathers again.

As September gave way to October Dick waited for news of his
posting to arrive, but everything had gone quiet and he began has-
tening the Admiralty again, by phone and letter. Whilst waiting for a
reply he visited 165 (Ceylon) Squadron at Church Fenton and flew
four missions over France with the RAF, escorting American and
British bombers on two of these raids. He kept no record of these
operations, beyond a brief note in his log book, and it is left to
Norman Hanson, who later flew Corsairs with Cork, to provide some

hint of what happened:

> "Dickie, I am sure would have submerged us evermore in fly-
> ing stories had he felt so inclined. Yet despite his fine record
> he wasn't a lineshooter. Persuading him to open up on his
> exploits was like extracting an obstinate molar, and great per-
> severance was called for.
> He did unbend one evening and held us spellbound with an
> account of a daylight raid carried out by the US Army Air
> Corps B 25s over Cherbourg docks. The bombers were
> escorted by RAF Spitfires, including one flown by Cork.
> As usual, German reaction was violent. Hordes of
> Messerschmitts rose to meet the threat and the escort fight-
> ers were soon busily engaged. Too many, unfortunately, were
> led astray by the Luftwaffe and became involved in dog fights
> far away from the bombers. Those who remained faithful to
> the B 25s found the going rough, so much so that the strike
> leader, a Brigadier General flying the lead B 25, sized up the
> situation and broadcast to the fighters 'Hey! It's rough out
> there fellas! Come on beneath us and stay out of the cold!'
> They did as they were ordered. Cork said that the magnifi-
> cent protection given was more than enough to keep the Bf
> 109s at bay whilst they enjoyed a breather."

> *Lt Cdr(A) N. Hanson RNVR.*

Other than this brief account, Cork remained silent, preferring understatement to self advertisement, as witnessed in a letter a few weeks
later:

> "Things have been very dull over here recently, nothing hap-
> pening at all, and the Germans seem to have packed up the
> war over France. I have been working with the RAF again,
> but there has been little around.
> Anyway at last I'm off on operations again, but not in your
> part of the world, unfortunately. I'm going in command of a
> wing of four squadrons, which should be amusing. I shall be
> most annoyed if ever I get shot down with about sixty air-
> craft behind me.
> There seems to be no one at home these days and the beer

and everything else is as poor as piss and very expensive. The American Army of Occupation rules London nowadays and as they have so much money can get anything they want. An American's idea of getting a taxi is to stand in the middle of the road and wave a pound note. A most objectionable people and absolutely covered in gongs, all of which mean nothing at all, pistol shooting and so on.

I recently bought a wizard golden Cocker puppy, which you can look after for me when you come home, as I cannot take him to sea with me. He is with a girl friend of mine called Pat Janssen at a place called Wilkenthroop Estate, Templecombe, Somerset. So look her up if you get back, she's got a nice young sister about your mark.

A happy Christmas, and have a drink on me. I got an extra two year's seniority the other day for meritous work, sounds good don't it."

Whilst life at Henstridge had some compensations, Dick became very aware of changes in lifestyle, unthinkable in pre-war years. With a massive build up of men and equipment, towns and cities around Britain became homes to thousands of seemingly wealthy young Americans, living off the 'fat of the land, whilst our boys fight the war'. It was an illusion, but it fostered much ill feeling and resentment. But it was a rapidly changing world, in which many struggled to find some semblance of order.

For men committed to battle, it seemed that those on the sidelines enjoyed all sorts of benefits, from positions of safety. As the fifth Winter of the war approached, stories of strike action in shipyards, coalfields and factories began to spread, although news reports were muted, if not devoid of any information. Dick and his comrades were aware of this increasing disaffection and saw a people and a country seemingly less worthy of their sacrifice. The frontline seemed to be the only place where unity of purpose might be found.

His time with 165 Squadron passed quickly and Cork returned to Henstridge hoping his posting notice might have arrived, but little had happened in his absence, much to his disgust. However, a chance encounter, one evening in the wardroom, sent him scurrying to a phone, seeking contact with staff at nearby Boscombe Down, where aircraft about to enter service were evaluated. In September they had acquired a Corsair and Dick asked if he might fly it. They agreed and on a very overcast October morning he flew his Seafire the short distance to Boscombe.

Even to an experienced pilot the Corsair could prove a difficult aircraft to fly and newcomers treated it with the greatest respect, as Norman Hanson recalled:

> "Each morning we heard dreadful tidings of pilots being killed in Corsairs. Then suddenly, when I felt there couldn't be any Corsairs left for us to fly, we found ourselves at Quonset Point. After supper on the first evening, the CO came across to me.
>
> 'Feel like a stroll, Hans?'
>
> We walked up to the hangar that had been allocated to us. There was an armed sentry on guard, but Eric told him to open up and turn on the lights. For some reason or other we headed up a flight of stairs leading onto a balcony running the length of the hangar. Just then the lights came on and there they were. Corsairs filled the hangar floor and I must say that, of all the aircraft I had seen, these were truly the most wicked looking bastards. They looked truly vicious and it took little imagination to realise why so many American boys had found it difficult, if not well nigh impossible, to master them especially in deck landing. We stared at them and hadn't a word to say.... I tried one of the typewriters, a beautiful machine. I found a sheet of quarto and typed; and what I typed was my last will and testament. I saw no reason why a Corsair shouldn't kill me when it could obviously kill so many other lads without any trouble.
>
> For one thing, they were damnably big fighters for their day. They had a vast length of fuselage between cockpit and the propeller which, together with a rather low sitting position and a not too clever hood (both later modified for the Mark II version), made for very poor visibility when taxiing and landing. It was pretty long-legged in the undercarriage department in order to give clearance to the great propeller, said to be the biggest ever fitted to a single engined fighter. To increase the clearance, which the undercarriage alone could never have achieved, the wings were of 'inverted gull' format, dipping downwards for about four feet from the wingroot at the fuselage, then rising sharply to the wingtip. Not for noth-

ing was it called the bent winged 'bastard from Connecticut'. "

The Corsair at Boscombe was a Mark I, like Hanson's and after the briefest of cockpit checks, Dick took off and, for 40 minutes, flew this strange machine, with its bent wings and birdcage canopy, back and forth across Salisbury Plain. After several landings, he taxied in and handed it back to the groundcrew, asking many questions of them and other pilots. He was not displeased with the aircraft, but appreciated the problems it could pose, for the unwary or the inexperienced. Yet its strangeness stayed in his mind and for the next few days he tried to put together as much information as he could about the type, including a hard to get copy of 'Pilots Notes'.

Cork realised that his command would be populated by experienced Corsair pilots, leaving him at a distinct disadvantage. With time so short he voiced this concern over his lack of experience on the type. In response the Navy changed the terms of his transfer from permanent to temporary. In effect they had placed him on probation, pending a successful conversion to Corsairs. So Dick's last few days at Henstridge were coloured by a tinge of bitterness and controversy. The Admiralty's attitude showed a basic ignorance of flying matters and acted as a snub to a man of immense experience and dedication. They misread his message, which highlighted the need to spend more time on Corsairs, or any other type for that matter, before leading them on operations. But there was little he could do, except fume at their 'stupidity'.

In reality, as he told friends, he was not displeased with his posting, but would have preferred a Seafire Wing, having spent so much time training others on the type. A feeling heightened by the arrival at Henstridge of 894 Squadron, fresh from Illustrious.

During December they would be joined by 887 and together form a Wing. As he departed, Dick looked with envy on such a posting, but at this late date there was little he could do and to the 15th Fighter Wing he went.

Henstridge was by then in the depths of winter, with rain storms sweeping the runways, making life cold, damp and unpleasant. Some brighter moments lit the gloom and his last days were spent organising and leading a flying display for Winston Churchill, home leave and a formal lunch at Simpsons, in the Strand, attended by many noteworthy personalities from the Battle of Britain. Dick met many old friends and was photographed by the Press, looking relaxed and happy, after the meal.

With this his time as an instructor came to an end. Whilst the 15th

Wing appointment was only temporary, he had no doubt that it would soon be confirmed and he would join Illustrious before the year was out. He displayed no apprehension about this posting and seemed determined to succeed. Some suspected that he might 'have seen too much war' and should have been rested longer, but realised that the man's very nature would not allow him to remain in reserve for long. In any case, as he was the first to admit, there were many others who had seen more action and were still operational, so why should he be different ?

On the eve of his departure, Captain Sparks, his CO at Dipper, called Dick to his office and thanked him for all his efforts. In his personal file he then wrote:

> "Lt Cdr Cork has conducted himself to my entire satisfaction. An outstanding pilot and an outstanding personality. He has done excellent work as the first Chief Flying Instructor at this station."

For 15 months he had kicked his heels, but now his moment had come. As he loaded up his tiny Austin car and headed along a mud splattered road towards London, the signs of war were all around him on Salisbury Plain, through Hampshire and Berkshire. The southern counties were now gripped by the build up of men and arms for the coming Second Front, and Dick picked his way home for a few days leave along roads thronged with transport and soldiers on exercise. Within a few short weeks he would leave Britain's shores for the last time, his memories of her once peaceful countryside and roads disturbed by images of war. He would not live to see her restored.

In the wake of his departure there remained vivid memories of a good friend and officer, which time has not coloured:

> "He was a remarkable man and I, and most others who met him, have been left with an indelible memory of his flying skill, his immense good looks, his charming modesty and his total unselfishness and generosity to those around him."

> *Mike Crosley.*

CHAPTER FIFTEEN

MUDGE ANDERSON

Having volunteered for service with the Navy, and each day reading of fresh setbacks in the war, Murray 'Mudge' Anderson expected early call up. But nothing happened and he was forced to 'kick his heels'. Finally, late in 1941, his wait came to an end. Posting instructions arrived and, after basic training and aircrew selection tests, he joined a troopship, with other recruits, sailing for England.

A pattern so familiar to hundreds of other young men, seeking to become pilots or observers, had begun and he found himself, one cold, snow filled January night, driven by lorry from Gosport to nearby St Vincent and dumped in front of one of its many barrack blocks. Norman Hanson later recalled the impression this establishment made on him and so many others:

> "St. Vincent was a naval barracks of the old style gloomy, for-
> bidding and ceding not an inch to comfort or reasonably gra-
> cious living. The Regular Officers were fine chaps but the
> RNVRs, with one or two exceptions seemed to me in my
> brief acquaintance of six short weeks to be a fairly bloody
> minded lot who probably resented the fate which found
> them a seemingly thankless task in pushing through an end-
> less procession of birds of passage.
> The Chiefs and Petty Officers, on the other hand, were an
> entirely different cup of tea. They were inured to discipline
> and knew all about the Navy from the age of 14 onwards....
> In the main they were more than friendly and anxious to
> teach; although the older ones found it difficult to believe
> that our eyes should sparkle more brightly at the thought of
> learning to fly than at the dubious advantages to be gained

from pulling a bloody heavy cutter around Clarence Docks
or mastering an endless list of bends and hitches."

Being so far from home, Mudge wrote to his family regularly
describing life in this new world. In so doing, the young New
Zealander kept a record of his life as he progressed through training
establishments towards China Bay and his tragic meeting with Dickie
Cork, A sad echo from a lost age:

Lee on Solent, 18/8/42.

"Dear Fritz,
Well I have a few minutes before I go on night guard over at
the hangars, so I guess this is the best way to fill them in.
This station has two nights duty watch and one night
ashore and I must admit I have slipped these last two nights
on the duty parade; both nights I have landed the armed
party. Such slipping is very bad form on my part. I have a
Tommy Gun to keep me company but even though it is a
handy weapon, a rifle is much easier to lug about. What
with an uncomfortable bed on the benches in the guard-
room between watches and the dawn standby, everyone is
liable to get a bit browned off with such a job when it is
not in his regular line. However, I guess it is quite important
even if it is not very exciting when nothing, except perhaps
a bit of fireworks up top, is going to happen (We hope!)
Tomorrow I am going to try and reciprocate this slight loss
of sleep by working a bit of an oracle and get my head
down for a while during the day shush! shush! don't tell the
Chief.
It amazes everyone the number of chaps who come back
here from E. F. T. S because they can't fly. Other courses
before us have been cut in half at this first flying school.
The part of the course which went to Elmden, in this country, have had several Poms dipped already and nowhere
near all of them have yet soloed! Most of the N. Zeas are
doing OK, but one or two are a bit doubtful. Ken is OK so
far and I have an idea he has gone solo, but would not be
sure about it. I'm sure he will do well. One N. Zeas on his
second solo lost himself good and proper so he landed on a

Bomber Command aerodrome and asked his way home. Just like asking a London 'Bobby' the way to Piccadilly.

While we were down at the RN Air Station, St Merryn, in Cornwall we were flying with a Fulmar Squadron doing their conversion course to British fighters after doing their training in the States. Most of us found it a bit strenuous jumping straight into the back seat of a first line fighter doing its stuff properly without any previous flying experience to break us in. I had two flights back in NZ, as you know, but I'm afraid they did not count for much when we were pulling out of dives at roughly 300 mph. This is inclined to shake you up quite a bit until you get used to it. But believe me it is great fun and I enjoyed it all right from the time we left the ground. I can only hope I can fly OK myself.

We were doing fighter tactics, air firing, aerobatics and low flying, with the usual formation stuff....The officers were a good crowd and wanted to know all about their beloved St. Vincent and very often spent the night with us down at the local. Several are N. Zeas but no one I know.

We spent our last evening at the 'Ring O'Bells', by way of a farewell to Cornwall and travelled to and from our camp in great pomp by using Padstow's one and only cab, which strange to say was an exceptionally beautiful car. I'll bet we disturbed the village folks equilibrium with our 'Hakas' after we had been 'slung out of the pub'.

One of the boys from the boat harbour is here at present waiting to go back to St Vincent, poor chap, to do his Observers Course, seeing that he can't fly. Ian Mckay is his name. I've just been told that the chap who landed on the Bomber Command aerodrome has been dipped, he is the first N Zeas in our course to miss...."

Throughout the summer months Mudge's course gradually progressed through elementary flight instruction and made ready for transfer to North America to complete training. By 1942 pressure on airfields in Britain was so great that a decision was made to move courses to Canada and the United States. Out there enemy action could not cause delays and vast resources existed to speed up the process of turning novices into pilots.

Shortly after arriving at the Naval Reserve Base in Michigan Mudge soloed:

"Friday October 2nd 1942

Dear Mum,
Well here is your snowy headed baby in the Ready Room after doing his first solo.
I just popped in the plane, did exactly as I had done with my instructor (with probable variations I was oblivious to) and got along famously. I had too much to do to think about the fact that I had to rely solely on my own judgement, and consequently had no misgivings whatsoever. I was up about an hour and a half all told, and in that time surprised myself no end by doing a dozen or so perfect landings. Although I must admit my air work was much sloppier than it was with the chief pilot yesterday, who passed me out as fit to solo.
My instructor was married last night and will not be back 'till monday, so if I get my other one and half hours solo tomorrow I guess I'll get sunday off and go to Detroit. Must be off now Mum. The flying is swell and providing a chap keeps his eyes open and the crate holds together there is no earthly reason why there should be any risk to it".

All my love to you,

Murray.

At each stage of training instructors checked his progress and each success was reported to his mother and sister in a steady stream of letters home. There were minor setbacks, but these were quickly overcome and, in March 1943, he faced the final hurdle before qualifying as a pilot. From the US Navy Air Station at Pensacola, Florida, he wrote:

British Flight Batt,
PO Box 395.
12th March 1943.

"Dear Fritz,
Just a few minutes to go before lights out, so I thought I would start a note to you.

A swell day today for me. I got through the hardest check
in the course so far and have just a week of ground school
to plough through before I get my little share of gold
braid.
Sat 13th. Ian and I have just been trying to get our clearance chits signed and Lefty has just been trying to get up.
They also got their 'upchecks' yesterday.
I guess we will be going into town for a while this afternoon, although I think it is going to be pretty warm, but
we can't get permission to wear our whites, even though
we have them.
The great Batten has been composing poetry of late and,
surprisingly enough, is making quite a fair job of it. He
creeps away to some secluded spot, between flights, and
mutters away to himself and if you go up to him and start
talking he grins, but tries to look serious and says. 'We
with the creative and delicate temperament of the poet
must have silence in which to perpetuate our immortal
lines', and goes on muttering and grinning. His last intel-
lectual enterprise was Spanish. They wear off after a while.
He says he gets inspirations.... "

Now a Sub Lieutenant (A), he felt that his status as an officer and avi-
ator was secure and happily posed in his uniform wings on left sleeve
for a series of snapshots that soon found their way home. It had been a
long wait, but worthwhile and he savoured the moment of success,
before passing onto the final phase of training conversion to front line
fighters, starting with the Grumman Wildcat:

British Officers Quarters,
US Naval Air Station,
Miami, Florida.
29th June 1943.

"Dear Fritz,
I have just written to Mum pretty well all the gen on the trip,
our designation at Pensacola and what I have seen of Miami
in the few hours I was ashore. The station, as far as I can
judge in these last couple of days is 'super duper'. Our rooms
are twice as big as at Pens and twice as well furnished (Brad

and I are together), the grounds are large, lawns and palm
trees everywhere. The Officers swimming pool is quite an
affair and the Officers Club is as good as any lounge in town.
All our chaps, who got through, are here, in various stages of
training. I guess you have gathered that I am on fighters.
We have been busy checking in lately and this morning did
another forty thousand foot pressure chamber test, which
Cutter and Chappell had to be taken out of half way through.
But the rest of us were OK...."

In September Mudge transferred to Lewiston, joining 732 Squadron,
an Operational Training Unit preparing pilots for frontline service. After
weeks of rumour, in which they endlessly discussed the aircraft they
might fly in combat, they finally came face to face with the Corsair and
the realities of squadron life:

Lewiston, Maine.
Monday 6th September 1943.

"Dear Mum,
Well I'm a busy man these days. Besides flying I am adjutant
of the Squadron and for the next two or three weeks will be
1st Lieutenant. The permanent Station Officer has gone to
Canada to marry a girl whom he met in South Africa. A long
way to come eh ! The adjutant's job is quite an undertaking,
but having the other one as well, without a typist is just a bit
on the rugged side. However, I was never so happy and it is a
lot of fun besides. I had no idea of anything a few days ago,
but am getting the run of things now and am a little less
snowed in.
On saturday I went to Brunswick drove the rickety old 'milk
waggon' to do some stuff for the CO. That night Bill Christie
had his twenty first. So we went to Poland Springs for dinner
and had a party in the lounge afterwards...."

Saturday 18th September 1943.

"Dear Mum,
I went up to Peterboro, New Hampshire last weekend, by bus
and came back as far as Boston by private car, then on up

Twisting and turning away from the convoy to avoid enemy bombers, Indomitable's defences were quickly overcome and explosions could be seen along her deck (top). Flames and the effects of HE claimed many lives, including 880's Hugh 'Boy' Cunliffe Owen (below right), whose father ran an aircraft factory producing Spitfires and Seafires (B. Cork).

With Pedestal over, and the heavily damaged Indomitable on her way back to Britain, the surviving pilots posed for press photographs. Never happy to be in the public eye Cork was persuaded to take part donning flying kit and sitting in one of the few undamaged Sea Hurricanes (Authors collection).

After a brief period of leave Cork was posted to 760 Squadron at RNAS Yeovilton as a flying instructor. Smarting at this perceived 'relegation' he nevertheless threw himself into these new duties, discovering an aptitude for the work. In 1942 the FAA had few pilots with such extensive fighter experience and the newcomers benefitted by this close contact with men such as Cork. In these photographs he demonstrates fighter tactics to men under instruction.

Cork, flying NX 957, when CFI at HMS Dipper, Henstridge, leads three other Seafires (ex-Spitfire MK V's) over Somerset in mid-June 1943 (B. Cork).

Cork with an unidentified Petty Officer and matelot, check the records of a 761 Squadron Seafire - Henstridge (Authors collection).

Cork poses in front of his Seafire (RJ - C), with an unidentified RAF pilot, whilst on secondment to Fighter Command's School of Tactics (Course No 9 - August 1944).

15th Fighter Wing 1943/44

By late 1943 Cork's efforts to be posted back to an operational unit came to fruition and he joined the 15th Wing (1830 and 1833 Squadrons). For the first few days he regularly flew Corsair JT 228 (6A), gradually building up his hours on the type, aware that his pilots had flown the American fighter for many months already (RAF Museum).

Cork photographed on the eve of joining the Wing (B. Cork).

Mike Tritton who arrived in November 1943 to replace Brian Fiddes in command of 1830 Squadron (Fiddes having been killed during a flight deck accident).

Mudge Anderson a young New Zealander posted to the Wing in April 1944 but killed on his way out to HMS Illustrious when his and Cork's aircraft collided at China Bay.

Gordon Aitken, Cork's wingman on a number of occasions, poses in front of his Corsair with riggers and fitters attached to the Wing (C. Facer).

Jack Parli, another New Zealander with the Wing, poses beside his Corsair, one of the few with 'nose' art applied (C. Facer).

Alan Booth (1833 Squadron) also flew as Cork's wingman a number of times (C. Facer).

With the war in Europe still absorbing most of the Royal Navy's effort few ships could be spared to fight the Japanese. Illustrious was the first carrier to arrive in the Far East, but to make any worthwhile contribution she needed support from the United States Navy. As a consequence USS Saratoga, with her Air Group, led by 'Jumpin Joe' Clifton (below left, joined Illustrious in March 1944. Unlike the British, her aircrew were very experienced and quickly revealed the learner status of their new allies (below right) (Authors collection).

Gerry Salmon (left) and Mat Barbour (right) both survived the Wing's early setbacks to serve through 1830/1833's entire commission on Illustrious (C. Facer).

China Bay as it appeared in the summer of 1944. On the morning of April 14th Cork came into land in almost total darkness from the far end, curving in from the right hand side, his approach masked from Flight Control by the rise in the ground and buildings atop it. Anderson's aircraft was stationed at the camera end of this lengthy runway and was seen to accelerate away as Cork circled. The collision occurred at the runway's mid-point (MOD).

A Corsair from 1830 Squadron practising a dummy deck landing in late 1943, a scene that captures the basic problem of getting the long nosed fighter onto the ground safely. Left wing held low on a turning approach, the pilot peering along the fuselage to catch sight of the runway - relying heavily on the guidance of a man on the ground. Add to this darkness, a flare path lit apparently to guide you home, no radio contact and the problems faced by Cork on April 14th become only too apparent (RAF Museum).

Though taken in June 1944 the scene captured here is typical of the days on board Illustrious just before Cork's death.

April 11th - Cork at China Bay

Corsair JT 269 with Cork's initials along its side. The tank farm that bordered China Bay is just beyond.

With pilots from 1830 and 1833 Squadrons acting as pall bearers, Cork and Anderson are carried to the cemetery near China Bay on April 15th.

here by train, getting in just in time to fly. I think Lt Flood
saw I was tired, so just sent me up to fool about doing some
aerobatics, which was decent of him. He is our fighter
instructor here and knows his stuff; he was in N. Africa with
the Fleet Air Arm Martlet Squadrons there.

Well then the fun started. I had an early night monday and
next morning we were told there were a number of Wildcats
(Martlets) at Philadelphia to be ferried up and we would
have to do it. We promptly went crazy back at the Ready
Room, then began dashing about getting things together in
our weekend bags. Christie, Baggy Woodwards, John Lee,
Laurie Allum and I set off for 'Philly' with the CO in the
Grumman 'Goose', an amphibious, flying boat affair. I was co-
pilot - main job winding up wheels after takeoff, but I didn't
mind as I flew it all the way and the CO just made the land-
ings and takeoffs. We refuelled at a little place called
Sandford, here in Maine, on the trip and met some of the
Corsair boys there who were in courses ahead of us (1830
Squadron).

We waited about in the morning for the weather clearance,
but didn't get it until noon, when the five of us got away, plus
Johny Apted who came up in a TBF, with McQueen, an
instructor, who was to lead us back as we had no radios. We
got off without any hitches, except that I had to get another
crate at the last minute as the one I had didn't have a left
brake, which I didn't know until I tried to taxi it. I had to
ground loop her to stop running into a line of parked planes.
Fun and games huh? We got as far as Quonset Point, Rhode
Island, where they grounded us for the night.

We were cleared early next morning and all got away to a
good start. Johny's ASI wasn't working, which fact didn't really worry him 'till it came to landing here, then it was just a
matter of damned good airmanship. I certainly wouldn't care
to land even a Moth by the seat of my pants. Yours truly had
his fun leaving Quonset; my arrestor hook came down in my
take off run and as you don't have your head in the cockpit
taking off I didn't know what the devil was holding her back.
So I just yanked and off she came, then I woke up to it, but
there was little I could do having my hands full elsewhere.
Today we had a chap here from the Admiralty, who is writing

a book about the Fleet Air Arm. I presented him with the worst Wildcat landing I have ever made. I hope he got a thrill out of it, if nothing else. Anyway he seemed quite pleased with his visit, and no doubt enjoys his travelling about for material. Maybe there is something in being an author, or should I call him a novelist, seeing he is writing about us?"

Whilst there was a serious side to their lives, carefully kept out of letters home, there was still some fun and they made the most of the opportunities that came their way. Yet with Christmas approaching squadrons were embarking for the UK and it took little imagination to realise that the Royal Navy was building up its strength to face the Japanese. Many of these young men would soon give up the relative calm of skies over Quonset and Lewiston, Brunswick and Norfolk for the more deadly waters of the Indian and Pacific Oceans. Before this happened there were a few more weeks of training to complete and Christmas to enjoy:

USNAS, Brunswick.

"Dear Mum,
Christmas afternoon, everything is secured for today and tomorrow so I'm having a quiet time sleeping etc. Last night Stan Buchan, Mat Barbour, Bill Christie, John Lee and I went over to Lewiston for a spot of fun, slept at the De Witt Hotel and came back this morning by bus. We all stuck together and had a lot of fun. Tonight seven of us 'Clueless Wonders', as our CO (Charlie Orange) puts it, are to go to a supper and evening in Brunswick to help keep up seven college girls' Christmas morale and also, no doubt, ourselves. Doc Davies, the Canadian Lieut. I told you about, has things organized and as yet we don't know what shape the party is going to take.
I got up for dinner today; quite a normal dinner except that the Mess was a little decorated and we had a few extras such as nuts and fruit to browse over.
One of the boys (Ian Grave) who has just turned 'Subby' (twenty) was married in Lewiston on thursday. We wish him luck but we think he was a bit hasty. She is a good looking girl, and seems quite nice to talk to, but we smell a mouse in the family's background and also in hers to a certain extent.

Exhibit A her mother went south on a vacation the day
before her daughter was married, because she didn't want to
lose her Pullman reservations. Hardly the thing, what, what?
Then, of course, there is the step sister who is the same age,
nearly, as our friend's wife. He had too good a start in England
to mess himself up over here. Still, no business of ours,
though a couple of his better friends had a yarn to him about
it, but it didn't change his mind and we hope he hasn't made
a mistake.

About half a dozen of the boys got time off to go over to the
wedding; Jerry Salmon was best man and Cliff Singleton gave
the bride away. I took a hop up at that time, so we did some
formation flying (in Corsairs) over the town. I took up three
and flew them line abreast, nearly, with me second from the
right, in the lead. The boys said it looked good and we arrived
right on the tick of time, and we did some slow rolls and
'upward Charlies'(slow rolls going straight up that-a-way). No
complaints from the locals yet. One has to be careful and use
the old top piece, leading a section, or flight, or your days as
such, if you get caught doing something you shouldn't
oughter, will be over. One of the boys in another squadron
got caught leading his flight under Bath Bridge and was put
under open arrest and Court Martialled here by big shots
from our HQ in Washington. He is a damned good flyer, but is
now a 'tail end Charlie', which is regarded as rather sticky,
although without responsibility.

So much for that angle of it, but you have to do something to
keep people from becoming bored with straight and level
and gentle turns, so I let them let off steam trying to follow
me in a tail chase and tell them off when they get out of line
then they're not nattering over the R/T 'Lets go down on the
deck Pink Leader' for which Pink Leader stops the above
penalty if he is caught.

For your information two of us have 'above average pilots' in
the COs (Lt Cdr (A). M. Godson RN) 'Clueless Wonder Book',
but don't breath a word Mum, you are the one and only to
whom I tell such. Someone might think I was boasting and
besides I might start making a mess of things any day, touch
wood. The thing I turn over in my mind is 'No over confidence pranks Anderson' when I'm flying and keep my mouth

shut on the ground. Thank you for a level head, I hope, Mum.
I did my first firing in these cabs the other day, strafing a buoy
out at sea. It is a great thrill to fire wing guns for the first time,
to feel yourself push forward in the straps as she slows down
and the whole shooting box jumps and jars 'till you think
she'll fall to bits. You can see the three tongues of flame coming from each wing, out of the corner of your eyes as you look
through the sights and keep her lined up, and the tracers hitting and the water churned up, just like it was in the movies.
There is very little else to tell just now Mum. It is as cold as
charity; 20 to 30 below, and feels twice as bad as Detroit ever
did, but I guess we'll survive OK. The last ten days, since I
wrote, have really been very quiet. Evenings by the fire in the
Officers Club, chewing the fat and talking shop, as we are supposed to do in our particular branch of this 'ere profession.
Plenty of sleep and all that sort of thing.... "

Having flown Corsairs for some 50 hours, and Wildcats for an additional 76 hours, Mudge was more than ready to deck land a fighter for
the first time. As 1944 dawned, and the weather improved, he finally
achieved this goal, having rehearsed it on land many times before:

Plaza Hotel,
101 West 58th Street,
New York.
30th January 1944.
"

Dear Mum,
Just arrived in town for the day with seven of the boys and I
have at long last landed on an aircraft carrier that was on the
27th on Chesapeake Bay in my Corsair. Quite an exciting business in these fast cabs of ours. Doc Davies batted me aboard. I
caught the second wire which is good but was well over to
port when it pulled me up. I took off again within a few seconds. There is nothing to the takeoff, but the amazing thing
about the landing is how quickly and smoothly, considering
you are stopped at about sixty in twenty yards, that the wire
pulls you up. It is a long story, this trip of ours to Norfolk, and
I'll write you all about it sometime later when I have more
time.

On the 28th we flew up as far as Quonset Point, RI, at 10,000 feet, with seven grand of solid cloud below us, so we saw no land or sea for 360 miles. We just bogged along the top of the cloud layer, then split up into four plane flights and let down through it. I was Blue Leader, so I formed up my four close as they could get to me and went on down through it (on instruments of course) and the others flew on me. I could see all three of them most of the time (amazing the perfect formation they flew hah, hah !), but just the last thousand it got as black as pitch, then whoof daylight and there we were near Nantucket and the rest of the boys coming through half a mile or so away.

Very amusing coming through stuff like that, when you're not quite sure how low the ceiling is (I think I heard someone say 'Thank C for that', when we came out), but I was going to go back up if we didn't get any results by five hundred feet hills and things, you know.

We landed at Quonset just before dark and went on up to Brunswick, via lunch in Boston (waiting for weather clearance) and back to New York next day.

I have just been down to HMS Sakar with my CBs from Brunswick, to get my orders, my gang and my dough, and now I'm going out to lunch, then a show at Radio City Music Hall (Walter Pidgeon and Greer Garson).

Incidentally, I had a busy day on my birthday, yesterday, but I was enjoying myself nevertheless…."

A single day's decklanding training would be all that Mudge would get before being posted 'overseas'. More were planned, but the requirement for qualified Corsair pilots grew so intense that there was insufficient time for more practise before embarking. In Spring and Summer this might have been possible, but during January and February, with the weather so poor, this proved impossible. Mudge and his comrades would have 'to catch up' when they reached their new squadrons.

On February 1st Mudge was assigned to the carrier HMS Ranee, and with a party of other young pilots, many of them from New Zealand, he embarked a week later. The novelty of being on a carrier, even though she was only used for ferrying, was immense, because it was a taste of operational life. In the hours before sailing, Corsairs were swung aboard by crane and lashed to the deck, tarpaulins over engines and cockpits to protect them from salt spray. Under cover of darkness she slipped her moorings and steamed out into the Atlantic, heading south to begin her long journey to the Indian Ocean, her course taking her via New Zealand:

> "In February or early March Mudge's carrier called in at Wellington. All the boys who lived there (as we did at the time) were allowed ashore every day. The men didn't know until they were well out to sea that their first port of call would be Wellington. What excitement for those boys, especially as most had been away for nearly two years.
> On the day of the ship's arrival in harbour my mother was watching her through a pair of opera glasses (which were all we had). Our house was on a hill and from the back gate we had a wonderful view of the harbour and wharves. Of course Mum had no idea it was Mudge's ship, but as she moored in the harbour, Murray was looking at her through his binoculars! He was allowed to take our brother, Dick, on board for lunch in the Wardroom; a great thrill for them both..."

> *Freda ('Fritz') Anderson.*

Ranee remained in port for a few days, her crew and 'passengers' taking the opportunity for leave around Wellington. To those entering the war zone and their families it was a poignant moment when most must have wondered whether they would see their loved ones again. Words of false comfort flowed, but casualty lists, published by newspapers every week, were a stark reminder that tragedy stalked their every move and aircrew were the most vulnerable. Mudge knew that he was joining a Corsair Wing on HMS Illustrious and guessed that she would soon be in action, but he kept this knowledge to himself and spent his last few days in New Zealand pretending, for his mother's sake, that he would soon be safely home. Yet her worst fears were soon be realised and within five short weeks he was dead.

CHAPTER SIXTEEN

WING LEADER

Dick had come a long way in the four years since walking through Greenwich's ornate gates and had achieved much in the process. Yet for every success there had been personal loss and, as he stood on the brink of his latest challenge, the weight of these losses hung very heavily on his shoulders. But the promise of a Wing gave him fresh impetus and he busied himself with preparations before assuming command on December 2nd.

Two days of briefings, in Whitehall, told him a great deal about his command and the extent of the task ahead. His main concern, though, was the squadrons and he avidly read reports on their organisation and pilots. However, he was dismayed to discover that the three squadrons would be reduced to two within days 1831 being broken up to furnish 1830 and 1833 with additional pilots and aircraft. Apart from this, their work up in the States had been fairly uneventful, with attrition rates seemingly no higher than usual; something of a surprise considering the Corsair's reputation as a 'pilot killer'.

Although each squadron had still to taste action for the first time, they had several experienced pilots amongst their number. After leaving 880 Squadron in 1943 Brian Fiddes went straight to the States to command 1830. Cork had not seen him since leaving Indomitable and looked forward to meeting him again. The task ahead was a daunting one and it was reassuring to have at least one 'friendly face' to rely on. 1833 had Lt Cdr H. A. 'Eric' Monk DSM and Bar RN as CO also a man of immense experience. Apart from this there seemed little else to work with, as he related in a letter on December 9th:

> "I'm sure we can iron out some of the problems, but time is short. Most of the pilots are new and sure to be as apprehen-

sive as we were at the same stage. At least when we were
learning we had an airfield to land on after a battle and not a
carrier's deck until Indom that is. Add to that the Corsair and
the problems begin to mount up.
With so much resting on our shoulders, I can't help thinking
we will get it all wrong and be sent 'home in chains'. Perhaps
I should have remained at Henstridge!"

Two days before taking command of the Wing, Cork was relieved to
discover that commonsense had finally prevailed in the Admiralty and
his posting was no longer 'temporary'. Nevertheless he was keenly
aware of the need to fly the Corsair as much as possible in the short
time available. But poor weather and administrative duties contrived to
keep grounded until December 10th. In the meantime he got to know
the men under his command:

> "Most of us had gone to the USA on what was known as the
> Pensacola draft to learn to fly. We were kept in the States
> after training to form squadrons on lease lend aircraft when
> they became available. COs and some more experienced
> pilots and all the ground crews were sent over from the UK.
> So the majority of the pilots, the Pensacola lot, had been in
> the States for about 18 months before returning in formed up
> squadrons early in November 1943. So we all knew each
> other very well and had got to know those who joined us
> from the UK."

S/Lt(A) G. Aitken RNVR, 1833 Squadron.

Dick was one of the last to arrive and, so, was something of a
stranger, although his reputation had gone before him. But in terms of
squadron life this did not matter too much, because the Wing Leader's
role was divorced, to a certain extent, from day to day business:

> "Dickie left Squadron COs to run their own shows. He
> planned Wing training, but again we led our own groups
> most times, although he would 'bounce' us from time to time
> to test our alertness and reactions."

Eric Monk.

With Fiddes and Monk in command, Cork could plan and direct operations; monitoring progress against his own high standards. This 'hands off' approach also allowed him time to fly a series of Mark I and II Corsairs, beginning with a one hour forty minute trip on December 10th. Though an immaculate pilot he found the Corsair a bit of a handful at first, as Gordon Aitken recalled:

> "The Corsairs were the first American planes Dickie had
> flown and British and American planes had completely dif-
> ferent braking systems. At first he did some funny things
> taxying. It was often that way the very experienced and the
> famous seemed to think that they could get by without
> reading instructions and, in Dick's case, he clearly didn't
> understand the Corsairs brakes, there was a control on the
> top of each pedal. He didn't know how to use them, so
> each time he wanted to turn left or right he ended up
> 'ground looping' in the other direction. It looked like a
> comic beginner. It didn't take him long to get it right, but
> caused amusement in the meantime. We smiled, he was
> human."

As Christmas approached, flying hours increased rapidly and he participated more and more in preparations for the Wing's first deployment on HMS Illustrious. During these few days the pilots saw his personality begin to emerge from behind the mask created by preconception and Cork's own sense of privacy:

> "What we knew about Dickie was that he had been lent to
> the RAF during the Battle of Britain and was Bader's No 2.
> He was awarded the DFC, but when he returned to the
> Navy they took it away and replaced it with the local cur-
> rency the DSC. At any rate Dickie wore two most enviable
> decorations at a time when campaign medals had not been
> thought about and hardly any one first line wore anything
> on his chest.
> Socially we did not mix. I was a Sub/Lieutenant and he a Lt
> Commander. Subs did not talk to the more exalted ranks
> except at work and that was mostly doing what we were
> told with the occasional, 'Aye Aye Sir.'
> I remember Dick as a private man, often to be seen standing

or walking by himself. I suppose it is the same with me. With 2,000 in the ship and 200 officers in the wardroom a little privacy meant a lot me."

Gordon Aitken.

"Dickie was a good leader, a real gentleman, good looking, large as life, not fussy or interfering. I liked him.
He was not a great party man and although Norman Hanson was a great pianist for wardroom sing songs neither Dickie, nor Mike Tritton or myself took part."

Eric Monk.

"He was a very good looking man, but not vain. He didn't 'throw his weight around', as did some RN officers. He was generally considered to be a good pilot though FAA ops were generally not so 'glam' as RAF ops, and of course did not get the publicity.
The Wing Leader's job was to coordinate the fighter squadrons into an effective unit for escorting bombers, low level bombing etc. So our paths didn't cross a great deal, but I did quite a bit of flying with Dickie, as did many others, as he put us through our paces."

Sub/Lt(A) C. R. Facer RNVR,
1830 Squadron.

After four years flying front line aircraft, Dick was more aware than most how quickly problems could arise, with little warning and from any quarter, exposing you to danger; whether novice or 'ace'. Experience taught you to look out for signs that something was going wrong, but occasionally even the best were caught out and, on December 16th, Dick was very nearly killed by a simple technical fault:

"On return to the UK, in Trumpeter, our aircraft were fitted with British R/T and oxygen and two forward facing scoops just to the rear of the cockpit, and one facing backwards under the aircraft, to counter Carbon Monoxide contamination from the engines exhaust. On one flight at Stretton

Dickie made an emergency landing feeling unwell. A blood
test was taken suspecting CO poisoning. The result was a
request to ask 'how long the person had been dead when the
sample had been taken'.
This had been something of a problem and we had lost one
pilot in the States on his first solo in a Corsair. I suspected
CO contamination and told my boys that I was going to use
oxygen at all times."

Eric Monk.

Although he made light of this incident, it had been a close run thing.
As he lost height and brought his Corsair into a very bumpy landing he
was slipping in and out of consciousness and had to be helped to sick-
bay for treatment. Being young and fit he soon recovered, but was
grounded for three days until headaches and nausea passed.

Despite modifications this problem was never completely eradicated
and some remedies owed more to Heath Robinson than Chance
Vought. On one occasion sticky tape was applied to cracks between
engine compartments and cockpits. It seemed to work, but such a temporary solution was no guarantee of safety and many pilots followed
Eric Monk's advice and used oxygen all the time to avoid accidents.

Stretton, in Lancashire, become the Wing's base for most of
December and they practised dummy deck landings whenever conditions allowed. With Illustrious exercising off the Scottish coast they
would soon be hitting her deck for real and these rehearsals were
essential, if casualties were to be kept to the minimum. But even this
could prove dangerous:

"Influenced to a certain degree by stories of death and
destruction on carrier decks, Illustrious sent down her batsman Johnny Hastings to give us a good work out. We did little
else during our short spell at Stretton.
Doing a touch down for Johnny one afternoon in a bit of a
cross wind, Monteith clipped a wingtip on the concrete runway at the moment of opening up to do another circuit....
Instead of cutting his throttle and making the best of a bad
job he pressed on. The great Corsair, under full throttle
careered across the grass bouncing on the end of the port
wing, which took a very poor view of such treatment.

It so happened that the NAAFI van had just rolled up to the
squadron with tea and scones. The CO and I were standing at
the office window, cups in hand, when we were astonished
to see a Corsair fly past - literally - the window, busily
engaged in completing a slow roll. As we looked at one
another, unbelieving, there came the most monumental crash
from our left. Monty had hit an earth revetment near the
office which had canted his aircraft on to one side, breaking
off a wing at the root.... Monty was clambering out. He was
looking somewhat vague....'What happened?' he asked, stum-
bling away with his parachute waggling behind him like
some monstrous bustle.... He hadn't a scratch."

Norman Hanson.

With their pilot safe an amused shake of the head seemed to be the
most appropriate response and, after raising an A 25 accident report
form, little more was said about the incident, though Monteith
remained the butt of many jokes for a few days more.

Next morning the Wing left Stretton for Machrihanish, on the southern tip of the Mull of Kintyre, off Scotland's west coast. A desolate spot
at the best of times, but, in a wet and windy December, virtually unin-
habitable, or so the young pilots reported in their letters home. But they
would stay for a short period only, waiting for Illustrious to finish trials
in the Firth.

Before leaving Stretton Dick selected a Corsair for his own use, a
Mark II, code JT 269. It was fresh from the manufacturers, via a British
factory, where it had been modified and painted in standard Navy camouflage colours. But this anonymous aircraft was soon made more distinctive. He remembered the way Douglas Bader had used his initials as
a call sign and had them painted on his Spitfire's fuselage, Dickie followed suit and 'RC' appeared in large white letters down each flank, as
soon as 269 had been assigned to him. Some may have seen this as
affectation, but he was no show off and its purpose was simply to
achieve quick recognition in the air. For the remainder of his life he
would fly 'RC' exclusively, borrowing JT 228 or JT 241, when his Corsair
was being serviced.

The chill, damp air brought with it a spate of colds and, in Norman
Hanson's case, bronchitis. He was consigned to hospital for four days,
during which the Wing continued its preparations. Deck landing train-

ing began in earnest, both squadrons spending time on an escort carrier, in preparation for Illustrious, now in the Clyde exercising with her
two Barracuda squadrons, 810 and 847, before the fighter wing arrived.

On his return from hospital Hanson was greeted by Cork with the
words:

> "The best thing for bronchitis is to get in a Corsair and fly. Up
> you go, cobber !"

Time was short and Hanson had to make up lost ground before
attempting his first deck landing, which would have to be in full view
of all his comrades on Illustrious. In his absence, to add to his worries,
four pilots from 1830 Squadron returned to Machrihanish, on
December 18th, carrying tales of disaster:

> "Illustrious had been suffering the onslaughts of Corsairs in
> their first attempts at decklanding. There had been far too
> many prangs and one of them had been fatal. Brian Fiddes,
> CO of 1830 Squadron, despite his experience, had made a
> bad approach to the deck and at the last minute had been
> given a wave-off to go round again. In manoeuvring a shade
> too violently to avoid hitting the island, he had clipped the
> port wingtip on the deck and had crashed over the side into
> the sea. Nothing had survived. He and his aircraft had sunk
> like a stone."

> *Norman Hanson.*

If an inexperienced pilot had died in such a way few would have
been surprised, but to lose a man, who had been on active since 1941,
was different. With days to go before she sailed, Cork, as Wing Leader,
and Illustrious's Captain, E. D. G. Cunliffe, known universally as 'Smiler',
had to report this loss to the Admiralty, recruit a replacement for Fiddes
and try to restore the confidence of their young pilots. On land there
would be the luxury of time and resources to correct these problems,
but Illustrious was heading for war and quick solutions were needed.

1834 Squadron, commanded by Lt Cdr(A) A. M. Tritton RNVR, had
been working up in the States alongside 1830 and 1833, but arrived in
Britain a month later. The 15th Wing desperately needed an experienced Corsair pilot to replace Fiddes and 'Mike' Tritton was an ideal

candidate. 1834 still had some way to go before embarking on HMS Victorious and so, at Cunliffe and Cork's bidding, he was transferred to Illustrious, arriving on Christmas Eve:

> "I was on leave and was told to join Illustrious at Glasgow without delay. I went up and got a tug to take me out it was the usual sort of coaster. They were frying kippers on a shovel and it smelt absolutely wonderful.
> As I arrived alongside the Captain and other senior officers were seeing someone important off and Bob Cunliffe was standing on the gangway when I came aboard. As I was only a two and a half ringer I was rather surprised to be met by the Captain and said, 'I've come to join Sir!', at which he smiled."

Lt Cdr(A) A. M (Mike) Tritton DSC and two Bars RNVR.

With Tritton on board the pressing need for an experienced commander was resolved, but Cork realised that this alone would not restore the Wing's lost confidence. With so much to be done in so short a time, he had to lead by example.

He began the process in a small way on December 26th, by leading the last five pilots from Machrihanish to Illustrious, including Norman Hanson, on his delayed first deck landing. Under Cork's guiding hand all went well; each pilot drawing strength from their Wing Leader's exemplary performance:

> "We took off to the west, Dickie immediately going into a wide, lefthand turn to enable us to join up on him. I latched on to his port wing as we swept low over Campbletown and out over the Firth. After a minute or two, across the fuselage of Cork's aircraft, I saw her; that great, beautiful ship, serene on a silver sea , a faint wisp of smoke above her island and only the suspicion of a feather of wake astern to belie her apparent immobility.
> Dickie put us into starboard echelon. I lifted slightly and skidded over him with rudder to fall into position on No. 2's starboard wing. After a sweeping turn to port, losing speed and altitude, we flew low up the ship's starboard side. Down undercarriage, down hook. About a mile ahead of the ship, Dickie broke to port, establishing the landing pattern. Seconds

later, I followed No. 2, carefully taking up an interval on him a practice which would become second nature. Now we were flying downwind, locking safety harness, locking open the hood, increasing the pitch, lowering flaps; first to ten degrees, then to 20. Now I was abeam of the stern of the ship. Turn 180 degrees to port; full flaps. Already Johnny was signalling for me 'Roger' as you go. A shade faster OK. Now come down, down, DOWN, damn you! CUT ! I chopped back the throttle, held the stick steady as a rock. Three seconds, then I was on the wire. My body lunged forward against the harness with the deceleration I was down.

It was the greatest moment of my life."

Norman Hanson.

Everything went well and before unloading the few possessions he bought with him, stowed behind the cockpit's armour-plating, he reported to Captain Cunliffe and Commander (Flying), Ian Sarel. Delivering a bundle of documents given to him by Terence Shaw, Commander (Operations), at Machrihanish. It was 15 months since he had last set foot on a carrier, but the surroundings, the noises and the smells soon struck a familiar chord. Within an hour, after consulting Eric Monk and Mike Tritton, he gathered the Wing together and gave them a pep talk, but the problem they were facing was a substantial one:

"The squadron (1830) was in a fair old mess and morale was nil and we had to stop them flying until we reached Ceylon, because we couldn't really afford to have any more machines smashed up. We'd lost one (Fiddes) and four or five more were damaged in deck landing accidents.
The problem was made worse by the number of New Zealanders. They were awfully nice chaps, but totally irresponsible. Tell them to do one thing and they did another and didn't come back as a consequence. It was a great shame. I got shot of them eventually gave them to Norman Hanson."

Mike Tritton.

1833, under Eric Monk, was in much better shape, reflecting his long, distinguished service. He was a hard task master, but his approach had consistently paid dividends throughout their work up period, though at times his easy going young RNVR pilots found him quite a handful. Nevertheless he had seen it all before, knew what they would face, and tried to prepare them as best he could for the coming traumas:

> "My service career started as a Boy Seaman, paid 9p a day in 1933. Ten years later I found myself an acting Lt Commander. After 1 year on operations in 800 Squadron on Ark Royal as a PO pilot I was commissioned and flew Wildcats with 882 and 881 Squadrons on Illustrious. After that I took on 1833."

> *Eric Monk.*

With 1830's disasters imprinted on their minds, Monk's pilots could so easily have succumbed, but his leadership and training brought them through:

> "Our brother squadron preceded us to the deck of Illustrious with disastrous results. I think there was fear in our hearts when we flew out to the carrier, but we landed on without incident. The disciplines and skills involved were considerable, but the satisfaction in mastering them was all the greater for that. In two years of flying from HMS Illustrious, with interludes in Ceylon, South Africa and Australia, I carried out seventy odd deck landings without a scratch. But naval aviation was a dangerous business and we all think of the lives lost.
> Of the fifty seven pilots who passed through the two squadrons twenty two lost their lives. Some were killed while landing on deck, some died in other flying accidents and the others were lost in aerial combat or were hit by anti-aircraft fire."

> *Sub/Lt(A) F. C. Starkey RNVR, 1833 Squadron.*

Illustrious sailed from Greenock on December 30th under a mist laden, grey sky and slipped down the Clyde, picked up her mooring and awaited nightfall. At first light they were well underway, the coast of Northern Ireland appearing on their starboard side, confirming rumours they were heading south for the Mediterranean and the Far East.

In the Irish Sea's sheltered waters, Illustrious's group gradually gathered together. The maintenance carrier, Unicorn, took up station, followed by three destroyers and seven frigates; the smaller ships burrowing their noses into the deep swell, sending water cascading over bows, forcing them down into the depths from which they pulled themselves clear, with painfully ponderous movements, only to plunge into the next wave. A few aircraft remained on Illustrious's deck, tightly lashed down, in case intruders were spotted submarines or aircraft but the sea was too rough for flying and these machines remained firmly on deck.

The fleet pressed on through the Bay of Biscay, to Gibraltar, without a break in the weather, but once the sea calmed a little, Barracudas began anti-submarine patrols and in fairly short order 847 Squadron lost two aircraft. The first ditched with engine trouble, killing its pilot and a second blew up, all three crew members perishing when its depth charges exploded shortly after take-off. The Corsair pilots could only stand and sympathize with these losses, but to Lt Cdr(A) J. Cullen RN, 847's CO, fell the unenviable task of writing to relatives and disposing of kit.

Passing through the Straits of Gibraltar, on January 5th, into the relative peace of the Mediterranean, 1833 began flying again. Illustrious was now within easy reach of land based bombers and fighters were kept at readiness, to scramble if a raid developed. Returning from patrol, Reggie Shaw mis-timed his approach and neatly severed his port wheel on a 4.5 inch gun. He just managed to struggle into the air and was ordered to Maison Blanche in Algiers, from where a Barracuda later collected him. But worse was to come. A JU 88 flew high over the Fleet, as they approached Alexandria, and the standby Corsair flight was scrambled. In his haste to get airborne Monteith failed to lock his wings properly in the 'spread' position and, when he raised the undercarriage, they folded up and his Corsair dropped into the sea, taking the young Scot to his death.

The remainder of the voyage passed quietly, except for one incident, which highlighted the tension spreading amongst Illustrious' crew. The limited space on a carrier's deck and the large number of aircraft made careful planning of movements essential. In normal circumstances everything ran smoothly, the Flight Deck Party martialling aircraft to meet flying serials, but occasionally things went wrong and tempers became frayed. In one episode a 'contest' developed as 1833 attempted to range one of its Corsair's on deck, against the wishes of the Flight

Deck Officer. Two teams, fore and aft, urged on by their respective officers, put their shoulders against the Corsair, which was trundled back
and forth, whilst a plaintive voice could be heard shouting, 'Get that
American rubbish off my flight deck!

The ship finally reached Ceylon on January 28th and the 15th Wing
flew ashore to China Bay, Cork flying JT 227, whilst his personal aircraft
remained on board:

> "We flew off the ship and landed at China Bay. As I taxied in
> behind Cork and switched off a very nice chap walked up,
> climbed on my wing and said 'Hello', and treated me like a
> long lost friend. Strange because I had never seen this guy
> before. 'My dear chap', he said, 'how lovely to see you'. I
> thought the man was stupid. Before you could say 'Jack
> Robinson', he'd rolled up my sleeve and given me a jab and
> said, 'That's okay. Right next one!' They had cholera there and
> so you got a jab even before you got your feet on the ground. I
> shall never forget it a brilliant bit of acting, because he treated
> everyone the same. 'How lovely to see you' and bang.... got
> you!"

> *Mike Tritton.*

In the twenty months since Dick's last visit much had changed and the
airfield had been expanded. There was still a single runway, but it was
now some 2,500yds long, linking Tambalagam Bay, to the south west, and
Malay Cove. There were dispersals on either side of the runway and
Catalina flying boats swung around their moorings in the harbour nearby, amongst a growing number of Navy ships. Set to one side there were
two large hangars, one a skeleton after the Japanese attacks of 1942, and
between them 'Flying Control'; a tall structure 500 yards or so away from
the runway.

Corsairs, with their poor forward visibility, had to adopt a landing tech-
nique ill-suited to China Bay one wing held low on a sharp turn to keep
the runway in view. On a carrier or an uncluttered airfield this was difficult enough, but here the problems were magnified. The Controllers, sitting so far back from the runway, could only catch sight of Corsairs, landing from the north east, within yards of touchdown; their approach being
screened by buildings and a rise in the ground. This could have been
overcome by resiting the control point or using radio transmitters, but

one was not planned and the other had yet to be installed. In the weeks ahead these deficiencies would have tragic consequences.

At the time Illustrious arrived the RAF still controlled the aerodrome, but were in the process of handing it over to the Fleet Air Arm. In this transitional period China Bay was home to a mixed bag of aircraft, from Liberators and Hudsons of 321 and 357 Squadrons, to Navy types of all shapes and sizes. Periodically carrier Air Groups would come ashore and be added to this complement.

Even though the Navy had their own Commander (Flying) at China Bay, in the form of Major R. C. Hay RM, a highly experienced pilot and officer, RAF officers had ultimate control. But, as events soon proved, this authority was rarely exercised effectively, as Captain Cunliffe recalled:

> "I was warned very early in the piece that we were poor relations at China Bay and heard many stories about the shoddy treatment handed out to my pilots when ashore. This they tolerated with good humour, but where it impinged upon their flying activities and their safety, they protested. Though there was little one could do, because the RAF chose to ignore our pleas. We could only look forward to the day when they departed and the Navy took control, but in March and April 1944 we were still in their hands and suffered because of it, facing unnecessary dangers as a consequence!"

Despite the RAF's poor support, Major Hay maintained a semblance of order and occasionally pulled up one of the Wing's pilots for some infringement of ground control rules, although pilots only saw themselves responding to poor RAF management:

> "When landing you usually flew past the Tower, for want of a better word. There was a square on the ground where various instructions were placed. 'T' gave you the instruction as to the direction in which to land. Quite often these markings weren't up to date and you looked around for other sources of information. On one occasion Ronnie Hay was rather short with me for taking the wind direction from the smoke of an old steam engine, instead of the 'T' and landing the wrong way. But it was easy to see that nothing else was coming."

Gordon Aitken.

"Whenever you came into land at China Bay you couldn't be
sure what to expect. Sometimes Flying Control helped, but
more often than not you had to make do without them,
watching carefully for any danger. In daylight this was okay,
although we often came in for criticism for 'taking the law
into our hands', but in the dark, and we did quite a bit of
night flying in March and April, things got very dicey indeed,
and there were a lot of complaints about the RAF's lack of
participation. The more jaundiced souls were quite sure the
'lazy b******s' couldn't be bothered to get out of bed...."

Colin Facer.

Once ashore Cork put into practice plans made during the long voyage to Ceylon. Free from the restrictions imposed by a carrier's deck,
the Wing ranged far and wide, exercising battle tactics under their
leader's guiding hand:

"As soon as we were installed on the airfield at Trincomalee
Dick set us to work. We were roused from our beds while it
was still dark and by the crack of dawn we were out over the
west coast of Ceylon, low flying or practising various forms
of formation flying. Then back for breakfast. For the first time
we used our Corsairs as true fighters, throwing them around
the sky, diving, climbing and turning to the outside limits.
Dickie set squadron against squadron and our dog fights
seemed to fill the sky above China Bay. It was all highly exhil-
arating. What is more, our fighters now became part of us, no
longer a machine we were pushing about the sky.
Dickie now set about turning us into fighters within the
meaning of the act. We practised flying as a Wing, both
squadrons together, in the manner of RAF Ramrods which
flew over northwestern Europe enticing the German fighters
to take to the sky and give battle. In this we were to be
unlucky for, at this stage of the war, the Japanese were
already feeling the lack of fuel and aircraft, and in our experience could be drawn into battle only when some cherished
prize was at stake. Cork, however, knew what he was doing
when he drove us on and on in low-flying exercises. Fighter
schools in our days didn't teach ground straffing as we would

have to fly in action. There, we had been taught to dive at the target from considerable height and to open fire when down to about 400 yards. After firing, we had to pull up sharply and disappear from the scene at high speed and low altitude.

Norman Hanson.

Against the Japanese these tactics could prove suicidal. Their short range anti-aircraft guns were very effective and could pick off an aircraft diving from height. To make matters worse a sharp pull out might see you dive into the ground, as the elevators struggled to grip the air. They needed different tactics and Cork showed them how best to survive:

"Cork had been fortunate enough to take part in some ground straffing attacks. With these recollections very much in mind, he led us day after day low-flying at treetop height the full width of the northern part of the island. Such fun it was too!"

Norman Hanson.

"We practised a lot together mostly from China Bay, sometimes in the dark, in the very early morning, and mostly at low level. At sea there was less activity, as a rule, in order to conserve engine hours and have as many aircraft serviceable as possible.
Dickie had a sense of humour. At that time of year low country Ceylon was hot and the very low level work in formation did nothing to cool us, especially with a hot sun shining through the perspex canopy. One afternoon Dickie beckoned us all in to close formation. My flying suit was soaking and sweat was pouring down inside my goggles and mask and there was no way I could relax.
Dickie trimmed his plane for straight and level, held the stick between his knees, pulled out a thermos flask and poured out a glass of iced lime juice. Smiling he held up his glass to each of us and drank it!
I flew as Dickie's wingman. Why I should have been I don't know, but at the time it did lead to some problems. All my

training in the States meant that we took off and kept close
in to the aerodrome, so we could keep in contact with each
other as we formed up.

I used to take off from China Bay after him, lost in the most
awful cloud of dust thrown up by his aircraft. By the time I
came out of the other side he had gone and couldn't be seen
anywhere. Eventually he came over the R/T, 'I'm over west of
you….!' Then I found out, towards the end, that he was going
out in a very wide circuit, whilst I kept in close to the airfield. He could see me, but I couldn't see him, so it took a
long time to form up and made a simple job very time con-
suming. It was just a difference in training. Whenever it happened and he went charging off in the general direction of
India I expected a rocket, but he said nothing when we landed…."

Gordon Aitken.

Occasionally during this work up period the squadrons re-embarked
on Illustrious, exercising with the Barracuda Wing or simply practising
deck landings. The Corsair pilots had grown accustomed to their aircraft and the number of accidents diminished, though occasionally
some tragedy would occur, a reminder, if one was needed, of their close
proximity to death:

"March 10th was a tragic day and no mistake. The party
opened up at 1030 when Alan Vickers did a bad bounce and
went headlong into the crash barrier. He was unharmed but
the aircraft was a bit of a mess. During the afternoon the
Barracudas put in a dummy torpedo attack on the ship. Scott
of 810 Squadron pulling out his dive to level out for his torpedo run, got into a high speed stall. He hit the sea with a
tremendous impact and disintegrated before our eyes. All
three crew being killed instantly.

If that was a bad day, the next was murder. Don Hadman hit
the barrier on landing and the rest of us flew around in circles waiting for the flight deck party to sort things out. I was
on next. I crossed the barrier, folded my wings and taxied
onto the forward lift. I had just switched off when there
came the deafening scream of tortured metal behind me. Alan

Vickers had drifted off to port on his approach.... he ignored all signals from Hastings to go round again; and Johnny had to jump for his life into the safety nets as Alan hit the port after group of 4.5 inch guns. He then careered up the port side of the deck until he crashed heavily into the great steel stanchion of No 1 barrier.

Then, without a spark of a warning and with the concussion of seething hot air, the main petrol tank went up in a great explosion. "

Norman Hanson.

Alan Vickers, whose neck may have been broken, died in the inferno and was joined by two of the brave men who rushed out to help him. The flight deck doctor, Ron Alcock, was blown by the explosion to the deck, with horrendous burns to head, face and arms, but survived. Dick, stationed on the bridge, inspecting his pilots at work, stood, with the Captain beside him, watching in horror as this, terrible scene unfolded below. Death by fire remained an unspoken fear of many pilots and to see such a dreadful scene enacted within a few yards, bought home all its ghastliness.

Bad days had to be endured, made tolerable by comradeship and the lighter moments friendship produced. But, as Norman Hanson described, the constrictions of life on board a carrier brought these horrors sharply into focus and magnified their effect:

"Life was lived, utterly and completely within a space of something like 10,000 square yards. Within this area we ate, slept, drank, chatted with our friends, attended church, watched films, took our exercise and flew, landed or crashed our aircraft. Friendships became, if anything, too close and the hurt the more painful for that very reason."

Cork kept his flying time to the minimum when afloat, but occasionally 'bounced' the Corsairs or Barracudas in classic fighter pilot style. For the rest of the time he observed, trained and planned, becoming a familiar figure on the bridge, where his friendliness made a lasting impression:

"He used to visit the Air Defence Position located above the

ship's bridge in line with the Flag Deck. I was then a young
Petty Officer Seaman with a gunnery qualification of AAI. I had
control of the lookouts and communication ratings to the gun
turrets. Lt Cdr Cork would visit the ADP when he wasn't flying. I
would lend him a pair of binoculars so that he had a clear view
of the flying operations going on.

He always asked me about the beer situation in the RN canteen
in Trincomalee, as we were rationed to 2 bottles per visit with
beer tickets issued daily to libertymen proceeding ashore. I used
to make him laugh at the ruses we used to do to get more than
two bottle, such as cutting numbers out of old calenders to hand
to the native barmen in the POs Bar. As long as the barman saw
a piece of paper with a number on it, they okayed the sale of
beer...."

William O'Neill.

Another with clear memories of Dick was Illustrious's Chaplain, E. D. G.
Fawkes:

"I wish I had known him longer, but in the few weeks left to
him our paths happily crossed on many occasions, sometimes
socially and other times when discussing pilots in his Wing. He
knew better than most the stress and strains they had to cope
with and did whatever he could to relieve the symptoms keeping a careful watch for those who might be getting 'twitchy'.
I remember our conversations and I sensed a terrible feeling of
isolation emanating from him. Of course, this wasn't uncom-
mon, but after four years of war Dick had seen more than most
and now seemed to shy away from close friendships. There was
little that anyone could do to overcome this restraint and I felt
impotent at being unable to help.

When Illustrious sailed for the Far East none of us knew how
long we would be away. The war against Japan seemed to stretch
into the future and the knowledge that we would be home in
15 months, 18 months or even two years, would have given us a
target to aim at. But we had to live with the uncertainty and this
depressed our spirits considerably. The aircrew felt this strain
more than most, because they came close to infinity each time
they flew.

Few, if any, expressed their fears in public, but in private they often gave voice to some very dark thoughts, except Dick, who remained guarded until the end, only occasionally giving brief, subtle glimpses of the shadows that hung over him. When he was so tragically killed I did wonder whether exhaustion ran deeper than was apparent and in some way contributed to his death. But he seemed so self-assured that my fears were calmed, yet they arose at frequent intervals when I witnessed other pilots being lost, whose condition was suspect and for whom danger no longer seemed to exist...."

There are few clues to judge the extent of Dick exhaustion. Certainly his pilots saw no signs of fatigue and found him ever eager to lead by example, as they later remarked, but his reserve and senior rank made it difficult for them to see through his outer shell. So we are left with memories of a good officer, busying himself with day to day activities, giving his best, with little thought for his own well being. As always he remained a thoroughly polished, professional naval officer.

For the most part his letters now betrayed little of his feelings. They were bland and noncommittal and seemed only mild attempts at reassurance. But in late March two long delayed letters arrived from England, forcing him to address an issue he had sought to forget.

In Canada, Isabelle's marriage had come to end and in the early months of 1944 she managed to get passage to Britain. Uncertain of her future, she sought to re-establish her life in war torn London, but, after so many years away, lacked contacts. In January Isabelle's mother wrote to Dick telling him of her imminent arrival, but this letter took two months to arrive. Dick quickly replied with a cablegram, fearing that his 'slow' response might be interpreted as a snub:

25th March, 1944

"Thank you so much for your letter of last January, which I have only just received.
Regarding Isabelle's return I'm afraid there is very little I can do, stuck out here, the other side of the world - however,I have written to a friend of mine in London and I'm hoping he can fix something more definite, but being so far away, it takes too long for everything, except the war, to happen - this includes the mail...."

Dick's note arrived in London within hours, but, in the meantime, Isabelle had already posted a letter to Illustrious and on March 30th Dickie replied:

HMS Illustrious,
30.3.44.

"My dear Isabelle,
I have just received your letter, which came as a tremendous surprise after all this time.
I'm so very sorry about your marriage, and I do wish it could have been happier still it is just as well to break it off and return to England. I'm sure your people will be most thankful to see you.
For my own part, really nothing has happened except the war, which becomes more and more tedious as every month drags by. Still I have no complaints, because I have a very good crowd of boys with me, a quite important job, and although by now through force of circumstances I am fairly senior, I am still allowed to fly on operations, which is the biggest thing.
When you married I thought the bottom had fallen out of every thing, but the old service custom of a wife in every port, taken with a fairly liberal quantity of our excellent gin or whisky, took away the extreme bitterness I felt at the time. Anyway I know that just in this very small job, there is no time for personal feelings, and the only thing that really matters is winning the war I was going to say staying alive, but even that is relatively unimportant nowadays.
If and when I get home it would be nice to see you. But do call on my Mother, if you have time; she would love to see you will probably find Brian has pinched my membership tickets for all the clubs in Town, so have a drink on me.
Well Isabelle I guess that's all for the moment look after yourself, and if you have a moment and can be troubled, I should like to hear how things go on.

Believe it or not,
Love,
Dickie."

Two weeks later, on the day that Dick died, this bittersweet letter arrived. In a reply, written and posted the same day, Isabelle, moved by his lack of concern for the future, sought to encourage him:

> "I am sorry more than words can express, that things turned
> out as they did for us. You always had such great faith, what is
> all this talk of keeping alive being unimportant, doesn't
> sound like you, although I can well understand how bitter
> you felt and rightly so in many ways, however it was fate...."

Her letter arrived too late for Dick to see and it was returned, unopened, by Chaplain Fawkes.

CHAPTER SEVENTEEN

SEE YOU SOON

April brought a new challenge, but first a major problem had to be addressed.

Before her first strike against the Japanese, Illustrious' squadrons had to build up their strength. In the weeks since her departure from Scotland, losses had taken a heavy toll of their numbers. Fresh pilots arrived, as did new aircraft, but some also departed, without warning, as Norman Hanson recalled:

> "I was about to take a Corsair to our 'workshop' carrier Unicorn for repair when Dickie Cork hailed me.
> 'Hello, Hans, where are you off to?' he shouted.
> 'Taking this cab to Unicorn for a mod,' I yelled back, trying to make myself heard above the engine. Dickie came up and climbed on the wing.
> 'When are you coming back?' he asked.
> 'Oh, I don't know, sir, sometime after lunch, I should think or whenever I can get a lift.'
> 'All right. It's just that there might be some interesting news for you when you get back, that's all. So long.'
> When I returned some hours later I met Eric Monk, packed up and ready to leave Illustrious for home. His period in command had come to an end and Captain Cunliffe had decided to bring his posting forward, to release him before action started in earnest. He had seen a lot of war by then and deserved a rest. We chatted for a few minutes before he wished me the best of luck and departed. I returned to the ship wondering what was

happening, but had to wait until the following morning to find
out. I was piped to report to the Captain, who in a three minute
interview told me I was taking over from Monk.
I was taken aback, though pleasantly surprised, and sought out
Dickie Cork for advice. In a less than brief interview he quickly
painted a picture of what had happened and added,
'You know the things I want you to do, Hans. All right off you go
and do them. Oh! and move into Monk's cabin forthwith, of
course.'

Monk's departure posed a number of problems, not least amongst them
a replacement, as Captain Cunliffe remembered:

"In a period of a few weeks the Wing lost two of its most experienced commanders (Fiddes and Monk) when it could least
afford it and a lot of extra responsibility fell on Cork's shoulders,
as a result.
I remember very clearly the discussions that took place between
Commander (F), Cork and myself. I took very careful note of all
that was said, realising that I had to make some very far sighted
decisions, but Cork made them for me by offering very sensible,
rational solutions. In both cases he put forward the names of
RNVR officers (Tritton and Hanson) as replacements and they
proved their worth in no uncertain terms in the months ahead,
fully vindicating his choice."

It was a difficult time to make such an important decision. But, faced
with a fait accompli, he had little room to manoeuvre and realised Hanson's
appointment was a gamble. Although a seasoned pilot, he had no combat
experience and so might prove a liability in the battles ahead that lay
ahead. But Cork was a good judge of character, placed faith in Hanson and
gave him his full support and encouragement in the days before his death.
Hanson repaid this trust in full with an example of leadership few equalled,
returning from the Pacific War, in 1945, still in command of 1833, with a
DSC as visible proof of his prowess.
As Monk departed, so Mudge Anderson's party arrived from New
Zealand, all eager to join a squadron. With Illustrious' programme uncertain,
and her sea time building up, their presence seemed to pass unnoticed
until Dickie Cork sought them out one morning. Remembering his early
days with 242 Squadron and Douglas Bader's example of positive leader-

ship, he spent time talking to the newcomers, giving advice and answering their questions. They found him a little formal, but were glad of his attempt to involve them in squadron life. However, as the days passed they began to wonder if they would ever reach the ship and waited impatiently for postings. Anderson need not have worried, his time had come. On April 13th he was finally assigned to the 15th Wing and ordered to take over a new Corsair and fly it out to Illustrious next day.

In the meantime Cork, Tritton and Hanson set to work, conscious that Illustrious would soon be working alongside one of the US Navy's most experienced Air Groups, operating from the decks of the Saratoga.

The Royal Navy would, in time, reinforce her Far East Fleet with a host of Fleet Carriers, but until the Summer of 1944 only Illustrious could be spared and she lacked sufficient punch to tackle the enemy by herself. The US Navy were aware of this shortfall and, following high level discussions, reinforced the British Fleet with Saratoga one of the oldest carriers still in service, but one that had fought long and hard through the Pacific. With an equally distinguished record, Illustrious' Captain should have had few qualms about his ship's ability to play a full role, but times had changed and she had to prove herself in a world of newer technology, alongside a ship that had already mastered these new techniques. It was a daunting prospect:

> "Cork came to Illustrious to knock a lot of raw pilots into shape; to show them how it should be done and to lead them in our first operations. We were the first carrier in that theatre and everyone was aware that the eyes of those at home and, more importantly, the Americans, would be on us. We were in company with the USS Saratoga and her Air Group made our efforts seem amateurish and clumsy by comparison. But that was their purpose and we quickly learned by following this example.
>
> Without Cork the gap between us would have been immense and impossible to breach in the short time we had. He had the drive and the ability to work the Wing most effectively and I can still see him striding up the flight deck to advise, cajole or just listen to the many young, inexperienced pilots under his command, who clearly had a great deal of respect for him and not just for the medals he wore."

Captain. R. L. B. Cunliffe RN.

Illustrious steamed away from Ceylon, her escorts snapping at her heels, to meet this famous old US carrier and found her with three destroyers ploughing across the Indian Ocean from Australia, her massive funnel hardly blowing any smoke. The two carriers turned onto a common course and sailed along parallel to each other exchanging signals and then aircraft, as senior officers flew aboard to greet their opposite numbers.

Having trained in the States, many of Illustrious' pilots were immediately at home with the Americans and quickly renewed old friendships, but others found their lack of reserve and spontaneity rather disconcerting, as Bob Cunliffe recalled:

> "Their Group Commander, 'Jumping Joe' Clifton, came on board in his Hellcat and made a perfect touchdown. I watched from the bridge as he jumped down from the cockpit and made his way across the deck. Within seconds he was up beside me, a sturdy hand thumping me on the back saying something to the effect of, 'Hiya, Captain, I'm mighty glad to know yuh! Say, you've got a mighty fine little ship here....' I was taken by surprise, but soon recovered to find that behind this hail and hearty exterior lurked a very fine officer."

If the British squadrons had any doubts about the quality of Saratoga's pilots they were soon dispelled by a crisp display of flying, described by Norman Hanson in his diary:

> "Thursday March 30th 1944
> This afternoon Sara shook us solid with a wonderfully coordinated dive bombing attack on a towed target, using 18 SBDs and 20 F6Fs. Beautifully executed, followed by a snappy land-on with no prangs!"

Next day they approached Ceylon and aircraft from both carriers flew ashore to China Bay, in preparation for a joint exercise. Cork and 'Fanny' Forde, 810's CO, quickly got together with Joe Clifton and his squadron commanders to work out tactics. In the meantime the air crew socialized and flew each others aircraft. Cork and Clifton exchanged machines and for an hour happily buzzed the airfield. But this breaking in period soon came to an end and the time came to rejoin their respective carriers to begin work in earnest.

The carriers would spend two weeks off the coast of Ceylon, their Air Groups working together in a number of dummy strikes against targets around the island. Trincomalee featured large in their plans, because it bore a close resemblance to potential Japanese targets and the harbour soon resounded to the howl of fighters and bombers racing in from over the sea, by night and day. The RAF at China Bay looked on from the 'wings', as the naval aircraft rehearsed around them, relying upon Major Hay to keep some semblance of order on the ground. Yet this was easier said than done, as the movements were not always to plan. A situation made worse by squadrons disembarking each time the carriers returned to harbour. Flying Control could not cope with these fluctuations and the problems experienced in February and March returned with added force, causing some disagreements and souring relations still further.

Having been used to operating by themselves, many Fleet Air Arm pilots found the addition of a second carrier disconcerting and struggled to find their feet in the midst of such large formations, particularly when the exercises took place at night or just before dawn:

> "The form up itself was an alarming experience. The carriers were packed inside the destroyer screen with barely room between them for a tight circuit. Whilst the first flights were circling the fleet, the next to take off were forming up in the carrier circuits. Having stumbled across the flight deck in pitch dark, tripping over the tethers, you squeezed into the cockpit encumbered by Mae West, parachute, dinghy, survival pack, and service revolver. If among the first off, your aircraft would be secured to the catapult. As dawn broke you were shot into the air. In minutes a blinding tropical sun rose above the horizon. In the briefing rooms the formup diagrams had been neat and tidy, fitting together beautifully. In the air there seemed to be aircraft everywhere, with a high probability of head on collisions...."

Fred Starkey.

Although the Corsair and Barracuda pilots were gradually learning these skills, there was still some way to go before they could equal Saratoga's performance. But time was running out and within a few days their first strike against the Japanese would go ahead. They tried hard, but results did not justify the effort expended and, on the eve of his death, Dick found himself defending his Wing's performance against a rising tide of criticism. However, in Joe Clifton he discovered an ally and one who smoothed ruffled feathers when exercises on April 13th went disastrously wrong.

After taking 1 hour and 50 minutes to accomplish 'even a semblance of a rendezvous', the British and American aircraft were running so low on fuel that they could do no more than turn back and land-on. In an effort to arrest this deterioration, Clifton called a conference on board Illustrious, attended by senior aviators from both ships. If there were any recriminations, they were swept away by the positive way in which Clifton addressed the assembled men and within a short space of time they were actively debating the problems, looking for solutions, benefitting from a cross flow of ideas.

The day had begun with the Corsairs operating from China Bay, but by nightfall they were back on board Illustrious. One last rehearsal was planned as the carriers made their way back to Ceylon, with the whole Wing participating, led, for the first time in several days, by Cork. Once the 'attack' was over the Wing would land at China Bay and stay there until Illustrious sailed for her first strike against the Japanese. Before briefings got underway Dick made his way to the bridge, to discuss the next day's activities with Bob Cunliffe:

> "For some reason we seemed to accept all the Barracudas lim-
> itations without question we knew they weren't much good
> as aircraft, so expected little from them. On the other hand we
> naturally demanded a great deal more from our Corsairs per-
> haps unreasonably so and were very conscious of any short-
> coming in their performance.
> Despite their best endeavours the 15th Wing didn't appear to
> be making progress. A dawn 'attack' against China Bay on the
> 14th would be their last chance to practice before sailing to
> face the Japanese at Sabang and Cork and I discussed at some
> length how best we could encourage the squadrons to give of
> their best. He had no doubt about their ability and convinced
> me they would stand the test of combat, when their turn
> came. But his feelings weren't shared by all on board and
> some were very sceptical about their prospects and Cork, as
> one would expect, stoutly defended his men."

During the last evening of his life, little was seen of Cork after a late meal. There were a few words of encouragement for a number of pilots, a couple of jokes about heavy landings and then he retired to his cabin.

Dick was roused early on the 14th with a bland, "Morning sir, briefing in half an hour", and handed a cup of tea. He shaved, washed and dressed. Donning his tropical flying rig, he made his way through the wakening ship, its motion and vibration informing him that Illustrious was moving quickly through the water. Climbing ladders, through deck levels, opening and closing watertight doors, he made his way up to the island and out onto the 'goofers platform', to observe activity on the deck beneath him. Apart from one young sailor, a rigger from his Wing, whose salute he acknowledged, he had the place to himself and watched in silence as mechanics clambered over the Corsairs, screwdrivers and spanners in hand, inspection hatches open and final checks underway. Some were wiping dampness from canopies with old rags, whilst others stood watching the ship steadily rising and falling in a heavy swell. The clouds were thick and black overhead, with only the vaguest glimmer of light striking the carrier's deck:

> "It was the sort of sky you expected witches on their broom sticks to appear from at any moment...."

> *Gordon Aitken.*

The thought of breakfast held little appeal and he made his way to the Briefing Room, where he found Chaplain Fawkes chatting to several pilots. Not wishing to disturb their conversation he waved and gave the Chaplain a cheery, "See you soon."; a greeting and a farewell.

After final briefings, in which emphasis was placed on the need for 'a good tight form up', Cork visited the bridge. Conditions were still poor and the cloud seemed even more oppressive, but after the previous day's debacle it seemed imperative to complete this final exercise. There followed a brief debate, in which concerns about forming up in thick, low cloud were voiced and it was agreed to cancel the drill, if conditions did not improve. Dick descended to the flight deck, momentarily losing his balance as his heel slid on a patch of oil, recovering, with a joke to the handlers about the state of the deck, before mounting his Corsair:

> "The aircraft were lined up on deck ready to take off for a joint exercise with planes from Saratoga. This was a dummy

run, in preparation for our first strike against the airfield and harbour installations on the Japanese held island of Sabang. The weather was dead calm and the ships could not find sufficient wind to allow us to take off for about half an hour."

Lt(A). W. K(Keith). Munnoch RNVR,
1833 Squadron.

"I was next to fly off after Dickie. It was still very dark and the clouds remained low and murky. Beneath us the sea stayed choppy. But even in the doldrums Illustrious could give us the required thirty knots over her deck, so it was decided that Dick would take off and test conditions."

Gordon Aitken.

"In darkness the Corsairs were prepared for flight and the air was full of noise and fumes as engines were started. Cork's aircraft headed the line on the port side of the flight deck. Conditions were very poor and, with hindsight, we should have called it a day there and then, but Commander (F) and Cork, who were communicating by radio, decided that we should test conditions to establish if flying was possible. Being the man he was he would not delegate a potentially tricky job to a less experienced pilot and made ready to take off.

It was 0600 hours and there was the faintest glimmer of light on the horizon, as the Corsair's engine was run up to full power. From the bridge I could just see Cork sitting upright in his cockpit, unrecognisable under helmet and goggles. He waved briefly to the deck party, released brakes and accelerated smartly away, his code letters, 'RC', being caught in the low gleam of light filtering through the darkness.

He swept over the bows, just as we pushed into a deep swell and dropped alarmingly towards the sea. From my position it looked bad enough, but from deck level he must have disappeared almost completely. I was on the point of ordering an emergency turn to starboard in the hope of avoiding the wreckage, but cancelled it as the Corsair staggered into the air. For a few minutes, whilst the Corsair slowly circled the ship,

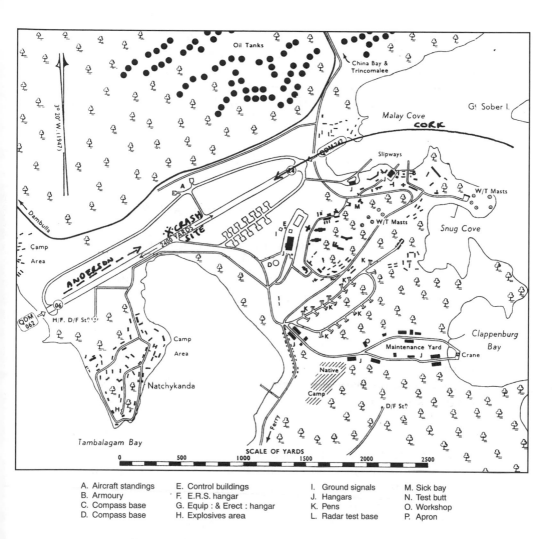

A. Aircraft standings	E. Control buildings	I. Ground signals	M. Sick bay
B. Armoury	F. E.R.S. hangar	J. Hangars	N. Test butt
C. Compass base	G. Equip : & Erect : hangar	K. Pens	O. Workshop
D. Compass base	H. Explosives area	L. Radar test base	P. Apron

Prepared by the Hydrographic Dept. of the Admiralty

The official drawing of China Bay as it appeared in April/May 1944, with Cork's flight path on the 14th superimposed. Flight Control ('E') is marked showing its poor position for spotting the Naval pilot's approach. Reports taken at the time imply the airfield was small, thereby enhancing the view that the pilots were even more foolhardy in their actions, because every signal would have been plainly visible. In reality the runway was huge and only the most precise and positive ground control could have maintained any order. Both these elements were absent on April 14th and even with the high degree of caution displayed by Cork proved insufficient to avoid the tragedy.

Commander (F) and Cork discussed conditions by radio and
decided that flying should be cancelled for the day. As we
were heading for Trincomalee, some 80 miles away, to store
prior to attacking Sabang, Cork decided to proceed to China
Bay, to stop a new pilot flying out to practice deck landings.
It was impossible to get either plane down, because the deck
was so crowded with other aircraft. With that the Corsair
turned away and headed towards land, its navigation lights
quickly extinguished by banks of cloud."

Captain. R. L. B. Cunliffe RN.

"Personally I was rather glad that the remainder of the flying
was called off, because of the darkness and the lack of a glimmer off a horizon and the difficulty of forming up with the
others under the conditions."

Gordon Aitken.

As Cork flew towards Ceylon, a lone Corsair, with Mudge Anderson
on board, was being made ready for flight at China Bay, packed with his
personal possessions. The previous evening he had been interviewed
by Major Hay:

"The airfield was normally closed between 1800 and 0800. As
Commander Flying, I personally briefed S/Lt Anderson and
the Duty Pilot a Flight Lieutenant RAF, that there was to be
no night flying and particularly no aircraft movement before
full daylight. I specifically ordered that there was to be no
flare path. As soon as it was daylight about 0645 or so the airfield was to be opened to allow Anderson to take off and
then closed until normal opening at 0800.
Thus the staff at Flying Control consisted of the Duty Pilot
and one airman plus the Crash Tender and crew. This was the
normal manning level for daytime operations."

Anderson taxied his Corsair from dispersal towards the south western end of the airfield and halted on hardstanding just off the runway.
Flying Control was not equipped with radio, so his only means of contact with the Duty Pilot, over a mile away, was by Aldis Lamp. A rigger

stood by watching the pilot manoeuvre into position, then climbed on the wing and asked Anderson whether he wanted to turn his navigation lights on. "No not necessary, I'm not taking off until daylight," he replied. Although the rigger had seen the danger of an unlit aircraft idling within feet of the runway, he could not overrule an officer and kept his silence. But with dawn only minutes away, and the airfield quiet, the rigger consoled himself with the thought that there was little danger.

There was a certain amount of impatience in Anderson's actions, prompted by news that he would have to be away smartly at first light, to avoid Illustrious' dummy strike on China Bay; due to arrive at 0700. As his rigger later testified, Anderson was eager to take off and began to tap his fingers on the control column impatiently, yet he stayed where he was, awaiting fresh instructions or sufficient light to see the runway clearly. Either way he would have only a few minutes to clear the area, before getting mixed up with the strike. But, of course, he had no way of knowing this operation had been cancelled and Cork would soon be over the airfield.

At this point the Duty Pilot decided to light the flare path, against Major Hay's orders. One can only assume that his actions were sponsored by concerns over the impending arrival of Illustrious' fighters. But whatever the reason, he decided to give Anderson every assistance in getting clear in good time. Later reports suggested that Anderson then moved onto the runway and started to taxy towards the far end, some 2,500 yards away, to get into wind before take-off. But the air was virtually still and with such a long runway before him there was more than enough space in which to get off the ground without the benefit off any breeze brushing the aerodrome.

As he swept towards China Bay, a little before 0630, Dick would have seen the flare path from some distance. As he approached, witnesses reported, he turned and circled the airfield, before joining the circuit. We shall never know how the flare path affected his actions over the next few minutes, but knowing China Bay's 'opening hours', he must have been surprised to see any night time activity, particularly when the airfield was about to be 'attacked'. Yet the briefings had specified no movement, except for Anderson's flight out to Illustrious at dawn. Perhaps he thought the flare path was for him? But as his approach seemed unannounced this was unlikely, unless a signal from the ship had reached Ceylon and been transmitted to China Bay by phone. He knew from his last call to Illustrious that they were trying to make contact, but had no way of knowing whether a message had been received.

Either way his experience dictated a degree of caution and his subsequent actions suggested a careful examination of the runway, before committing himself to a landing:

> "I was on duty amongst the fuel tanks to the north and west
> of the aerodrome. I had been there for over two hours and
> was due to be relieved at 0800 hours. It was still very dark
> when I heard the sound of an aircraft circling in a wide
> sweep before approaching from over Clappenburg Bay, curv-
> ing in sharply onto the end of the runway. I couldn't tell the
> type, but clearly saw its lights flashing. I thought it was going
> to touch down, but it remained at about thirty or forty feet
> and passed along the full length of the runway. From the way
> its lights swung up and down it seemed as though he was
> having a look around to see what was happening below.
> I can't say I saw any signals from anyone on the ground as he
> passed, but that doesn't mean there weren't any. A light point-
> ed towards him would have had a narrow arc, so unless
> flashed directly at me would probably have stayed hidden
> from my view. All I can say is that for he last hundred or so
> yards of his descent the aircraft and the main hangars were
> in a direct line with me and I saw no signal.
> As he passed beyond the end of the runway the aircraft
> banked to the left and went into another circuit, disappearing
> from view around the headland adjoining Tambalagam Bay."
>
> *L/Cpl A. E. Watson.*

As L/Cpl Watson looked down from the raised ground on which the tanks were situated, a young Aircraftsman was making his way, by bike, around the perimeter track to the dispersal point just vacated by Anderson:

> "Arrangements at China Bay always seemed a bit amateurish,
> probably because it was a backwater most of the time. The
> only time it livened up was when a carrier arrived and flew
> its aircraft ashore.
> I always liked the look of the Corsair and took an interest in
> them whenever they were about. By this stage of the war I
> had seen most RAF types and so was very familiar with more

conventionally shaped aircraft. So the Corsair, with its rather brutish looks always caught my eye and I invariably stopped to look when one was about.

On the 14th I was cycling from my mess to start work on a Hudson, over on the far side of the aerodrome. Passing the end of the runway I heard an engine gently ticking over and, as I got closer, saw the familiar shape of a Corsair. It had no lights on, but wasn't on the runway, so seemed in no danger.

I passed within a few feet and the pilot gave me a wave. The Navy boys were a grand lot of lads and were always happy to chat, but on this occasion the noise made it impossible to communicate.

I cycled on a few yards when the sound of a second aircraft approaching cut through the noise of the first just behind me. I looked to my right and saw a machine a couple of hundred yards away, heading directly towards me, over ground to the right of the runway its wings dipping from side to side as though the pilot was having a good look around. I just made out the shape of a Corsair and noted that its undercarriage was up and flaps down. I stopped and it passed directly overhead turning sharply to port the back draught hitting me with some force. In the distance Flying Control were flashing a green light. He swung out over the bay, his left wing down, describing a sharp curve around the headland.

I remained where I was expecting him to reappear at the far end of the airfield, with some concern because the Corsair behind me, acting on the 'green', had moved forward, swung left and was moving down the runway preparing to take off."

Aircraftsman. R. W. Williamson.

In the absence of any communication with China Bay, Cork clearly exercised caution in his approach, sizing up the potential risks and dangers. After two months operating from the place he knew the layout and the poor standards of control and so flew down the runway, off to one side, looking for problems, before making his final approach. His sudden appearance undoubtedly took the Duty Pilot by surprise and he must have emerged, on his sharp, carrier landing approach, without warning from behind the northern most hangar, giving the Duty Pilot insufficient time to find his Aldis lamp and signal. As he passed down the runway Dick would have looked to see the landing square directly in front of Flying Control, so would have been glancing in the right direction to see a light, if it were being flashed. If a red had been seen he would surely have aborted any attempt at landing.

The Duty Pilot was suddenly faced with an unforeseen problem. Two aircraft and no communication with either, except an Aldis lamp. To make matters worse one was out of view and might reappear at any moment, from either end of the airfield, whilst the other could be anywhere on the runway. By rights Anderson should have been in a safe position, awaiting sufficient light to take off, but having lit the flare path, against orders, the DP had encouraged him to move onto the runway and, in darkness, he would see no sign of this unlit aircraft to know where it was. The potential for collision was obvious and must have loomed large in his mind and with only seconds to make a decision the DP decided to give Anderson a 'green', sending him onto the runway, from a position of safety. To make matters worse the 'green' was flashed as Cork banked sharply to port over Anderson's head and could have been misconstrued as a signal for the Wing Leader to land.

Even if Anderson had taxied down the runway all might have been well, there was, after all, nearly one and a half miles of concrete ahead of him. With his Corsair laden with fuel and ammunition, Cork required no more than 800 yards to land safely and would have been off the runway, on his way to Flying Control before the New Zealander's aircraft reached a midpoint on the runway, and a collision avoided. But this was not to be. Acting on the sharp promptings of the green flashing lamp, Anderson accelerated away:

> "The Corsair paused for a few seconds, but, spurred on by another 'green', moved forward, quickly picking up speed. Although my view was restricted by dust and the poor light, I could see that it followed a straight course and didn't swing from side to side as long nosed fighters did when taxiing. He was going for a takeoff.
> I can't be sure, but I seem to recollect seeing navigation lights at the far end of the runway as another aircraft touched down. But it was only for a moment, then was lost.
> Seconds later there was a most dreadful crashing sound, then silence, followed by a sudden 'whoosh' as petrol ignited."

Aircraftsman R. W. Williamson.

"The aircraft (Cork's) reappeared for the second time from the edge of Clappenburg Bay behind a small hill on which there were a number of accommodation blocks. His turn seemed even sharper than the first, but this time he continued down, touching the runway fifty yards in from its end. Once again I saw no signals from the ground. He de-accelerated rapidly and trundled along in a straight line, or so it seemed from the pattern set by his lights, which half way along appeared to move to the left in a turn (towards Flying Control).

At this point there was a most sickening 'crunch' and then, a few seconds later, fire. I looked on with horror, my face seeming to glow with the vivid orange light flooding across the airfield. I stood there transfixed, my shadow looming over me, reflected back by the oil tank behind me. The fire seemed to rage for a some time, lasting long enough for dawn to have broken."

L/Cpl. A. E. Watson.

Even with two aircraft on a collision course, Flying Control could still have dictated events by firing a red flare from their Very Pistol, but in their panic they 'could not find it'. Instead the Duty Pilot reported flashing a red on his Aldis lamp, but, in appearing from the blind spot behind the hangar, there would only have been a few seconds before touch down in which it could be seen. A pilot of Cork's experience would not ignore a clear signal such as this and one can only assume he did not see it or it was not sent, as stated by the Duty Pilot.

As shock subsided and movement returned, the few witnesses to this tragedy sprang into action:

"My instinctive reaction was to cycle straight down the runway, to the crash, though I'm not sure what I could have done to help I had no firefighting gear or clothing. But if there was a chance of pulling someone clear I might have been able to help. As I got close, the heat was intense and kept me well away, but in the vivid light of the fire I could see the roundels on the fuselage of one aircraft.

I was one of the first to arrive and was surprised to find no crash tender about, but it eventually turned up, though there

was little they could do to douse the flames and in any case
the occupants were beyond help.

I hung around for a half an hour until ordered back to work
by a Flight Lieutenant, to whom I tried to give details of what
I had seen. He was uninterested and took no notes...."

Aircraftsman. R. W. WIlliamson.

Meanwhile the airfield's organisation came to life, as Major Hay
recalled:

"I was in my cabin at the time of the accident and was called
to the scene by field telephone, arriving about fifteen minutes after it had happened. It was then light enough to drive
without lights. I asked a lot of questions, but no one can say
what the second aircraft type was, where it came from and
who was in it. I am told that the pilot ignored a red Aldis,
continued his approach, landed, colliding with the other
Corsair at the midway point of the runway. Both aircraft had
exploded. Death to both men had been instant.

In the aftermath of this accident I am nominated President of
the Board of Inquiry, but because of my involvement as
Commander (Flying) I tried to avoid this appointment, but to
no avail. The RAF appointed a Squadron Leader as their representative he was not very helpful...."

With daylight the full extent of the tragedy was apparent, but sadly it
was a common sight on wartime airfields. As the wreckage cooled, the
runway was cleared and the few pitiful remains of these two young
men were removed, but identification proved impossible, everything of
note having perished in the fire. Only with Illustrious' arrival in the
afternoon, could some of the pieces be fitted together, as Norman
Hanson reported:

"As we came through the boom and sighted the signal station
we were greeted with quickfire flashes, telling us that the
runway was out of use because of a bad crash. Though I
believe I was the first to put two and two together, I claim no
pride. Our arrival in port only confirmed what I had surmised
already as an appalling tragedy.

No wonder the shore station had ben lacking in detailed information, for both men had been burnt beyond recognition."

By nightfall the inquiry was well underway, armed with details provided by Illustrious' officers, but in amongst this sea of officialdom more poignant duties had to be fulfilled and the day ended with casualty reports being passed to the Admiralty. Three days later telegrams arrived in Burnham and Napier, on opposite sides of the world, recording the death of two much loved sons.

CHAPTER EIGHTEEN

AFTERMATH

In the rush to get Illustrious ready for sea the immediacy of war allowed little time to stop and remember lost friends.

By first light, on the 15th, Dick's kit had been packed and sent ashore for transport home to England, whilst most of Mudge's possessions had been destroyed in the crash. Captain Cunliffe composed two letters, one to each family; Chaplain Fawkes adding a postscript two days later, providing some reassurance after the first bombshell had hit. Yet words, whether written or spoken, could provide little comfort.

There was little enough left of either man to bury, but this did not matter and the funeral, although symbolic, was moving none the less. Air Groups from Illustrious and Saratoga turned out to honour these two gallant men; pilots from Dick's Wing carrying the coffins, both covered by Union flags: "

> "We headed the parade, which included a guard, and officers and men from the ship's company.
> We marched to a point a short distance from the cemetery, where the coffins were waiting and reformed the band in front, whilst the mourners followed. We then marched the remaining distance in slow time playing Chopin's Funeral March.
> As Chaplain Fawkes finished the service we played 'Abide With Me' the guard fired a volley, then a bugler sounded the 'Last Post' and 'Reveille'. As we marched back to Illustrious we carried on playing.... "

V. R. Foster RM.

"I was one of the bearers at the funeral and carried Dickie Cork's coffin. It wasn't a pleasant experience and one I will never forget. It was a typical hot sunny day and the large number of Blue Bottles swarming around us made things most unpleasant."

Keith Munnoch

"It was the saddest of occasions, with little or nothing to lighten the gloom. It just seemed a terrible bloody waste to be burying two young men so far from home.
Between us we had already seen a fair bit of death and destruction and would see a good bit more before it was over but each death still had the power to shock...."

Colin Facer

"I had the sad duty of presiding over the funeral and was moved to see so many men from both ships lining the route to the cemetery. The brightness of the light and the whiteness of their uniforms seemed in some strange way to make everything more melancholy.
After a brief service we laid them to rest under the shading trees. Rifles cracked out a last salute and in a very sombre mood we marched away from the cemetery, leaving the gravediggers to their duty, whilst the Royal Marine Band tried, unsuccessfully, to lighten our gloom.
Not for the first or last time did I contemplate the waste of it all, and the belief that we were burying the best of them came to the fore, those who after the war would be so sorely needed."

Chaplain E. D. G. Fawkes.

On Illustrious the sadness and shock at losing these men had to be put to one side. With her first strike only four days away action had to be taken to fill the void created by Cork's untimely death. In a little under four months the Corsair Wing had lost its three senior commanders now, as senior man, Mike Tritton was appointed Wing Leader and 1830's commander a dual role he filled, with distinction, until Illustrious returned to UK waters in 1945.

By April 15th the accident inquiry had interviewed the main characters involved in the collision and had begun the process of establishing circumstances, apportioning blame and recommending ways in which similar accidents might be avoided in future. As Major Hay later reported, responsibility for the accident was apportioned between Cork, the Duty Pilot and Anderson:

> "It was clear that the Duty Pilot had lit the flare path against orders and Anderson had taxied down the runway, in an unlit aircraft against instructions.
>
> We established that Cork arrived over China Bay in the pre-dawn glow, saw the flare path and after one complete circuit decided to land. He made no visual request to airfield control ie. flashing his call sign in morse. Flying Control had no idea what sort of aircraft was in the circuit and stated that he flashed his Red Aldis lamp at the aircraft continually. You can imagine his horror when the aircraft appeared on its final approach. Of course at this crisis Flying Control should have fired a Red Very cartridge, which no one could fail to see and is a mandatory refusal for any landing.
>
> So Cork, either not seeing or ignoring the Red Aldis, continued his approach, landed and collided with the other Corsair at about the mid-point of the runway. Both aircraft exploded and fire raged.
>
> Cork was in error as follows:
>
> > He failed to signal his request to land, by flashing his identity.
> > He failed to spot or act upon the continuous flashing Red Aldis lamp.
> > He landed without receiving the essential Green Aldis.
> > Without seeing positively this Green light, no landing is permitted.
>
> The Duty Pilot (RAF FL/Lt) was in error by:
>
> > Lighting the flare path against orders.
> > Failing to fire the Red Very signal.

The Sub Lt was in error because he taxied his aircraft in the dark without navigation lights being switched on.

During these investigations the RAF representative, a Squadron Leader, was not very helpful and I had to add one of my conclusions, which he refused to support ie. the failure of the Duty Pilot to fire a Red Very light when it was obvious the unknown aircraft was committed to a landing.

I and many others attended the funeral. Illustrious' band played good marching music on the way back from the funeral and afterwards we were all glad to hit the bar and try to drown the memory of a terrible two days...."

Major Hay was placed in an invidious position by the RAF. He was Commander (Flying) and was himself vulnerable to criticism over the accident. But they insisted that he should head the inquiry and, of course, he was in no position to refuse, the accident having involved two naval aircraft. Yet others, trusting his impartiality and judgement, saw his selection as demonstrating an unprejudiced attitude by the RAF, as it seemed likely that the Duty Pilot's lack of action had led to the deaths. But without either Corsair pilot to tell their stories the inquiry was limited in its scope and its conclusions reflected this lack of information, spreading the blame between the two pilots and Flying Control.

In wartime, where such accidents were commonplace, there was not the luxury of time to ponder these issues and investigations were, by necessity, muted. It was by no means a 'whitewash', but, with these constraints, its scope for detailed evaluation was limited. As a result its findings did a great disservice to Cork and Anderson, who were robbed, by death, of a means of redress. Yet close examination of events on the 14th points to inadequate RAF control, a lack of supervision, disregard of orders by Air Force officers, who should have been controlling activities on the ground, and an almost breath taking indifference to the lives and well being of aircrew operating from China Bay. In normal circumstances these limitations might have remained hidden, but the sudden and unexpected accumulation of events on the 14th, soon revealed the parlous state of affairs at China Bay. It was Cork and Anderson's misfortune to be in the wrong place at the wrong time and become the unwilling victims of a hopelessly inadequate system.

Major Hay, did not witness the accident, so could only record events as they were reported to him. In the circumstances his conclusions were a model of impartiality. Yet the inquiry's findings failed to reveal the full extent of what had happened and amongst Illustrious' officers there was much disquiet and some indignation, when the report's findings reached their ears:

> "I was not satisfied with the official report of Cork's death and questioned it on our return from Sabang, but to no avail. The ground controllers were absolved of any real blame and it seemed that Cork was held up as the main culprit. This angered me at the time and continues to do so now. The controllers at China Bay failed in their duty, showed near criminal negligence and two young men died as a result. The prevailing attitude seemed to be 'let the dead take the blame, they are unlikely to answer back'. Whilst those who should have known better allowed their judgement to be coloured by the well worn phrase 'these things happen in war', as though this could excuse incompetence."

> *Captain R. L. B. Cunliffe RN.*

> It was total incompetence. In half light or darkness there should have been someone on the runway with a Very Pistol. Given a well ordered situation two aircraft on the runway at once (one taking off and the other landing in opposite directions) shouldn't have been possible...."

> *Mike Tritton*

> There was little doubt that the controllers were responsible for the accident, yet our chaps were found 'guilty'. For weeks we had to make do with the poorest support one could imagine and daily, it seemed, things got worse. The RAF saw us as interlopers and dealt with us in a very slip-shod way as a result. I can only think that this attitude, coupled with inadequate resources and incompetence on April 14th led to these deaths. Some even thought that control was unmanned at the time or, worst still, the Duty Pilot was asleep...."

> *Colin Facer*

Anger at such unnecessary losses is understandable, but the impartial might consider it misplaced; none of those expressing anger having witnessed the accident. Yet they could point to Cork's exceptional ability as a pilot and his experience, reasoning that someone of his quality would not throw life away so contemptuously. Contrary to the official reports he displayed great caution when approaching China Bay circling once, before doing a low pass down the runway, observing movement on the ground.

Knowing the routine at China Bay, limited 'opening-hours', the landing square in front of Flying Control, he would not have expected control to be manned or to receive any signals from them. Yet if they had signalled a 'red', as the Duty Pilot reported, Cork could not have missed it as he would have been looking directly towards the landing square in front of Flying Control, for any information about landing conditions, as he made his first pass along the runway.

Some argued that the Corsair's unusual configuration, with the pilot sitting far back behind a massive, barrel shaped nose, might have contributed to the accident sighting its lack of forward visibility, when landing or taxying as evidence. In truth it did not help, but at China Bay it was a short coming that only came in to play on the 14th when coupled to Flying Control's position in relation to the runway and other buildings in the vicinity.

According to eyewitness accounts Cork curved in sharply on both approaches to the runway, appearing each time from behind a hangar and a natural rise in the ground, topped by several large buildings. With all these visual restrictions, the Corsair would have been hidden from control's view until almost on the ground. After so many months of operating these types of aircraft, controllers should have appreciated the difficulties, but on April 14th they were not expecting a Corsair to land and were badly compromised by its sudden appearance. Cork may have realised this, hence his caution, but control failed to respond and then made matters worse by flashing a 'green' at Anderson, 'ordering' him to take off.

The Inquiry placed little emphasis upon the part played in the collision by the flarepath, but its role was crucial. Without it there seems little doubt that Anderson would have stayed where he was, away from the runway in safety, and Cork would have kept circling until instructed from the ground to do otherwise. Despite its importance, the Duty Pilot offered only a weak explanation of his actions. One can only imagine that he intended to get Anderson airborne before the expected 'strike' from Illustrious arrived. But, when faced with two deaths, he fell back on the simple explanation that it was lit to allow Anderson to taxy down the runway and so take off in to wind. But with dawn so close and the air so still there was little to be gained and much to be lost by traversing 2,500 yards of runway; even the most heavily laden Corsair would require 800 yards to get into the air.

The use of the flarepath was central to the accident, but this mistake might have remained unpunished if the Duty Pilot had kept control and provided clear, unambiguous signals to both pilots. Certainly Cork's sudden appearance would have taken him by surprise, but the Wing Leader gave him every opportunity to exert his authority, by passing low in front of him. Evidence suggests he made no effort to signal Cork, who must have assumed that Flying Control was unmanned and come in to land, after visually checking the runway, unaware of the danger ahead, a danger created by the Duty Pilot himself.

The inquiry placed great importance on Cork's apparent disregard of signals flashed by Flying Control, but here one comes back to the quality of the man himself. He was no amateur and had survived four years of war with hardly a scratch. His record was unblemished, so why should he suddenly ignore all the basic rules of airmanship? In truth he did not and, in the absence of any instructions from ground controllers, took a positive, but cautious approach to an airfield seemingly closed, yet lit up by its flarepath. Believing it closed and seeing nothing to the contrary, he adopted a standard landing pattern and set his Corsair down, having visually checked the runway as he curved in to land. Yet his caution went unrewarded, an unlit aircraft having been ordered into his pathway.

There is little evidence to support the view that the Duty Pilot flashed a 'red' at Cork, yet it seems possible that he might have seen the 'green', flashed at Anderson. Dick was immediately above him at the time, turning to port to begin another circuit. If this was the case, the positive way he circled the airfield and came in to land can be explained.

With so few witnesses to the accident coming forward or sought, the inquiry could only reach conclusions favouring the survivors and no amount of questioning could change this. But not everyone's voice was heard and accounts, suggesting a different train of events, remained hidden for many years.

Armed with more information, given time to question more fully, one can only presume the Board of Inquiry would have exonerated the pilots and placed the blame more fully on those who were truly responsible. But they did not have the luxury of time and could do no more than sift very onesided 'evidence'. As a consequence Cork took the lion's share of the blame and an exceptional record was irrevocably blemished. As a separate report concluded, "his rashness in landing against instructions from the ground resulted in the death of an innocent party, an experienced Wing Leader and the loss of two valuable aircraft, at a time when Illustrious was about to commence attacks on the Japanese". It is small wonder that Captain Cunliffe objected to the way events were portrayed and sought to protect the reputation of such a gallant officer.

Set against the immensity of war, these deaths were a small incident, but events cannot always be viewed in such a broad way. The effect of tragedy maybe limited to a small circle of family and friends, whilst the world, in general, marches on, but in that circle tragedy encompasses all.

Dick's parents had lived with the possibility of losing either son and now their worst fears were realised. The 'telegram boy', became the innocent bearer of this terrible news and on April 17th, he delivered the sealed, buff envelope to the Cork household, with its appalling announcement enclosed, 'LtCdr R. J. Cork has been killed in a flying accident....'

After the first shock had passed, the Admiralty wrote a brief letter of condolence, which immediately caused Dick's father to respond. 'Killed in action' was a term which raised few questions, but 'killed in a flying accident' created doubt and sponsored the need for explanation 'what happened, who was to blame?', On May 3rd 1944 Vice Admiral Monroe replied:

> "I have now obtained the information received regarding the death of your son on 14th April.
> The circumstances appear to be that Lt Cdr Cork landed on a runway at the Royal Naval Air Station China Bay, against the ground signals, and collided with another aircraft while landing. Both aircraft burst into flames.
> I very much regret to be the bearer of such particularly sad news, and as your son was the only occupant of the machine I fear we shall never know why a landing was attempted against the red lights.
> Death would certainly have been instantaneous under such circumstances, so your boy would have known no pain...."

One might have expected the Navy to temper a letter of condolence with some compassion. But underlying this tact there is the clear accusation of recklessness, a disregard of orders and sole responsibility for the accident. From the information available they knew this was a gross distortion of facts and one can read in their words the edict, 'let the dead take the blame'.

In their grief Dick's parents were persuaded that their son had thrown his life away needlessly and must have suffered additional anguish as a result. Sadly neither lived long enough to know that he bore little or no responsibility for the accident.

EPILOGUE

In the months after Dick's death, China Bay witnessed a flood of air-craft transitting, on Fleet Carriers, to the Indian Ocean, then the Pacific as the Allies tightened the noose around Japan's neck. Even giant B 29's flew to attack the enemy from its single strip in August 1944. But, with capit-ulation, activity quickly subsided and the world moved on, leaving only scattered remnants to remind visitors that men had once lived and died on its hard, concrete surface. Days full of hope and days of great endeav-our merged into memory, recalled by few and forgotten by most.

Dick and Mudge Anderson remained side by side in St Stephen's ceme-tery, bearing silent witness to these changes and in time their remains became the responsibility of the War Graves Commission. Exhumation followed in the late 1940's and a short journey to a new cemetery com-menced, a gathering together of dead comrades-in-arms, guarded by a concrete cross honouring their sacrifice.

Asked to choose words to adorn their son's gravestone, Dick's parents chose the simple, but moving epitaph:

"Greater love hath no man ...."

His dedication to the Fleet Air Arm and the Navy had been exception-al by any standards, but this is praise he himself would have undoubted-ly denied, preferring the quiet satisfaction of a job well done. It was an attitude that many considered important, because it treated all partici-pants equally, no matter how small their contribution. In this way I am sure Dick would have agreed with Mike Tritton when he said:

"You need to be very careful about creating a hero, because there were so many people who broke their necks or sur-

vived who were just as good as anyone else. Dick had been
lucky, had gained a lot of experience and achieved a lot in
the process. But like so many people in those days you
went from being an amateur to a professional in a compar-
atively short time. You couldn't survive if you didn't...."

There are now only a handful of people left who remember Dick
and the number continues to diminish yearly, with sad regularity. But
when the war ended there were very few survivors anyway. By 1945
50% of those who had flown with 242 Squadron in the Battle of
Britain were dead, only four pilots from 880's 'Pedestal' complement
were still living and the 15th Fighter Wing had lost 22 men out of 57.
Although a small number, in terms of wartime casualties, the attrition
rate was alarmingly high and it took little imagination for a pilot to
work out their diminishing chances of survival. Yet Dick chose to go
back on operations when he could justifiably have said, 'no more',
and found himself a 'safe' posting. But this was not his way.

Like many servicemen he had grown tired of the war and looked
forward to its end, but he was encouraged to carry on by promotion
to Wing Leader and saw some possibilities in the months ahead. He
also knew there was a limit to his time with Illustrious; a heartening
fact, when set against the general uncertainty amongst the remainder
of the crew, who faced the prospect of an unlimited tour in the Far
East. Dick had been told he would remain Wing Leader during the
early strikes, withdrawing once the Corsair pilots had gained experience in combat. All being well he could be back in England by
Autumn, fresh for a rest and further promotion, but he knew that his
return home would herald an end to operational flying a period
already extended by extensive canvassing of those with power to
decide these matters. So he must have faced the future with a mixture of emotions. It had been 'a good run', but was now coming to an
end.

There was the vague prospect of staying in the Far East, flying
Corsairs for some months more, but in April '44 the Navy awaited the
results of their first attacks against the Japanese before committing
themselves to any tactical change. Yet, even at this stage, it was
realised that over the target fighters and bombers would need 'on the
spot' control, adjusting attacks to suit changing conditions. The RAF
had tried this tactic with some success and late in 1944 the Navy followed suit establishing Air Coordinators.

Cork's name had been 'pencilled in' for this job. With his death the Navy looked for another officer to fill this demanding role and, in late 1944, appointed Major Hay, late of China Bay.

Throughout the long years Dickie stayed loyal to the memory of lost friends. He wrote regularly to their families, offering whatever support he could, but, as he related in a letter in March 1944, 'words of sympathy and encouragement have a very hollow ring' revealing words that betrayed his own feelings. Though dead for over three years, Cork still felt Arthur Blake's loss very keenly and described his thoughts in a letter written days before his own death:

> "So much has happened since Arthur's death, but it seems like only yesterday that he came trotting across to my Hurricane, at Rochford, blood on his face, smiling broadly, with hardly a care in the world! It all seemed so much simpler then. Everything is much more complicated now. What would he have made of it if he was still here? Probably shrug his shoulders and head for the nearest bar, with a shout of 'Why worry!'...."

After four years of war Dick had not given up the battle, but he faced the prospect of being a survivor from a 'bygone age', surrounded by people to whom 1940 was history. By 1944 there were few pre-war contemporaries in front line squadrons and the list of dead friends stretched alarmingly over the years, leaving him isolated. The war had taught him how to use his special skills, but it could not teach him how to cope with the loneliness of being a survivor and by April '44 he was finding this obligation increasingly hard to bear. Back in England things had been bad enough, little of the country he had known untouched by war, so he had placed great hope in the unchanging nature of operational flying. But even here the old order had disappeared, removing the rock to which he could cling. He was adrift in a fast changing world and so placed great faith in more stable elements to see him through, his sense of responsibility and an instinct for survival. Neither let him down, but fate contrived a set of circumstances, on April 14th 1944, over which he had no control.

High above London on that April morning, pilots saw few landmarks through the thick clouds that covered the capital. But to the north, beyond barrage balloons, they could see American bombers streaming vapour trails behind them as they clawed their way skywards, turning en masse over the North Sea towards targets in Germany, their regular destination for many months now. With D Day so close, other squadrons of silver and olive painted B17s and B24s flew south, around London, over Surrey, Kent and Sussex, to bomb targets in the invasion area.

Unseen at night, RAF bombers droned over England's East Coast, heading for the Baltic, before turning south to attack the enemy's cities an assault now two years old, yet still unable to force a decision. By dawn tired aircrews reached home, their eyes alighting on familiar, safe scenes, clouded by the knowledge that another moonlit night would see them return.

In a scene unchanged since 1917, trains marked their routes around and through the capital, with whispers of steam, but now the emphasis was on transporting men and munitions to staging points along the south coast, not casualty clearance to hospitals in the Home Counties. London was still a rallying point, but now the centre of activity had shifted to airfields and ports, as the build-up to D Day gathered momentum. On the city' s western perimeter Burnham sat on the sidelines of these preparations, but heavy goods traffic over the Great Western Railway nearby, left few in any doubt that something was in the air.

From the innocence of pre-war Britain had risen an armed camp that would soon reach out and strike a death blow against Nazi Germany. But in this moment of triumph the Cork family found little to celebrate, having lost a son and son in law in the conflict, and seen so many other familiar young men killed along the way. There would be a victory, but for this and thousands of other grieving families it came too late to be of value.

RNC Greenwich 1979
to Limpley Stoke 1998

The End